TALKING TO PATIENTS 900

History Taking in Chinese Medicine

Xie Fang & Xie Zhufan

TALKING TO PATIENTS 900

History Taking in Chinese Medicine

FOREIGN LANGUAGES PRESS

First Edition 2016

ISBN 978-7-119-09553-0

Published by Foreign Languages Press Co. Ltd
24 Baiwanzhuang Road, Beijing 100037, China
http://www.flp.com.cn   E-mail: flp@cipg.org.cn
Distributed by China International Book Trading Corporation
35 Chegongzhuang Xilu, Beijing 100044, China
P.O. Box 399, Beijing, China

Printed in the People's Republic of China

Foreword

With the rapid development of communication and transportation technologies, geographic distance is no more an insurmountable barrier to the exchange of ideas between people in different regions of the world. Modern communication has more or less covered all the places where there are human inhabitants. With telephone or Internet connection, people can communicate with each other spontaneously. Transportation tools such as planes, cars, trains and ships can take us to almost every corner of the world to meet people, and talk to them face to face. The convenience of communication has encouraged people to crave ever-higher levels of communication. In fact, in-depth cultural and ideational communication has become a necessity of life in modern times. However, when people really get serious about a different ideation or culture, they might have to confront the really big barrier — a gap in mentality. Language, which is supposed to be a bridge of communication, has become so crucial that it needs to be maintained, updated or even rebuilt, in order to overcome the gap.

Traditional Chinese medicine (TCM) is a treasure which has safeguarded the survival and prosperity of the Chinese nation from generation to generation. It has long been the vehicle for ancient Chinese philosophical ideas and experiences in the prevention and treatment of diseases, but remains to be fully cultivated. It is incumbent on us to demonstrate the strength of TCM to the rest of the world and promote the relevant cultural exchanges so as to make TCM accessible and beneficial to more people. Among many approaches, the most direct one is to create an environment for TCM doctors to treat more patients with different cultural backgrounds, and allow them to regain their health via TCM. Many licensed TCM doctors have opened clinics worldwide, and people have come to China from different regions of the world, seeking TCM treatment. Under such circumstances, communication between TCM doctors and patients has become the key to the success of not only the treatment but, more importantly, cultural exchanges. This book is intended to help doctors communicate with patients in appropriate English.

TCM, which originated several thousand years ago, has been inherited along with its old-fashioned or even outdated language expressions. TCM terms and habits of expression first developed during the periods of the *Internal Classic* (5th~3rd centuries BC) and *Treatise on Cold Damage Diseases* (196~204 AD), and most of them are still current. Many terms which might have been household words or phrases in ancient times have been either abandoned or given new meanings during the long historic evolution of the Chinese language. Indeed, these terms are often puzzling even to modern Chinese, not to mention those who were raised with different cultural backgrounds. So, interpretation of these expressions in languages other than Chinese is definitely a tremendous challenge.

For the past 30 years milestone achievements have

been made in the field of translation of TCM terminology. A standard TCM nomenclature has been established, and many TCM classics and textbooks have been translated into English. However, there is still a missing link in the communication between doctors and patients: The ways of expression and terms used in textbooks cannot be used directly in conversation with patients who do not understand TCM or who simply have no medical knowledge at all. Doctors need to convert these traditional technical terms into modern colloquial words. So, while the standardization of English translations of TCM terminologies provides a reference for communication among TCM professionals, the efforts we have made in this book are aimed at establishing a reference for communication between professionals and nonprofessionals. In others words, we are trying to supply this missing link.

As everyone knows, the first thing to do for any doctor faced with a patient is to collect information related to the latter's illness. In TCM inspection, listening-smelling, inquiry and palpation—the so-called four examinations—are the means to collect such information. Inquiry, equivalent to medical history taking in Western medicine, is an important approach for collecting information about symptoms. However, the information achieved via inquiry may very likely be subjective, and patients with different cultural backgrounds may describe the very same symptom differently. They may either perceive the same symptom from different angles, or describe it with different habitual expressions. In particular, the Chinese have established a tradition of symptom description which may conflict with those of people from other parts of the world. Some expressions are difficult to understand for Westerners. For example, 渴不欲饮(kě bù yù yǐn), which literally means "thirst with no desire to drink," does not seem to make any sense at all, because in English the word *thirst* already denotes the feeling of wanting a drink. However, such an expression is a traditional TCM technical term, and TCM doctors know that *thirst* in this case actually refers to dryness in the mouth. As an important symptomatic description of pattern identification, 五心烦热 (wǔ xīn fán rè) *vexing feverish sensation in the palms of the hands, soles of the feet and chest* is another confusing term for Westerners. In Western medicine, fever is defined as a body temperature above 37.2℃ or 99℉. Local fever may appear in the case of inflammation, and thus is always accompanied by swelling and pain. How can one have a feverish sensation involving five localities far away from each other without actual rise of body temperature?

Obviously, it is very difficult to establish an effective communication between TCM doctors and patients if both hold on to their own habits or traditions. Some sort of converter is needed, so that different expressions can be converted into a version readily understandable to both. On the one hand, symptoms have to be converted in language that a TCM doctor uses daily for diagnoses. On the other, the patient needs to know what his or her doctor is asking about.

Only in this way can doctors obtain accurate and useful information from their patients. However, conversion of the way of describing illnesses and symptoms from one culture to another is indeed a tough task which involves in-depth understanding and accurate comprehension of both TCM and Western medicine, as well as other cultural aspects such as linguistics and logics. Therefore, some mistakes and errors in this book are unavoidable. Nevertheless, we hope that it may bring more professionals in the field to help us refine and expand our work in the future.

We have selected 75 illnesses and symptoms that meet the following criteria simultaneously: a) those that are commonly complained of by patients in the course of general TCM practice; b) those that can be effectively treated with TCM; and c) those that require inquiry as the major approach to pattern identification (clinical diagnosis required for TCM treatment).

In order to make this book practical and handy, we have categorized those selected illnesses and symptoms in accordance with *Ten Inquires in Rhyme*, a modified version of the *Chapter of Ten Inquiries in Complete Works of Jingyue* (1640):

"Cold and heat, and then sweats; head and body, urine, feces;
Food and drink, chest and belly; deafness, dry mouth classified clearly;
Chronic illness and then its causes; take medicine and see what changes;

Menstrual period is a must for women, late, early, hypo or hyper should be determined;

Questions on illnesses of children, smallpox and measles to be detected before they happen!"

Contents

Introduction

In Chinese medicine, inquiry is a vital tool for doctors to collect information from patients. Indeed, it may be the only tool when certain conditions or states of an illness are involved, including its occurrence and development, treatment history and subjective symptoms, as well as the patient's dietary and life habits. Those conditions or states are critical pieces of information upon which doctors rely to uncover the syndrome patterns involved. In particular, in the absence of any objective signs during the early stage of a disease, subjective symptoms (which can only be ascertained through inquiry) become the major clues for a doctor when suggesting treatment. Therefore, inquiry is often the first resort for a doctor of Chinese medicine in clinical practice.

In order to achieve reliable information, doctors should avoid by all means using medical terms that are unfamiliar to patients, especially those who have no or only limited knowledge of Chinese culture. Although no unified wording can be referred to, there are definitely universal guidelines for doctors when making inquiries of patients with different cultural backgrounds. In such cases doctors should strive to make the patients understand the inquiries clearly and accurately, while demonstrating care and respect for their cultures. At the very least, doctors should try to avoid giving such patients any impression of impoliteness or intent to offend.

Generally speaking, doctors need to be clear about the chief complaint first. And then, inquiries should be focused on the present symptoms that are strongly associated with the chief complaint, followed by inquiries about past and family medical history, as well as life style and previous life experiences.

Inquiries Centered on Chief Complaint

The term chief complaint denotes the most noticeable pain(s) or other symptom(s) and physical sign(s) displayed by a patient, which drive(s) him or her to visit a clinic. It includes the nature, extent and duration of the chief symptom(s) or physical sign(s). "Wandering pain of the limb joints for two weeks," "severe dizziness for a day," "recurrent edema of the lower limbs for a year" are typical examples of a chief complaint.

The following are the commonest expressions used when starting to inquire about the chief complaint of a patient:

1. Good morning (afternoon, etc.). I'm Dr. xx. I would like to ask you a few questions about your illness. What is bothering you right now?
早上好（下午好……），我是XX医生。我问一下您的病情可以吗？您现在有什么不舒服？

2. Hello, my name is Dr. XX, how can I help you?
您好，我是XX医生，有什么我能帮助您的吗？

3. Good morning (afternoon, etc.). Sit down, please. What's troubling you?
早上好（下午好……），请坐，您哪里不舒服？

4. Please take a seat. What's wrong with your baby?
请坐，您的孩子怎么了？

Doctors also need to obtain information on the duration of a present symptom or physical sign if it is not included in the feedback to inquiry. The following are three examples:

5. (If a patient comes to a clinic for a fall injury:) When did it happen?
（如患者因跌倒摔伤来就诊）这是什么时候的事？

6. (If the chief complaint of a patient is pain:) How long have you had this pain?
（如患者的主诉是疼痛）痛了多久？

7. (If the chief complaint of a patient is palpitations and shortness of breath:) When did you start to notice these symptoms?
（如患者的主诉是心悸气短）您是从什么时候发现这些症状的？

Inquiries Concerning Present Illness

The term *present illness* denotes the detailed conditions of pain or other sufferings of a patient enunciated during a visit to the clinic, i.e. all symptoms of the disease that the patient is suffering at present. In many cases of Chinese medical practice, identification of the chief symptom that a patient complains of is actually identical to the diagnosis of the disease he or she is suffering from; in other words, the name of the disease comes after its chief symptom. For instance, sleeplessness (insomnia), wheezing (asthma), epigastric pain (stomachache) are both chief symptoms or chief complaints of patients, and at the same time the names of the relevant disorders. Apparently, diagnosis of a disease in Chinese medicine does not provide sufficient information about the corresponding pathological changes, so Chinese medical doctors can seldom determine the proper treatment merely on the basis of disease diagnosis. In most cases, they need to collect all the relevant information about the disease including its accompanying symptoms, because each symptom is the reflection of a pathological change. Then, they need to rationalize the connections among all the symptoms in accordance with Chinese medical theory, and come to a conclusion on the pathology—including location, nature, and mechanisms—of the disease. Such so-called syndrome differentiation or pattern identification is a necessary step before any treatment is recommended to patients. So in the eyes of Chinese medical doctors, any symptom is a piece of evidence that might be crucial to the final conclusion. Accordingly, inquiry concerning the present illness is aimed at obtaining such evidence.

Chapter One
Fever

Fever can be divided into two categories: fever resulting from external contraction and fever resulting from internal injury. The former, which is due to the contraction of pathogenic factors from the environment, is characterized by acute onset, short course and intense heat (high temperature), and accompanied by other symptoms of exogenous febrile diseases such as chills and thirst. Fever resulting from external contraction is usually excessive in nature. On the other hand, fever resulting from internal injury, which is due to disharmony of *yin-yang* and *qi*-blood of the viscera and bowels, exhibits the features of gradual onset and prolonged course. It is often accompanied by deficiency symptoms of chronic diseases, such as weight loss, fatigue and listlessness. In most cases, fever resulting from internal injury is of the deficiency or deficiency-excess pattern. Clinically, to patients who suffer from high fever and those who suffer from low fever, doctors need to apply different approaches of inquiry.

High Fever

High fever is often a reflection of the conflict between healthy *qi* and invading external pathogenic *qi*. Exuberance of *yang* constitutes the main mechanism. In clinical practice, fever resulting from external contraction is usually excess-heat in nature. Doctors need to identify whether the exterior or the interior portion of the body, as well as which viscus or bowel is involved in these pathological changes. This is the key to finding out whether the patient suffers from chills in order to distinguish between exterior and interior syndrome patterns. A chilly sensation is bound to appear as long as an external pathogen invades the exterior part of the body. So, "if chills do not disappear, the exterior syndrome also remains."

High fever involving the interior is commonly encountered in the syndrome patterns of lung heat, stomach heat, bowel excess, gallbladder heat, dampness-heat of the spleen and stomach, dampness-heat of the large intestine, and dampness-heat of the bladder.

Typical approaches of inquiry:

8. How many days have you had this fever?
您发烧（发热）几天了?

9. Did you feel chilly at the beginning?
开始时发冷（恶寒）吗?

10. (If yes:) Are you still feeling chilly?
（如是）现在还发冷吗?

11. Do fever and chills hit you alternately? Or do chills hit you first and then fever?
您的发烧和发冷是交替出现的还是从最开始发冷之后就一直发烧了?

12. Have you taken your own temperature?
量过体温吗?

13. What was the highest temperature?
最高时多少度?

14. Do you have fever all day long or does the fever fluctuate? For example, is there no fever in the morning, but fever in the afternoon?
是整天都发烧还是有起伏? 比如上午不烧，下午才烧?

15. Do you have a stuffy or runny nose? Any soreness or pain in the throat?
有没有鼻塞流涕? 咽喉疼不疼?

16. Do you have dryness and a bitter taste in your mouth?
口干口苦吗？

17. Do you feel continually thirsty during the fever?
发烧的时候一直都口渴吗？

18. (If yes:) Do you have a desire for cold or hot drinks?
(如果口渴)想喝冷水还是热水？

19. Do you cough up sputum?
咳嗽吐痰吗？

20. Is the sputum white and thin or yellow and thick?
痰是白的稀的还是黄的稠的？

21. Have you had any bowel movement since the fever started?
发烧以来排过大便吗？

22. Did you sweat during the fever?
发烧时出过汗吗？

23. (If yes:) Did the sweating bring down your body temperature?
（如出过）出汗后体温下降了吗？

24. (To patients with fever and jaundice:) When did you realize that your eyes had turned yellow?
（对于出现黄疸的发热患者）您什么时候开始发现眼珠发黄了？

25. Have you felt nauseous and vomited?
感到恶心吗？呕吐过吗？

26. (To patients with fever and diarrhea:) Have you noticed any blood and/or pus in your stools?
（对于发热兼有腹泻的患者）您有没有注意到大便中有脓血？

27. Do you still have the urge to empty your rectum right after a bowel movement?
有里急后重的症状吗？

28. (To patients with fever and dysuria:) Do you feel pain during urination?
（对于有发热兼有排尿症状者）您排尿时感到疼痛吗？

29. (If yes:) What kind of pain is it?
（如感到）是什么样的疼痛？

30. How many times do you have to pass water (urine) each day?
您每天要排尿多少次？

31. Have you noticed any change in your urine?
您注意到尿液有什么变化吗？

32. Is your urine bloody?
尿里带血吗？

33. Have you had any trouble with urination before?
您以前有过排尿异常吗？

Low Fever

Low fever refers to a subjective feverish sensation with only mild elevation of body temperature, normally in the range of 37.5℃ to 38℃. Differentiation of syndrome patterns of low fever routinely starts from that between deficiency and excess. If a deficiency pattern is confirmed, the next step is to distinguish its subtypes, such as *yin* deficiency, *yang* deficiency and *qi* deficiency. Similarly, whether it is caused by *qi* stagnation, blood stasis or dampness-heat must be identified if pathogen excess is confirmed to be the basic character.

Typical approaches of inquiry:

34. You say that recently you have developed a chronic low fever. Did you just feel that you had a fever or did you actually take your own temperature with a thermometer?
    您说近来天天发低烧，是自己感觉发烧，还是用体温计量出来的?

35. (If taken with a thermometer:) Do you remember what the highest temperature was?
    (如果是用体温计量的)您还记得最高是多少度吗?

36. How many days have you had the fever?
    您这样发烧多少天了?

37. What triggered the fever originally? Has the fever been high? Or has it been low since the very beginning?
最初是什么原因引起的？有没有发过高烧还是始终就是低烧？

38. Does your fever come at a regular time every day?
您每天发烧的时间有规律吗？

39. (If yes:) Does it come in the morning or in the afternoon?
(如果有规律)是上午发烧还是下午发烧？

40. Is your daily high temperature maintained at the same level?
每天的热度有大的变化吗？

41. Do you feel really hot and want to wear less when your temperature goes up?
体温升高时，您是否的确感到发热而想减少衣着？

42. Do you feel cold and want to wear more even when your temperature goes up?
有没有体温升高，您反而感到寒冷，想多穿点衣裳的情况？

43. Where do you feel hot the most? All over your body, in the middle of the chest, or in the palms of your hands and soles of your feet?
您感觉发烧在身体什么部位最明显？全身、胸口、手心、脚心？

44. Do you sweat easily? Do you sweat even after very slight exertion?
容易出汗吗？有没有一动就出汗的现象？

45. Does an emotional change affect your temperature? Do you get upset easily?
情绪对您的体温有影响吗？您容易生气着急吗？

46. Does the fever affect your appetite?
低烧对您的食欲有影响吗？

47. Does the fever affect your body weight?
低烧对您的体重有影响吗？

48. Do you feel dry in the mouth when you have fever? Do you want to drink much water?
您发烧时感到口渴吗？想不想喝水？

49. Have you experienced a situation in which you only want to gargle with water but do not want to swallow it?
有没有只想含口水却不愿下咽的情况？

50. Did you ever vomit water out right after drinking it?
有没有咽下去又立刻就吐出来的情况？

51. Besides low fever, do you have other symptoms, for example, any pain in the body?
除低烧之外同时还有其他的症状吗？比如身上有哪里疼痛。

Common Cold and Flu

Among all the cases of external contraction, common cold and flu are the most frequently encountered. Apart from fever, patients who suffer from colds or flu may also experience other symptoms, such as stuffy or runny nose, sneezing, headache and aversion to cold. It is not difficult to identify the ailment, but syndrome differentiation is needed. The answers to the following inquiries may provide doctors with important clues for making the correct diagnosis. The syndrome patterns of colds and flu include wind-cold, wind-heat, summer heat-dampness, and *qi* deficiency.

Typical approaches of inquiry:

52. Do you have a fever?
    您发烧了吗?

53. Have you taken your own temperature? Please let me take it again for you now.
    自己量过体温吗? 现在再给您量一下体温吧。

54. Do you feel chilly or hot?
    您自己觉得身上发冷还是发热?

55. Are you intolerant of wind?
    怕风吗?

56. Is your nasal discharge thin and clear or thick and sticky?
您流的鼻涕是清稀的还是粘稠的?

57. Do you feel dryness in the mouth?
嘴里干吗?

58. Do you have soreness in the throat?
喉咙疼吗?

59. Have you sweated?
身上出过汗没有?

60. Do you have a heavy cough?
咳嗽得厉害吗?

61. Do you cough up sputum?
咳嗽有痰吗?

62. (If yes:) Is the sputum whitish or yellowish?
（如有痰）痰是白的还是黄的?

63. Is the sputum thin or thick? Is it easy to expel?
痰是稀的还是稠的? 容易喀出吗?

64. Do you feel dizzy and groggy? Do you have tightness in the chest and nausea?
有没有感到头部昏昏沉沉，沉重发胀，胸口烦闷，想要呕吐?

65. Does the illness affect your general health a lot or not much? Do you feel tired all the time?
患病以来，是觉得对身体影响不大，还是影响很大？经常感觉疲倦乏力吗？

66. Are you particularly susceptible to catching colds?
您比别人容易感冒吧？

67. Each time you caught a cold, how many days did it last?
以前每次感冒，几天能好？

Chapter Two
Abnormal Sweating

There are two abnormal sweating situations: no sweating when it is called for, and sweating when it is not called for. The presence or absence of sweating is a useful piece of information for the identification of syndrome patterns. For example, the exterior syndrome of an external contraction may further be identified as exterior cold type if the patient does not sweat at all. Therefore, the doctor needs to inquire about sweating if a patient suffers from external contraction with the symptoms of fever and chills. It may also be necessary to examine a sweating condition by touching the patient's body surface with a hand.

Abnormal sweating commonly encountered in non-febrile cases includes spontaneous sweating, night sweats and local sweating (sweating in specific bodily regions).

Spontaneous Sweating

Spontaneous sweating refers to excessive sweating during the daytime without such obvious factors as hot weather, too much clothing, emotional stimuli or physical exertion. It occurs in patients with either *qi* or *yang* deficiency. In patients with *qi* deficiency, sweating is aggravated by even minimal physical exertion, and is accompanied by other symptoms of *qi* deficiency, such as listlessness, shortness of breath and reluctance to speak. Spontaneous sweating due to *yang* deficiency is marked by intolerance of cold and cold limbs.

Typical approaches of inquiry:

68. Does your sweating have anything to do with the environmental temperature? Do you sweat even when the weather is cold?
您出汗多与气候冷热有关系吗？天气冷时也容易出汗吗？

69. When do you sweat? In the daytime or nighttime?
一般是什么时间出汗？白天还是夜间？

70. Does your sweating have anything to do with wearing too much? Do you still sweat when you wear less?
您出汗多与衣着过多有关系吗？少穿些还照样出汗吗？

71. Does your sweating have anything to do with physical activities? Do you sweat even without physical activity?
您出汗多与体力活动有关系吗？不活动时也出汗吗？

72. Are you particularly intolerant of wind while sweating?
出汗时特别怕风吗？

73. Do you feel chills with cold extremities (hands and feet) while you are sweating?
您是否一面出汗，一面又感到寒冷、手脚发凉呢？

74. Are you usually lethargic and tired, or even reluctant to speak?
您是否平时感到精神疲惫，连话都懒得说？

Night Sweats

The term *night sweats* denotes sweating that occurs during sleep and stops after awakening. This is usually caused by *yin* deficiency with exuberant fire, but may also be encountered when the heart blood is insufficient.

Typical approaches of inquiry:

75. You say that you sweat during sleep. Does that happen every night?
您说您夜里睡觉时出汗，是每天夜里都这样吗?

76. Do you sweat because you use too many blankets? Do you still sweat even with a lighter covering?
是不是被褥太厚了，少盖些也出汗吗?

77. Does sweating continue after you wake up in the morning?
早上醒来还继续出汗吗?

78. Do you take a nap during the daytime? Do you sweat during the nap?
白天睡午觉吗? 睡午觉的时候出不出汗?

79. Besides sweating during sleep, what other discomfort do you experience? Do you have palpitations and sleeping problems?
除了盗汗，还有没有别的不舒服? 有没有心悸失眠等症状?

80. Do you have a burning sensation in the palms of your hands and soles of your feet, or fever in the afternoon?
有没有手脚心发热或下午感到发热?

81. (To female patients:) Are your periods normal?

（对女性病人）月经正常吗？

82. (To male patients:) Do you often have wet dreams?
（对男性病人）常有梦遗吗？

Local Sweating

Local sweating usually appears in the head, face, chest, hands, feet, armpits or genital area. Head and face sweating may occur in normal individuals under certain circumstances, for example, when eating dinner. Morbid sweating of the head and face is often encountered in those with *yang* deficiency. Local sweating in the thoracic region is due to either heart-spleen *qi* deficiency or heart-kidney *yin* deficiency. Sweaty hands and feet irrelevant to emotional stress may be a sign of dampness-heat in the spleen and stomach or deficiency of *qi* and *yin*. Morbid axillary and genital sweating are also most likely caused by *yin* deficiency or dampness-heat. Sweat due to *yin* deficiency is odorless, but not that due to dampness-heat.

Typical approaches of inquiry:

83. You say that you often sweat from the head. Does it have anything to do with diet, such as hot and spicy

food, hot beverages or alcohol?
您说您的头部特别容易出汗，出汗和饮食有关系吗？比如吃辛辣的食物、喝热饮或饮酒。

84. Besides head and face sweating, do you feel thirsty or emotionally upset?
除了头面汗多，有没有心烦口渴等不适？

85. Besides chest sweating, do you also experience palpitations, sleeping problems, soreness in the lower back and weakness in the knees?
除了前胸汗多，有没有心悸失眠、腰膝酸软之类的症状？

86. Do you sweat a lot from the palms of your hands and soles of your feet? Does it happen whenever you are nervous? Do you still sweat after you calm yourself down?
您的手脚心汗多吗？与精神紧张有没有关系？心情平静的时候也出汗吗？

87. Besides sweating a lot from the palms of your hands and soles of your feet, do you have other symptoms, such as tiredness, lack of energy and decreased appetite?
您除了手脚心汗多之外，还有没有什么别的症状，比如疲倦乏力、食欲减退？

88. You are aware of excessive sweating in the armpits. Are you also aware of a bad smell along with it?

您的腋下多汗，有没有不好闻的气味?

89. Do you sleep soundly and have a normal appetite?
您的食欲和睡眠正常吗?

90. You say that you sweat often from the genital area. Is it accompanied by urinary problems?
您诉说阴部多汗，是否伴有排尿的症状?

Chapter Three
Pain

Pain is the commonest symptom encountered in clinical practice. About half of the patients who consult doctors are complaining of pain. Nevertheless, the causal factors are multifarious. Both external contractions and internal injuries may give rise to pain. In some cases, pain occurs with the development of a primary injury or illness such as a bone fracture, and subsides immediately after healing takes place. Pain due to conspicuous causes as such is not discussed in this chapter.

All the causes of pain can be summarized into two categories. One is blockage of the visceral organs and meridians by pathogenic factors, leading to obstruction of *qi* and blood flow. In such cases, in accordance with the rule "Wherever there is obstruction, there is pain," the pain is excessive in nature. The other is the insufficiency of *qi* and blood or deficiency of *yin* essence, either of which impairs the nourishment of the visceral organs and meridians. This time, another rule applies: "Wherever there is undernourishment, there is pain," and the pain is deficient in nature.

When inquiring of a patient who complains about pain, the questions should be raised in such a way as brings forth the necessary information on the location, nature, intensity and duration of the pain. In addition, doctors also need to learn whether the pain can be relieved by cold or heat, as well as whether it can be alleviated or exacerbated by pressure.

Patients usually complain of pain in accordance with its location, such as headache, shoulder pain, epigastric pain, hypochondriac pain, abdominal pain, lumbar pain (lumbago), or joint pain (arthralgia).

The quality of pain varies in different diseases or syndromes caused by different mechanisms. Distinguishing the nuances among pains may help doctors find out the corresponding causal factors or mechanisms. However, pain is a subjective symptom, and doctors can only rely upon inquiries to get an idea of the type of pain according to the description given by the patient. In many cases, doctors may need to guide the patients or give them hints when the latter find it difficult to give a proper description. The following are the pains of different qualities frequently encountered in clinical practice:

(1) Distending pain refers to pain that is accompanied by a fullness or distending sensation. It is most likely due to *qi* stagnation.

(2) Pricking or stinging pain refers to pain that is similar to the sensation when something sharp goes into the skin. It is an indicator of blood stasis.

(3) Both scurrying pain and wandering pain refer to pain that occurs without fixed location. But there is a fundamental difference. The former normally occurs in the thoracic and abdominal regions, in which pain travels here and there with no fixed location; the latter often occurs at the limb joints, in which the pain repeatedly changes its location from one joint to another. It is most commonly encountered in wind-dampness arthralgia.

(4) Fixed pain refers to pain that occurs at a fixed location. It may occur in the thoracic and abdominal regions due to blood stasis. It may also take place at the limb joints in the case of cold-dampness arthralgia.

(5) Cold pain refers to pain that is accompanied by a sensation of coldness, which can be alleviated by warmth. It may be due to either obstruction of the meridians by pathogenic cold or deficiency of *yang qi*. The former is excessive in nature, while the latter deficient.

(6) Burning pain refers to pain that is accompanied by a burning sensation, which may be alleviated by cold and aggravated by heat. It is often due to either invasion of the meridians by pathogenic fire or exuberant fire in *yin* deficiency.

(7) Colicky pain refers to a sharp, stabbing pain. It is most likely due to either blockage of *qi* flow by excessive pathogenic factors, or slowing of *qi* flow by pathogenic cold.

(8) Dull pain refers to pain that is slight but long-lasting. It is often due to deficiency of essence and blood, leading to undernourishment.

(9) Weighty pain refers to pain that is accompanied by a sensation of heaviness. It is most likely due to impediment of *qi* flow by pathogenic dampness.

(10) Dragging pain usually occurs at a major pain point connected with pain in the adjacent areas. Since the tendons are believed to be responsible for connection between adjoining areas, and the liver governs the tendons, dragging pain is often associated with liver problems.

(11) Hollow pain refers to pain accompanied by a sensation of hollowness or emptiness. It most commonly occurs in the head due to deficiency of *qi*-blood and essence that causes undernourishment of the tissues.

Headache

As one of the commonest symptoms, headache occurs in very many diseases, both acute and chronic. Here, however, headache is discussed only when it is taken as a patient's chief complaint.

The locations of headaches may include the forehead, as well as the temporal, parietal and occipital regions. Headache caused by external contraction is characterized by sudden onset with a sensation of pulling, throbbing, burning, distending or heaviness. On the other hand, headache caused by an internal injury often makes a patient suffer from a sustained intermittent pain with a slow onset. The sensation of the pain may be hollow, dull or muddy, and the headache may be induced or aggravated by mental and physical stress.

Headaches due to external contraction can be further classified into wind-cold headache, wind-heat headache and wind-dampness headache; and those due to internal injury into liver-*yang* headache, *qi*-deficiency headache, blood-deficiency headache, blood-static headache, and phlegm-turbidity headache.

Typical approaches of inquiry:

91. How long have you been suffering from headaches?
您患头痛多久了?

92. Do they take place suddenly or gradually?
是突然发生的还是慢慢发生的?

93. Which part of the head does the pain come from? Can you point it out to me?
您的头部都有哪里疼痛？指给我看看可以吗？

94. Can you describe your headache? For example, do you feel as if your head were pin-pricked, or as if tightly wrapped with a piece of cloth? Is the pain sharp or dull?

能够形容一下头痛的感觉吗？比如说，像锥刺那样，像用布紧裹那样，是剧烈疼痛还是隐隐作痛？

95. Do weather changes affect your headache? Does your headache get more serious on windy or rainy days?

您的头痛与天气有关系吗？刮风下雨会不会使头痛加重？

96. Is there any correlation between your emotions and headaches?

情绪对您的头痛有影响吗？

97. Do your headaches affect your emotions or your emotions affect your headaches?

是头痛影响您的情绪，还是情绪影响您的头痛？

98. Besides headache, do you have pain elsewhere, such as a sore throat or joint pain?

除了头痛之外，身体还有其他部位的疼痛吗？比如咽痛、关节疼痛。

99. Besides headache, do you feel dizzy with blurred vision?

除了头痛还有头晕眼花的症状吗？

100. Have you ever suffered from a head injury?

头部受过外伤吗？

101. (If yes:) Please describe the injury in detail.
（如果受过）请具体描述一下外伤的经过。

102. Do you sleep well at night? Does your headache affect your sleep?
您夜间睡眠好吗？头痛有没有影响睡眠？

103. Have you noticed any change in your physical condition? Do you suffer from fatigue or unwillingness to participate in physical activity?
近来您的体力有没有变化？有没有感到疲倦乏力，不愿意活动？

104. Does physical exercise alleviate or aggravate your headache?
活动活动身体对您的头痛有影响吗？是使头痛减轻还是加重？

105. Do you feel nauseous during an attack of headache?
头痛发作时有没有恶心、想要呕吐的感觉？

Shoulder Pain

Shoulder pain refers to the pain that comes from a shoulder joint and its surrounding tissues. Shoulder pain usually impedes the activity of the arm, and any forced action of the arm is bound to aggravate the pain. Its common causes include wind-cold affection and phlegm-dampness invasion. It can also be caused by a sprain that leads to blood stasis.

Typical approaches of inquiry:

106. How long have you had this shoulder pain?
您的肩痛有多久了?

107. Does it hurt badly? What kind of pain is it? Slight, dull, pricking (or stinging) or sharp?
疼得厉害吗? 怎么个疼法? 微痛? 隐痛? 刺痛? 还是剧痛?

108. What caused your shoulder pain? Was it coldness or an injury?
最初是怎么疼起来的? 是因为受凉还是由受伤引起的?

109. (If caused by cold:) How and when was the shoulder exposed to coldness?
(如与受凉有关)是怎样受凉的?

110. (If caused by an injury:) How did you injure the shoulder?
(如与受伤有关)是怎样伤着肩膀的?

111. When did it happen?
这是什么时候的事情?

112. Does the shoulder pain have any impact on the movement of your arm? Try to raise your arm.
肩痛对手臂的活动有影响吗？您把手臂向上抬一下试试。

113. Do you feel cold in that shoulder?
患侧的肩部有寒冷的感觉吗？

114. Have you ever applied a hot compress to that shoulder?
有没有试过热敷？

115. (If yes:) Did the hot compress relieve the pain?
（如果敷过）热敷有用吗？

116. What other treatments have you had? Did they help?
有没有用其他方法治疗过？有效吗？

Epigastric Pain (Stomachache)

Stomachache, or epigastric pain, refers to the pain occurring in the upper abdomen adjacent to the precordial region. The main mechanism involves invasion of the stomach by pathogenic cold, injury of the stomach by improper food intake, dysfunction of the stomach due to emotional disorder, and weakness of the spleen and stomach. Invasion of the stomach by cold may induce congealment, and hence pain. Dietary irregularity and improper food intake, including excessive consumption of greasy and sweet food, may lead to stagnation of undigested food in the stomach, hindering the function of *qi* and resulting in stomachache. Anger or depression may hurt the liver, giving rise to *qi* stagnation. Disordered liver *qi* may affect the stomach, leading to stomachache. Internal injury due to overstrain, or weakness of the spleen and stomach due to a prolonged disease may lessen the *yang* of the middle energizer (the spleen and stomach), leading to undernourishment of the stomach. As a result, pathogenic cold is generated internally in the middle energizer, and hence the pain of deficiency cold. Furthermore, long-term stagnation of *qi* usually results in blood stasis. Both *qi* stagnation and blood stasis may impede the function of the middle energizer, leading to stomachache.

In summary, stomachache can be generally classified into deficiency and excess patterns according to the pathomechanisms. Obstruction or stagnation of the *qi* function belongs to the excess pattern, and the resulting pain appears by the rule of thumb: "Wherever there is obstruction, there is pain." On the other hand, deficiency of the spleen and stomach indicates lack of nourishment. Deficiency-pattern pain occurs because "wherever there is undernourishment, there is pain."

Typical approaches of inquiry:

117. (To patients with recent onset of acute stomachache:) When did the stomachache start?
（对近期急性发作者）您的胃痛是从什么时候开始的？

118. Was there any obvious cause for your stomachache? For example, catching a cold, taking a large amount of cold drinks, overeating, or getting into an argument with someone.
您的胃痛有明显诱因么？比如受寒了，或喝了大量冷饮，或暴饮暴食，或因为和人吵架了。

119. Can the stomachache be alleviated by drinking hot water?
喝点热水能使胃痛减轻吗？

120. Does it help to alleviate the pain to warm your stomach area with a hot-water bag?
胃脘部热敷（例如用热水袋）能使胃痛减轻吗？

121. Is the pain alleviated or aggravated when you press the stomach area with your hands?
用手按压胃脘部能使胃痛减轻还是加重？

122. Do you feel nauseous? Have you vomited?
想吐吗？吐过吗？

123. (If yes:) What did you vomit, undigested food or acid fluid? Did you feel better after you vomited?

（如曾呕吐）都吐了些什么？是未消化的食物还是酸水？吐后胃痛有没有减轻？

124. Do you belch often?
打嗝吗？

125. (If yes:) Is there any foul breath along with the belches?
（如打嗝）打嗝时有酸臭的气味冒上来吗？

126. (To patients with chronic stomachache:) Do you have a lot of pressure at work? Do you take meals at regular times?
（对长期慢性患者）您的工作紧张吗？有固定的时间进餐吗？

127. Do you drink alcohol often?
您经常饮酒吗？

128. (If yes:) What kind of alcohol do you drink? And how much do you drink each time?
（如饮酒）喝什么酒？每次喝多少？

129. Do you eat hot and spicy food on a regular basis?
您经常吃辛辣的食物吗？

130. Does your daily diet include a lot of food that is difficult to digest?
平日的膳食中不好消化的食物多吗？

131. Can you describe your stomach pain? Is it a dull pain

that lasts off and on, a burning pain that runs like a fire, or a distending pain that gives you both pain and a stuffiness or fullness sensation?

请您形容一下胃痛的感觉：丝丝拉拉地隐隐作痛？火烧火燎地烧灼疼痛？满闷痞塞地胀痛？

132. Does heartburn or acid reflux come along with your stomachache?

胃痛是否伴有烧心泛酸等症状？

133. Do you have a dry mouth and throat with a burning sensation in the chest, palms of your hands and soles of your feet? Do you also have constipation?

有口燥咽干、五心烦热的情况吗？大便干燥吗？

134. Does your stomachache have anything to do with emotional changes? Is it aggravated whenever you are upset?

胃痛与遇到烦心的事情影响心情有关系吗？每次烦心的时候是不是加重了？

135. Have you ever vomited blood or have you had tarry stools?

有没有吐过血或排出过黑色发亮的大便？

Abdominal Pain

Abdominal pain refers to pain that occurs in the region below the epigastrium and above the pubis. Doctors need to rule out abdominal pain from surgical conditions first. Abdominal pain from non-surgical conditions is usually comparatively mild with mild tenderness and a soft abdomen, and occurs without fixed location. Abdominal pain from surgical conditions, however, is severe, and occurs at fixed location with obvious tenderness, muscular tension and rebound tenderness. In the case of female patients, doctors also need to look into the possibility of gynecological pain, which is associated with menstruation, vaginal discharge, pregnancy and childbirth. Only abdominal pain stemming from internal medical conditions will be discussed here. Improper food intake, emotional disorder and cold-catching are the common factors inducing abdominal pain from internal medical conditions. Clinically, it may be classified into the following syndrome patterns: cold obstruction, dampness-heat, deficiency cold, food stagnation and *qi* depression.

Typical approaches of inquiry:

136. How long have you been suffering from abdominal pain?
您的腹痛有多长时间了？

137. Have you ever suffered from the same pain before?
以前发作过吗?

138. Did it happen suddenly or gradually?
是慢慢发生的还是急剧发生的?

139. Is the pain alleviated when you press the abdomen with your hands?
用手按压腹部能不能使腹痛减轻?

140. Is the pain alleviated when you warm the abdomen with a hot pad?
用热的东西焐焐腹部能不能使腹痛减轻?

141. Do you feel dryness in the mouth? Do you have an urge to drink water?
口干吗? 想不想喝水?

142. Have you had the experience of having a dry and bitter mouth but not wanting to drink water?
有没有口干口苦，却不愿意喝水这种情况?

143. Are you intolerant of a cold environment? Are your hands and feet always cold?
您怕冷吗? 手脚是不是凉的?

144. Do you want to relieve the bowels when you have abdominal pain?
腹痛起来想不想大便?

145. Do you feel relaxed in the abdomen after a bowel

movement, or do you still feel the urge to evacuate?
大便后觉得腹部轻松了，还是仍然感到里急后重？

146. Is there a strong stool odor?
大便有没有特别酸臭的气味？

147. Can you find undigested food in the stools?
有没有许多未消化的食物？

148. Is your abdominal pain alleviated or aggravated after taking food?
吃点东西能使腹痛减轻还是加重？

149. Does your abdominal pain have anything to do with emotional changes? Is it aggravated when something or someone bothers you?
腹痛与精神情绪有什么关系吗？有没有一生气着急腹痛就加剧的情况？

150. Besides pain, do you also have abdominal fullness?
除了腹痛之外，腹胀吗？

151. Do you belch or break wind very often?
有没有嗳气、矢气(放屁)之类的症状？

152. Is your pain alleviated after you belch or break wind?
嗳气、矢气(放屁)之后，腹痛能减轻吗？

Hypochondriac Pain

Hypochondrium refers to either of the superolateral regions of the abdomen, lateral to the epigastric region, and overlying the costal cartilages. Pain occurring in one or both hypochondriac regions is called hypochondriac pain, and is different from chest pain and epigastric pain. Since both the liver and gallbladder meridians pass through the hypochondriac regions, hypochondriac pain is closely associated with liver and gallbladder disorders. Clinically, hypochondriac pain is often caused by emotional stress that leads to liver-*qi* stagnation and even blood stasis, or by either exogenous or endogenous dampness undergoing heat transformation. In all those cases, the pain is due to obstruction of *qi*-blood flow, and hence is excessive in nature. On the other hand, hypochondriac pain can also take place when liver *yin* is deficient due to chronic disease or overexertion and fatigue. In those cases, the pain is due to undernourishment, and hence is deficient in nature. Generally, *qi* stagnation produces distending or scurrying pain, while blood stasis often leads to severe or stabbing pain. As for patients with the deficiency pattern, the pain is mostly chronic and dull.

Typical approaches of inquiry:

153. Please point out the painful area.
请您指出疼痛的部位。

154. It is hypochondriac pain (pain in the ribs). Is the pain on both sides or only on one side?
您这个是胁痛。您是一侧疼还是两侧都疼?

155. How long have you had this pain?
疼痛的时间有多久了?

156. Is it getting worse, better, or staying the same?
是越来越重，还是逐渐减轻，还是没有变化?

157. Can you figure out how the pain started? For example, did it start after a fit of temper?
您能回忆起开始疼痛有什么明显的诱因吗? 比如说是不是与人争吵生气后开始疼的?

158. Can you tell me what the pain feels like? Is it stabbing, distending or scurrying pain? Or just a mild dull pain? Is it fixed in location or does it often move?
您能描述一下疼痛的感觉吗? 是刺痛，胀痛，窜痛，还是隐隐作痛? 是固定在一点上还是常有移动?

159. Is the painful area tender when you press it?
痛处有明显的按压痛吗?

160. Do you feel better when pressing the painful area?
用手按压能使疼痛减轻吗?

161. Is the pain persistent or on and off?
是持续疼痛，还是时轻时重?

162. Is it worse during the day or during the night?
一天之中，是白天疼痛较重，还是夜间疼痛较重?

163. Besides the hypochondriac pain (pain in the ribs), do you have any digestive problems, such as nausea and vomiting?
除胁痛之外，有没有消化方面的障碍，例如恶心呕吐?

164. Does your mouth feel dry and bitter?
感到口干口苦吗?

165. Is there any change in your general condition? Are you feeling weaker? Have you had dizzy spells?
全身状况有什么变化吗? 是不是愈来愈虚弱? 感到过头晕吗?

Lumbago (Lower Back Pain, Low Back Pain)

Lumbago refers to pain in the lumbar region. The causal factors of lumbago are either exogenous or endogenous. The exogenous factors include pathogens like wind, cold, dampness and heat, as well as trauma. The subsequent lumbago is excessive in nature. The endogenous factors include aging and chronic illness, both of which may lead to consumption of kidney *qi*. Lumbago thus caused is deficient in nature. Lumbar pain due to bony lesions of the lumbar vertebrae is outside the category of lumbago, and hence it is often necessary to take an X-ray film of the lumbar vertebrae for diagnosis.

Typical approaches of inquiry:

166. How long have you had this lumbar pain?
您患腰痛多久了?

167. Can you remember how the pain started? For example, after catching a cold, following an injury, due to excessive fatigue, and so on.
知道初起的原因吗? 比如说受凉，受伤，过劳等等。

168. Have you had an X-ray taken of your lumbar vertebrae (lower back bones)?

您照过腰部的X光片吗？

169. Can you describe the pain? Is it a stabbing pain or dull pain or just soreness?
能描述一下是怎么个疼法吗？刺痛？隐痛？酸痛？

170. Do you feel cold or hot in the painful area?
腰痛的地方是发凉还是发热？

171. Is the pain limited to the lower back? Any involvement of other joints?
是单纯的腰痛吗？其他关节也疼吗？

172. Is the pain related to weather changes? Is it worse in cold or hot weather? How about on rainy days?
您的腰痛与天气变化有关系吗？天冷时加重还是天热时加重？阴雨天会不会加重？

173. Are you able to move your lower back? Can you try to move it now?
能活动活动腰吗？请您活动一下看看。

174. Does the pain get worse when you move your back, or the other way around?
活动之后腰痛是减轻还是加重？

175. What happens when you press the lower back with your hands? Is the pain alleviated or aggravated?
用手按按能有效吗？是能使腰痛减轻还是越按越痛？

176. Does the lower back pain affect your walking?

腰痛影响您走路吗?

177. Do you feel your legs are as strong as before while walking?
走路时两条腿和以前同样强劲吗?

178. Is the lumbar pain still there when you lie down?
躺着休息的时候还腰痛吗?

Arthralgia (Joint Pain)

Arthralgia refers to pain in one or more joints, the latter of which may occur simultaneously. A variety of causes may lead to arthralgia. Wind, cold or dampness may invade the body when healthy *qi* is insufficient. Those pathogenic factors may stay in the body for a long period of time to generate heat. When wind, cold, dampness or heat blocks the meridians that control the joint(s), the flow of *qi* and blood to the relevant joint(s) is blocked, and arthralgia occurs. Clinically, doctors need to distinguish among those pathogenic factors and the degree of insufficiency of healthy *qi* (liver-kidney deficiency or *qi*-blood deficiency).

Typical approaches of inquiry:

179. How long have you been suffering from joint pain?
您的关节疼痛已经多久了?

180. Did it start suddenly or gradually?
起病急不急?

181. What triggered the pain? Did you catch a cold or become exposed to a windy environment? Or did you ever get drenched by rain? Or was there any other reason?
关节疼痛是怎么引起的? 受风受寒了? 被雨淋着了? 还是由于什么其他的原因。

182. In which joint or joints do you feel the pain?
都有哪个或哪些关节作痛?

183. (If there is pain in multiple joints:) Is the pain fixed at one location or does it move?
(如有多处关节疼痛)疼痛是固定的还是到处移动的?

184. Do you feel better with a hot compress? How about a cold compress?
患病的关节是敷热毛巾舒服些还是敷冷毛巾舒服些?

185. Is massage of the painful joint helpful? Do you feel better when pressing or rubbing it? Or does the pain get worse if you do so?
痛处能用手按揉吗? 揉揉按按能减轻疼痛, 还是越按揉疼痛越重?

186. There is no redness or swelling of the joint now. Was it reddened and swollen at the outset?
您现在的患病关节不红不肿，开始时红肿过吗?

187. Do you feel feverish?
身上有发热的感觉吗?

188. Are you intolerant of a windy or cold environment?
怕风吹吗? 怕冷吗?

189. Can you move the painful joint? Please try to move it.
疼痛的关节能活动吗? 请您动动看。

190. Is the pain alleviated or aggravated after the movement?
活动后疼痛是加重还是减轻?

Chapter Four
Head, Body, Chest and Abdomen Complaints

Dizziness

Dizziness refers to a vexing sensation of unsteadiness accompanied by blurred vision and a feeling of movement within the head, or an illusion that either the environment or one's own body is revolving. Dizziness may be caused by a variety of factors, such as emotional disturbance, improper diet, hemorrhage, trauma or overstrain. It takes place in the brain. The mechanisms involve insufficient nourishment of the brain, which is caused by deficiency of *qi* and blood or deficiency of liver-kidney *yin*, and upward invasion of the head by liver *yang*, phlegm-fire, or static blood.

Typical approaches of inquiry:

191. How long have you been suffering from dizziness?
您患头晕的毛病多久了?

192. Is this the first time, or has it happened before?
是第一次发作还是过去也发作过?

193. How would you describe your dizziness? Do you have a sensation of fainting, blurred vision or spinning (vertigo)?
请您具体描述一下您的头晕症状，是仅仅感到头部昏沉，看东西昏花，还是觉得天旋地转?

194. Besides dizziness, do you have any other discomfort, for example, headache or ringing in the ears?
除了头晕还同时感到有什么其他不舒服么，例如头痛、耳鸣?

195. Do you also feel any tightness in the chest or nausea?
有没有同时感到胸闷恶心?

196. Is your sense of taste normal? Have you ever felt your mouth to be dry and to have a bitter taste?
嘴里的感觉和往常一样吗? 有没有觉得口干口苦?

197. Do you have any idea of the cause(s) of your dizziness? Is it because of anger, fatigue or any other reason?
您认为您的头晕是什么原因引起的？因为着急生气？工作过于劳累？还是什么其他的原因？

198. Have you ever had a blow to the head?
头部过去受过外伤吗？

199. Do you drink alcohol regularly? Do you think that the dizziness has something to do with that?
您平时饮酒吗？这次头晕和饮酒有没有关系？

200. Does dizziness affect your sleep?
头晕发作后对睡眠有影响吗？

201. (If yes:) How is your sleep affected? Do you feel lethargic or sleepy during an attack of dizziness? Do you sleep peacefully or is your sleep disturbed by stressful dreams?
(如果有的话)是怎样影响的？是昏昏沉沉想睡觉吗？睡得踏实吗？是不是常做噩梦？

202. Do you have a mild temper, or are you easily upset?
您平时的脾气好吗？容易生气着急吗？

203. Has there been any change in your temperament since you started to suffer from dizziness?
患病以来脾气有什么变化吗？

204. Do you have such symptoms as night sweats and a burning sensation in the palms of your hands and soles of your feet?
有没有盗汗和手脚心发热的症状?

205. Do you have such symptoms as memory loss, soreness in the lower back and weakness in the legs?
有没有感到记忆力减退和腰膝酸软的症状?

Deafness and Tinnitus

Deafness refers to partial or total loss of hearing. Tinnitus refers to the perception of a sound where there is no sound in the environment. It may sound like a cicada chirping, a bell ringing, water running, or wind blowing. Of course those are the traditional Chinese descriptions for the quality of tinnitus, which may simply be replaced by hissing, ringing, roaring, or buzzing, respectively. Since tinnitus is usually associated with loss of hearing, or acts as an a priori manifestation of deafness, deafness and tinnitus are discussed together here.

A variety of factors may lead to deafness or tinnitus, via different mechanisms. Pathogenic wind-heat caught during external contraction may invade the auricular orifice, leading to deafness or tinnitus. Anger damages the liver, and so does depression, as they induce liver fire. Liver fire due to either anger or depression may move upward to invade the ears, resulting in tinnitus and deafness. Excessive consumption of alcohol and/or greasy food may induce aggregation of dampness to form phlegm. Stagnant phlegm may turn into fire, and the resulting phlegm-fire may move up and obstruct the ears, leading to impaired hearing and tinnitus. Constitutional weakness, malnutrition due to a prolonged disease, or excessive sexual activity may exhaust the kidney essence, leading to deficient vitality in the sea of marrow (the brain), and consequently tinnitus and deafness. Fatigue and improper food intake, including excessive intake of cold food, may damage the spleen and stomach. Consequently, impaired transformation and transportation ability of the spleen or spleen *yang* deficiency may occur. The former may lead to insufficient supply of *qi* and blood to the auricular orifice, while the latter may lead to insufficient power to transport clear *qi* up to the ears.

Typical approaches of inquiry:

206. How long have you been suffering from tinnitus (hearing noises in your ears)? Did it happen suddenly or gradually?
您感到耳鸣多久了？是突然出现的还是渐渐发生的？

207. Has your hearing ability been affected?
听力有影响吗？

208. (If yes:) Is your hearing ability seriously affected?
(如果有)影响很明显吗?

209. What is the noise like? Is it a hissing sound, or a roaring one like waves breaking on a shore?
耳鸣的声音音调高还是低? 像夏天的蝉鸣还是像潮水那样的轰鸣?

210. Do you hear the noise all the time? Or is it intermittent?
耳鸣的声音是始终如一的，还是有时轻有时重?

211. Is there any difference in the noise between daytime and nighttime? Is it worse at night?
白天和晚上一样吗? 晚上是不是会加重?

212. Did you also have flu symptoms when you first experienced tinnitus?
耳鸣刚开始时有没有感冒的症状?

213. Does it have anything to do with your emotions? Does the attack become more intense when you get upset?
耳鸣耳聋与心情有关系吗? 有没有恼怒生气之后加重的情况?

214. Does loss of hearing or tinnitus have anything to do with your body positioning? Do you suddenly feel hollow when you stand up from a crouching position, while the ringing in the ears and deafness

become worse?

耳鸣耳聋与体位有关系吗？有没有发生过蹲下站起来的时候耳朵里会突然感到空虚、耳鸣耳聋加重的情况？

215. Do you have a blocked sensation in your ear(s), with dizziness, oppression in the chest and coughing with mucus?

耳朵里有没有堵闷的感觉，伴随头昏沉重、胸闷咳嗽多痰的症状？

216. Do you have a sensation of fullness or pain in your ear(s)?

耳朵里发胀或者耳朵里疼痛吗？

217. Does loss of hearing or tinnitus have anything to do with tiredness? Do you feel chronically tired?

耳鸣耳聋的轻重和劳累有关系吗？身体感到倦怠吗？

218. Do you have dizziness with blurred vision or a sore lower back and limp knees?

有没有头晕眼花，腰膝酸软的症状？

Aphthae (Oral Ulcers)

Aphthae are small ulcers in the mouth. There are two types of aphthae: excess and deficient, caused by excess-fire and deficiency-fire, respectively. As a rule of thumb, excess-fire is commonly found in acute cases, and deficiency-fire in chronic ones. Excess-fire is transformed from the overwhelming heat accumulated in the spleen and stomach, which results from the habitual intake of hot and spicy food, and/or alcoholic beverages, as well as barbecued and fried food with strong flavors. *Yin*-deficiency fire normally results from obsessive worrying, and can also be found in the late stage of febrile diseases. In addition, aphthae may also be attributed to spleen-stomach *qi* deficiency, which occurs in those suffering from overfatigue or long-standing maladies.

Typical approaches of inquiry:

219. Did you suffer from any oral ulcer before? Is this the first time or does it happen frequently?
您以前患过口疮吗？这是第一次，还是以前也常常发生？

220. Does it hurt badly? Does it affect your chewing and swallowing food?
疼得厉害吗？影响不影响您吃饭？

221. Have you noticed any particular cause for the ulcer? For example, any unpleasant experience or stress at work that disturbs your rest.
这次长口疮有什么明显的诱因吗？比如说，生活上有不如意的事情或工作特别紧张，影响休息。

222. Can you describe your diet? Do you like hot and spicy food? Do you drink alcohol regularly? Do you eat barbecued food often?
能否说一下您的饮食习惯：喜欢吃辣椒吗？经常饮酒吗？常吃烧烤吗？

223. Does the ulcer affect your sleep?
口疮影响您的夜间睡眠吗？

224. Besides pain, do you have any other abnormal feelings, such as thirst and a craving for cold beverages?
嘴里除疼痛外还有没有其他的感觉，比如口渴、想喝冷饮？

225. Do you have a burning sensation, especially in the palms of your hands and soles of your feet?
有没有发热，特别是手心脚心有没有发热的感觉？

226. How about your bowel movements? Do you often experience constipation or diarrhea?
大便的情况如何？稀软还是干硬秘结？

227. How is your urination? Is it normal? Is the amount reduced, or has the color turned dark?
小便呢？和平时一样，还是尿量减少、颜色加深了？

Gingival Swelling and Pain (Painful Swollen Gums)

Gingival swelling and pain or painful swollen gums refers to redness, swelling and pain of the tissue surrounding the bases of the teeth but without ulceration. Gingival swelling and pain results from fire (heat) , which can be divided into two categories: fire of excess type and fire of deficiency type. The first may be derived from the pathogenic heat in an external contraction of wind-heat, or from stomach heat due to excessive consumption of hot and spicy food. The second originates in the kidney when there is deficiency of kidney *yin*.

Typical approaches of inquiry:

228. How long have the gums been swollen and painful?
您的牙龈肿痛几天了?

229. Was the onset acute or gradual?
是逐渐发生的还是突然发生的?

230. How is the pain? Is it just some endurable mild pain, or an intense pain that you cannot stand?
您的牙龈疼到什么程度? 是只有一点轻疼, 可以忍受, 还是剧烈疼痛, 难以忍受?

231. Do you have any symptoms of infection (external contraction), such as fever and chills?
您有没有发热恶寒之类的感染症状?

232. Do you like hot and spicy food?
您平时喜欢吃辣的吗?

233. Did you eat hot and spicy food just before your gingival pain started?
发病前有没有吃辛辣的食物?

234. Do you feel thirsty and have a craving for cold water or other cold beverages? Are you constipated? Is your breath foul?
您有没有口渴想喝冷饮，大便秘结，口气臭秽等情况?

235. Do you have dizziness, tinnitus, a sore lower back and limp legs, or heat sensation in the chest, palms of your hands and soles of your feet?
您平时有没有头晕耳鸣、腰酸腿软、五心烦热?

236. How about night sweating?
有没有夜间盗汗的症状?

Oppression in the Chest (Chest Tightness)

Oppression in the chest or chest tightness refers to a feeling of obstruction, stuffiness or fullness in the chest. It is usually encountered in excess syndromes and induced by wind-cold or pathogenic heat externally, or by stagnant *qi* and static blood retained in the chest internally.

Typical approaches of inquiry:

237. How long have you been suffering from chest tightness?
您感到胸闷有多久了？

238. Did it start suddenly or gradually?
是突然发生的，还是逐渐发生的？

239. Is your chest tightness serious? Does it bother your breathing just a little bit, or do you have a serious discomfort as if your chest were heavily compressed?
您的胸闷严重吗？只是感到呼吸有些费力，还是很难受，胸膛好像被重物压住了那样？

240. Was there any cause for the tightness, such as a bout of anger?
发生胸闷有什么诱因吗？比如发生了让您愤怒的事情。

241. Have you caught a cold recently? Did you get a fever with chills? Did you cough and have difficulty in breathing?
最近感冒了没有？有没有发热恶寒的症状？有没有咳嗽气喘的症状？

242. Do you cough up sputum (mucus)?
有痰吗？

243. Besides tightness, do you have any pain in the chest?
除了胸闷，胸部疼痛吗？

244. (If yes:) Do you feel the pain in front of the heart or in the lateral side(s) of the chest?
（如有胸痛）是心口部位疼痛还是侧胸部疼痛？

245. Do you also have dizziness and blurred vision along with chest tightness?
胸闷的时候感到头晕眼花吗？

246. I have noticed that you often let out a long deep breath. Do you feel relieved afterwards?
您不时地叹气，是不是长出一口气，胸闷就能减轻些？

Angina Pectoris (Chest Impediment with Heart Pain)

Angina pectoris is called chest impediment with heart pain in Chinese medicine. It refers to a condition marked by brief paroxysmal attacks of smothering discomfort or pain in the middle of the sternum or left submammary area. In mild cases, patients occasionally feel short and mild discomfort in the chest, described as heaviness, smothering, choking, or dull aches. In severe cases, sharp, fleeting pain or intense, suffocative pain is complained of.

The main mechanism involves the impediment of the heart vessel by turbid phlegm, static blood, stagnant *qi* or congealing cold, when healthy *qi* is insufficient. In clinical practice, doctors need to rule out epigastric pain, chest pain and hypochondriac pain. Stomach pain usually occurs in the upper abdomen, and is characterized by a sensation of distension, prolonged duration and local tenderness. Chest pain is often exacerbated by deep breathing, exercising, or turning the body, and is accompanied by respiratory symptoms such as coughing and panting. Hypochondriac pain occurs mostly on the right side and is characterized by tenderness beneath the ribs.

Typical approaches of inquiry:

247. Can you point out the location of the pain?
请您用手指点一下疼痛的部位。

248. Does your pain have anything to do with breathing or turning of the body?
疼痛与呼吸或转动身体有关系吗?

249. Is it connected with coughing?
与咳嗽有关系吗?

250. Is the pain fixed at one location, or does it move?
疼痛的部位是固定不变的还是变来变去不固定的?

251. Is the pain localized at the precordial area and behind the sternum, or does it radiate to other areas?
疼痛只限于胸骨后和心前区，还是向他处放散?

252. (If it radiates:) Which part of the body does it radiate to?
（如放散）都放散到哪里?

253. Is the pain intense? Can you describe the pain? Is it dull, smothering, bloating, burning, stinging, squeezing, or stabbing?
疼痛发作时疼得厉害吗? 请您形容一下疼痛的感觉：隐隐作痛，闷痛，胀痛，灼痛，刺痛，绞痛，痛如刀割。

254. Do you know the cause of each attack? For example, fatigue, emotional agitation, weather changes, or

windy or cold environment?
每次心痛发作有什么诱因吗？比如身体劳累，情绪激动，天气骤变，遇到风寒。

255. Does the pain often attack you on rainy days?
遇到阴雨天会不会容易发病?

256. Do you sweat during an attack?
心痛发作时出汗吗?

257. Are you prone to sweating? Do you sweat even when the weather is not hot at all, when you do not wear enough, or when you are not doing any physical exercise?
平时容易出汗吗？天气不热，衣着不多，不运动时也会出汗吗?

258. Do you have palpitations or shortness of breath?
有心悸气短之类的症状吗?

259. Do you have a burning sensation in the palms of your hands and soles of your feet? Do you sweat at night?
平时有没有手脚心发热和夜间睡眠中盗汗的情况?

260. Are you especially intolerant of coldness? Are your hands and feet usually cold or warm?
平时比别人怕冷吗？手脚经常是热的还是凉的?

261. Do you normally cough up mucus?
平时咳嗽吐痰吗?

Palpitations

The term *palpitations* denotes the awareness of abnormally rapid and strong beating of the heart which leads to uneasiness. Palpitations can be subdivided into fright palpitation and fearful throbbing. Fright palpitation is ascribed to fright or anger, and is characterized by paroxysmal attacks. Fright palpitation is a mild symptom, with the sufferer normally in good health. Fearful throbbing is not caused by fear, but the awareness of severe heart palpitations usually alarms the sufferer. Persisting throughout the day, fearful throbbing can be brought on by fatigue, and even a little overstress may lead to a strong reaction. Fearful throbbing is a severe symptom, and the sufferer is usually in poor health.

Palpitations are either excess or deficient. Deficiency-pattern palpitations are caused by impaired nourishment of the heart due to deficiency of *yin* and *yang* including *qi* and blood. Excess-pattern palpitations may be attributed to disturbance of the heart by sluggish flow of *qi* and blood due to phlegm-heat, retained fluid or static blood.

Typical approaches of inquiry:

262. How long have you been suffering from palpitations?
您感到心悸多久了？

263. Did your first attack of palpitations come suddenly or gradually?
是突然发生的还是渐渐显现的?

264. Have you noticed any cause for your palpitations? For example, have you ever been extremely frightened or extremely tired, or up all night for many days?
发生心悸有什么诱因吗? 比如说受了惊吓，过于劳累，或者接连熬夜，没有睡好觉。

265. Is there any change in your physical condition? Are you as energetic as before? Or do you feel tired?
体力有什么变化没有? 和以前一样精力旺盛吗? 有没有感到疲倦?

266. Is there any change in your mental condition? Are the palpitations making you listless?
体力有什么变化没有? 和以前一样精力旺盛吗? 有没有感到疲倦?

267. Have you had anything wrong with your chest? For example, have you had a choking sensation in the chest or a chest pain?
胸口有什么异常的感觉吗? 比如说胸口发闷或者有时候感到疼痛。

268. Do you sleep normally at night? Do the palpitations make you sleepless or awaken you with nightmares?
夜间睡觉好吗? 有没有因为心悸而失眠，或者做噩梦?

269. In comparison with the past or with others, are you particularly averse to cold or heat? Normally, are your extremities (hands and feet) cool or warm? Do you always have a feverish feeling in the palms of your hands and soles of your feet?

与病前比较或者与其他人比较，您是怕冷还是怕热？平常时，您的手脚是凉的还是手脚心发热？

270. Do you have any change in sweating? Are you more liable to sweating than before?

出汗有什么变化吗？有没有比以前容易出汗？

271. (If so:) Do you sweat in the daytime or at night?

（如果出汗多了）是白天活动时容易出汗，还是夜间睡觉时出汗？

272. (If sweating during sleep at night:) Does the sweating stop as soon as you wake up?

（如果夜间睡觉时出汗）醒来是不是就不出了？

273. Is there any change in the volume of your urine? Has your daily volume of urine increased or decreased?

小便有变化吗？比以前多了还是少了？

274. Besides palpitations, do you have any other problems? For example, dizziness or constipation?

除心悸之外，还有什么其他不适吗？比如说头晕目眩或者大便秘结。

Cough

Cough is the most commonly encountered symptom in lung diseases. It is due to failure of *qi* to descend and be diffused in the lung and the consequent reverse upward movement of *qi*. Dysfunction of the lung may also be induced by disorders of other viscera.

In clinical practice, doctors need to know the details about the coughing that a patient complains about, such as its onset, duration, time, rhythm, quality of sound, and other accompanying symptoms as well as exacerbation factors. Except for the quality of its sound, which may be distinguished by listening, other information needs to be acquired via inquiries. Of the accompanying symptoms, expectoration of sputum is the most relevant.

There are two main categories of cough-cough caused by external contraction and that due to internal injury. The former is acute with short duration of illness, and may be accompanied by chills, fever, and runny nose. The latter is, on the other hand, chronic and recurrent, and may be accompanied by shortness of breath. Clinically, externally contracted cough can be classified into wind-cold cough, wind-heat cough, wind-dryness cough and lung-heat cough. Accordingly, cough due to internal injury can stem from lung *qi* deficiency, lung *yin* deficiency, accumulation of phlegm-dampness in the lung, and liver-fire invasion of the lung.

Typical approaches of inquiry:

275. How long have you been suffering from coughing? Did it happen before?
您咳嗽多久了？以前有咳嗽的老毛病吗？

276. (In an acute case with no history of recurrent cough:) Is your coughing caused by a flu? Did you have a stuffed-up and running nose before the coughing started?
（对于新近发病，过去无反复咳嗽的患者）您的咳嗽是不是感冒引起的？咳嗽之前有没有鼻塞流涕的症状？

277. (In a case of flu:) Do you have a fever? How about chills and sweating?
（如有感冒）发烧了吗？全身发冷吗？有没有出汗？

278. Do you have a dry, itchy or sore throat? To what extent is your throat sore? Does it hurt when you swallow?
喉咙发干、发痒，还是感到疼痛？疼到什么程度？咽东西疼吗？

279. Do you cough to expel mucus (sputum)? Does the mucus (sputum) come out easily?
有痰咯出吗？容易咯出吗？

280. Do you cough up a lot of sputum?
痰多吗？

281. Is your sputum thin or sticky (viscous)? Is it white or yellow in color?
痰是稀薄的还是粘稠的？是白色的还是黄色的？

282. Have you coughed up blood or bloody sputum?
有没有痰中带血的情况？

283. Have you experienced dryness in the mouth, nose, lips and throat? So dry that drinking water is not helpful at all?
有没有感到口、鼻、唇、咽全都十分干燥，连饮水也无济于事？

284. Does your chest hurt when you cough?
咳嗽时胸痛吗？

285. (In a chronic recurrent case:) Is your cough persistently recurring? (Does your cough come and go repeatedly?) Does it seem to be getting worse?
（对于长期反复发病的患者）您的咳嗽是反复发作的吗？是不是越来越重？

286. (In the case of repeated aggravation:) Was there any reason for the aggravation each time? For example, do you easily catch a cold even when there is only a mild change of weather?
（如果是反复加重）每次加重有什么诱因吗？比如说，您特别容易感冒，天气稍有变化，您就会感冒。

287. Does the coughing fit come back when you are tired,

angry or worried?
身体劳累了或者生气着急了会不会使咳嗽再犯?

288. When do you cough the most heavily during the day?
一天之中什么时候咳嗽最重?

289. Have you had a weight loss accompanied with your coughing ?
除了咳嗽之外，体重有没有减轻?

290. Does your cough change with your emotions?
咳嗽的轻重与情绪有关吗?

Dyspnea (Panting)

Dyspnea or panting refers to difficult or labored respiration. In severe cases, the patient has to breathe through the mouth, with the shoulders lifted and the nostrils flaring, and is unable to lie flat. In clinical practice, doctors need, first of all, to distinguish between deficiency and excess patterns of dyspnea. The excess pattern is characterized by acute onset, coarse, deep and prolonged respiration with particular difficulty in exhalation. The deficiency pattern shows the common features of gradual onset, shortness of breath relief with deep inspiration and worsening with physical activity, and weak voice. Dyspnea of the excess pattern normally takes place in the lung, where accumulated pathogenic *qi* impairs the ventilating function. Obstruction of the lung by wind-cold, phlegm-heat, or phlegm turbidity is commonly encountered. Dyspnea of the deficiency pattern occurs in the lung and/or the kidney. In other words, deficiency of either the lung *qi* or the kidney *qi* may lead to dyspnea. Dyspnea may also be induced by retained fluid that attacks the heart and the lung. In this case, both palpitations and dyspnea are the chief complaints of the patient.

Typical approaches of inquiry:

291. How long have you been suffering from dyspnea (difficult or labored breathing)? Did it start recently, or a long time ago?
您患气喘病多久了？是最近几天才有的，还是已经很久了？

292. (In acute cases:) Did you catch a cold right before you found trouble breathing?
（对于新病气喘者）发生气喘之前有没有受凉感冒？

293. (If the patient caught a cold:) Did you have fever with chills?
（如曾感冒）当时有没有恶寒发热？

294. Do you still have a fever? Are you sweating?
现在还有没有发热？身上出汗吗？

295. Do you cough to bring up mucus (sputum)?
您咯痰吗?

296. Is the amount of sputum large? Is it easy to cough up the sputum?
痰量多还是少? 容易咯出来吗?

297. Do you feel relieved right after you cough up sputum? Or do you still have a blocked feeling in the chest afterwards?
痰咯出来是不是立刻就痛快了，还是仍然觉得胸中不爽快?

298. (In chronic cases) Are you apt to sweat with no obvious cause? Do you find that you cannot tolerate a windy environment? Do you easily catch colds?
（对于久病气喘者）您平时常出虚汗吗? 是不是害怕吹风? 容易感冒吗?

299. Do you have a sore lower back and limp legs? Are your hands and feet always cold?
您平时感到腰酸腿软，手脚发凉吗?

300. Do you often have palpitations?
您经常感到心慌心跳吗?

301. (In cases of edema of the lower limbs:) How long have you been suffering from edema of the lower limbs? Did edema come along with difficult breathing?

（对于下肢浮肿者）您的腿肿多久了？与气喘同时发生的吗？

302. Did you notice any change in your urine volume at the onset of edema?
腿肿的同时，小便量有变化吗？

Wheezing (Asthma)

Wheezing, also called asthma, refers to a condition marked by paroxysmal episodes of labored breathing accompanied by a whistling sound. The main reason is the presence of retained phlegm in the lung. The onset is usually precipitated by a change in weather, improper food intake, emotional disorder or overfatigue. When the retained phlegm is agitated, blockage of the air passage with spasm occurs, and hence the wheezing (asthma). To identify its syndrome patterns, doctors need to distinguish between cold phlegm and heat phlegm in acute cases, and determine whether there is deficiency of the lung, the spleen or the kidney when dealing with patients at the stage of remission.

Typical approaches of inquiry:

303. Is this the first time you have suffered from such an

asthmatic symptom? Or has it happened before?
您是第一次发生哮喘，还是以前就曾经发作过?

304. Is there an obvious cause that you know of for the wheezing? For example, catching a cold in cold weather or eating something unusual? Or have you ever suffered a mental trauma or become overtired?
您发生哮喘有什么明显的诱因吗? 比如天气凉，受寒了? 吃了什么特殊的食物? 精神受了什么刺激? 身体过于疲劳?

305. Are you allergic to anything?
您对什么东西过敏吗?

306. (To patients suffering an attack:) Do you feel cold or hot now?
（对于发作期的患者）您现在觉得身上发冷还是发热?

307. Do you have mucus in your throat? Can you cough it up easily?
喉咙里有痰吗? 容易咳嗽出来吗?

308. (If not:) Is it because there is not much mucus or because it is too sticky to bring up?
（如不易咳出）是因为痰少还是因为痰稠不容易咳出?

309. Are you thirsty? Do you have a desire to drink cold or hot water?

口渴吗？想喝凉的还是热的？

310. (To patients in remission:) Are you often short of breath? (Do you often experience shortness of breath?)
（对于缓解期患者）您平时感到气短吗？

311. Do you have a sputum problem all the time? Is it a lot?
您平时有痰吗？痰多吗？

312. Do you catch cold easily?
您容易感冒吗？

313. Is your wheezing connected with colds?
每次哮喘发作与感冒有关吗？

314. How is your appetite in general?
您平时的食量如何？

315. Are you prone to diarrhea?
容易腹泻吗？

316. How is your physical condition when you are not wheezing?
您不犯病时体力如何？

317. Do you have a sore lower back and limp legs, dizziness, or tinnitus?
您有腰酸腿软，头晕耳鸣的症状吗？

Acid Reflux (Acid Regurgitation)

Acid reflux or acid regurgitation refers to a condition in which the acid content of the stomach flows backward up the esophagus and the pharynx, followed by re-swallowing of the gastric contents, leading to a sour taste in the mouth along with heartburn, a burning feeling in the lower part of the sternum. Acid reflux may be induced by emotional changes as well as improper food intake. Clinically, patients with liver *qi* invasion of the stomach, food stagnation, or cold-dampness obstruction often have such a complaint.

Typical approaches of inquiry:

318. How long have you been suffering from acid reflux? Does it happen frequently?
您犯吞酸的毛病有多久了？常犯吗？

319. Do you know what caused the acid reflux that you are now suffering from? For example, was there anything unpleasant at work or in your everyday life, that upset you? Did you eat or drink too much?
这次犯病有什么诱因吗？比如说工作和生活上发生了什么令您生气的事情，或是饮食上有过暴饮暴食等。

320. Besides acid reflux, do you have any other digestive problems? For example, have you had an impaired appetite sometimes, or even total loss of appetite?

Have you suffered from belching, sometimes with foul breath?
您除了吞酸，还有其他消化方面的症状吗？比如不想进食甚至厌食，嗳气甚至嗳气酸腐。

321. How is your appetite? Does acid reflux affect it?
您的食欲如何？吞酸影响您的食欲吗？

322. Do you have any unusual feeling in your stomach? For example, a replete or burning sensation?
胃里有什么异常的感觉没有？比如闷胀或烧灼的感觉。

323. Do you have a dry mouth or throat? Do you have a bitter taste in your mouth?
有没有感觉到口干咽干，甚至口中发苦？

324. Do you feel any discomfort in your rib areas (hypochondriac regions)?
胸胁部有什么不适没有？

Eructation (Belching)

Eructation refers to the act of expelling gas noisily from the stomach out through the mouth. Occasional belching, especially after meals, is not a pathological symptom. However, frequent belching may result from liver *qi* invasion of the stomach or deficiency of spleen-stomach *qi*. Belching with the release of an unpleasant odor is often due to food accumulation in the stomach. Belching is different from hiccupping. The former originates in the stomach, producing a sound that lasts longer, while the latter comes from the pharynx and larynx, producing a sound that is sharp and short.

Typical approaches of inquiry:

325. How long have you been suffering from frequent belching (burping)? Did it start recently, or has it been like that for a long time?
您频繁嗳气（打嗝儿）多久了？是新得的病还是长期就有？

326. Normally, do you belch (burp) only after meals, or regularly without any reason?
一般是吃完饭后嗳气（打嗝儿），还是平时就时常嗳气（打嗝儿）？

327. Is your belching accompanied by an odor, such as sour and fetid?
打嗝儿有没有气味？比如酸味、臭味。

328. How do you rate your appetite from "very good" to "poor"?
饮食情况怎么样？是食欲很好，还是不想吃饭？

329. Do you have any discomfort in the epigastric or hypochondriac regions (in the stomach or rib areas)?
胃脘胁肋这些部位有什么不舒服吗?

330. Is your discomfort alleviated after belching (burping)?
嗳气（打嗝儿）之后不舒服的感觉能减轻吗?

331. Do you have normal bowel movements? Do you have constipation or expel stools that are abnormally smelly?
大便正常吗? 有没有便秘或者大便的气味异常酸臭?

332. Is there any change in your general health condition? For example, do you feel tired easily?
身体情况有变化吗? 比如感到疲倦乏力吗?

Epigastric Upset (Gastric Discomfort)

Gastric discomfort refers to an unpleasant feeling somewhat between hunger and fullness or between pain and comfort in the epigastric region. It often occurs with other symptoms such as belching, acid reflux, nausea, retching, and epigastric pain. Improper food intake, stomach heat, stomach cold, as well as disharmony of the liver and stomach may all induce epigastric upset or gastric discomfort.

Typical approaches of inquiry:

333. How long have you had discomfort in your stomach?
您感到胃里不舒服，嘈杂不安有多久了？

334. Do you know what triggered off the discomfort? Overeating or eating spoiled food? Or did it start as a result of an emotional disturbance?
有什么诱因吗？暴饮暴食，吃多了？吃变质的食物了？还是因为什么事情生气了？

335. Does your stomach discomfort have anything to do with food temperature? Does it get worse after eating cold food and better after eating warm food? Or just the opposite?
您胃里嘈杂不舒服的感觉和饮食冷热有关系吗？是吃冷的东西加重，吃热的减轻，还是相反，吃冷的感觉好些？

336. Besides discomfort in your stomach, do you have acid reflux?
除了嘈杂不舒服之外，向上反酸吗？

337. Do you feel nauseous? Have you ever vomited?
感到恶心吗？有没有吐过？

338. (If yes:) Did your stomach feel better after vomiting?
（如呕吐过）呕吐过后胃里有没有舒服些？

339. Do you often belch? Is there unpleasant breath when you belch?
打嗝儿吗？打上来的嗝儿有没有不好闻的气味？

340. Has anyone complained that you have foul breath? Or have you found that you have foul breath by yourself?
自己或者别人闻到您口中有臭味吗？

341. Besides stomach discomfort, do you feel oppression or fullness in the chest? Or do you have a pain in your rib areas?
除了胃部不舒服外，胸中有没有感到胀闷，两胁有没有疼痛？

Nausea

Nausea refers to the unpleasant feeling of an imminent desire to vomit. Both stomach cold and stomach heat may induce nausea. Nausea induced by the former usually lasts for a long time, during which deficiency manifestations appear. Nausea induced by the latter demonstrates the opposite characteristics: short course with no deficiency manifestations. Nausea in the case of stomach *yin* deficiency is often followed by violent vomiting, and usually occurs in patients at the late stage of a febrile disease or after major surgery. Any food or drink may be immediately vomited up upon intake.

Nausea in the case of disharmony of the liver and stomach results from invasion of the stomach by stagnant liver *qi*. It may be accompanied by the symptoms that manifest liver *qi* stagnation, such as a sensation of oppression in the chest, hypochondriac pain, bitterness in the mouth, and dryness in the throat.

Nausea in a case of dyspepsia is usually attributed to gluttony. Patients who suffer from dyspeptic nausea usually have a history of overeating and overdrinking. Besides nausea, other dyspeptic symptoms may appear, such as belching with foul breath and acid reflux.

Typical approaches of inquiry:

342. How long have you been suffering from nausea?
您感到恶心有多久了?

343. Did it happen suddenly or gradually?
是突然发生的，还是逐渐发生的?

344. Is there any obvious reason for your nausea? For example, did you get into an argument or a fight and get upset or even furious? Or did you eat improper food or overeat?
出现恶心的症状有什么明显的原因吗? 比如说病前曾与人生气争吵，或暴饮暴食吃坏了。

345. Did you vomit? Was your vomiting violent?
呕吐过吗？吐得厉害吗？

346. Besides nausea, do you also have a stomachache? Do you have other symptoms such as acid reflux and stomach discomfort?
除了恶心，还有胃痛吗？还有吞酸、嘈杂这类的不适吗？

347. Has your nausea anything to do with the warmth or coldness of food and drinks? For example, do you feel better after taking warm soup or a cold drink?
与饮食冷热有关系吗？比如说喝点热汤舒服些呢，还是喝点冷饮好些呢？

348. Has there been any change in your appetite? How do you describe the change? Is it a mild reduction or a total loss of appetite?
对食欲有影响吗？怎么样的影响?是稍有影响还是影响严重，根本不愿进食？

349. Do you have any abnormal sensation in the mouth, such as a bitter or sour taste?
嘴里感觉到有什么异常的味道吗？比如苦味、酸味。

350. Are your stools loose or hard and dry?
大便是稀溏的还是干结的？

Retching

Retching is vomiting without vomitus or only with a little amount of mucus. Retching is different from both nausea and vomiting. Nausea is merely the feeling of being about to vomit, producing neither sound nor vomitus, while vomiting produces both. Retching, however, only produces a sound. Retching results from a failure of stomach *qi* to descend, occurring in patients with stomach heat, stomach cold, liver depression, or food stagnation.

Typical approaches of inquiry:

351. When did you start to feel nauseous? Did you vomit? Did anything come out?
您是什么时候开始想吐的？吐了没有？有东西吐出来吗？

352. What do you think is the cause? Is it because you ate some contaminated food or because something unpleasant made you upset?
您认为是什么原因引起的？是因为吃了不干净的食物，还是因为有什么事情影响了您的情绪？

353. Do you feel dryness in your mouth while retching? Do you have an urge to drink water?
感到口渴吗？想不想喝水？

354. Do you have any discomfort in the pit of your stomach?
心窝处有什么不舒服吗?

355. Do you have any discomfort in your stomach? Do you have any abdominal pain?
肚子难受吗? 疼吗?

356. Is there any special odor accompanying retching? For example, any unpleasant sour odor?
有没有特殊的气味干呕上来? 例如酸臭的气味。

Vomiting

Vomiting refers to involuntary oral expulsion of gastric contents, which is induced by reversed upward movement of stomach *qi*. Very often, nausea precedes or accompanies vomiting.

A variety of factors may induce vomiting, such as contraction of the six external pathogenic factors, internal injury, improper diet, disharmony of emotions, and weakened functions of viscera and bowels. Vomiting occurs in both excess and deficiency syndrome patterns. In the excess patterns vomiting is induced via the invasion of the stomach by external pathogenic factors, improper diet, retained phlegm-fluid, stagnant *qi*, etc. In the deficiency patterns, the stomach loses proper nourishment due to deficiency of *qi*, *yang*, or *yin*. In any case, vomiting is caused by disharmony of the stomach functions that makes the stomach *qi* move upward in a reverse manner.

Typical approaches of inquiry:

357. How long have you been suffering from vomiting?
您从什么时候起开始呕吐的?

358. How many times have you vomited?
您吐过几次?

359. (In acute cases occurring in winter:) Do you have a cold? Besides vomiting, do you have chills and fever? Do you have any headache or body pain?
(对于冬日新发的病例)有没有感冒? 除呕吐外还发冷、发烧、头痛、身痛吗?

360. (In acute cases occurring in summer:) Have you caught heatstroke (acute discomfort due to summer-heat)? Besides vomiting, do you have fever, headache and general malaise?
(对于暑夏新发的病例)您有没有中暑? 除呕吐外还感到发烧头痛，全身不适吗?

361. (In acute cases in general:) Did you eat anything unusual, for example, contaminated food or food that

you are allergic to?
（对于一般新发的病例）您吃了什么特殊的食物吗？比如不干净的食物或者让您过敏的食物。

362. (In acute cases in general:) Did you eat too much of some food? Was it cold or warm?
（对于一般新发的病例）是不是什么东西吃多了？是凉的还是热的？

363. (In chronic recurrent cases:) Do you expel a large quantity of vomitus every time you vomit? Do you vomit part of the gastric contents or do you have to empty your stomach completely?
（对于长期反复呕吐的病例）您每次呕吐出来的东西多吗？是吐一部分，还是必须全部吐空？

364. Do you feel thirsty after vomiting? Are you able to drink water shortly after vomiting?
吐过之后感到口渴吗？能够立刻喝水吗？

365. Do you know the cause of the most recent vomiting? Was it that you were upset? Did anything unpleasant happen before the vomiting?
您知道这次呕吐是什么原因引起的吗？是不是因为生气着急引起的？呕吐前有什么不愉快的事情发生吗？

366. (To women of child-bearing age:) When was your last period?
（对于育龄女性）您上次来例假是什么时候？

Chapter Five
Changes in Appetite and Abnormal Taste in the Mouth

Anorexia (Loss of Appetite)

Anorexia or loss of appetite refers to lack of a desire to eat or subjective feeling of insipidity with reduced food intake. Anorexia occurs frequently along with spleen and stomach diseases. There are many factors that may induce anorexia, one of which is emotional disturbance, which may induce liver stagnation that invades the stomach, leading to anorexia. Overeating or intake of food that is hard to digest may also lead to anorexia via dyspepsia. Long-term over-consumption of greasy and sweet food may injure the spleen and stomach via aggregation of dampness-heat, and result in anorexia. Anorexia may emerge as a sequel to other diseases. For example, in the late stage of febrile diseases, even after the elimination of pathogenic heat, consumption of stomach *yin* may give rise to intractable anorexia. Long-term fatigue may hurt the *qi* in general, particularly spleen and stomach *qi*, and eventually lead to anorexia. In the most serious case, patients may not feel hungry at all. Prolonged deficiency of spleen and stomach *qi* or long-term intake of improper cold food and drink may lead to deficiency-cold of the spleen and stomach, which in turn exacerbates anorexia. Prolonged deficiency of spleen *qi* may also hurt kidney *yang*, leading to a complex syndrome in which anorexia occurs along with the symptoms of kidney *yang* deficiency.

In summary, the syndrome patterns of anorexia commonly encountered clinically include liver-*qi* invasion of the stomach, dampness-heat accumulation in the spleen and stomach, deficiency of stomach *yin*, *qi* deficiency of the spleen and stomach, deficiency-cold of the spleen and stomach, *yang* deficiency of the spleen and kidney, and dyspepsia.

Typical approaches of inquiry:

367. When did the anorexia start?
您的食欲从什么时候开始减退的，有多久了?

368. Do you feel that the food you liked before is tasteless or tastes insipid now, and does not whet your appetite? Or do you feel that you do not want to eat at all?
您是胃口变了，感觉过去喜欢吃的东西淡而无味，不合您的胃口了？还是根本不想吃饭？

369. What made you anorexic? Did you ever overeat to the point of stomach pain?
最初是什么原因引起的？是不是因为某一次吃多了，吃坏了胃？

370. Did you have a liking for greasy food? Did you take it often?
您以前是不是特别喜欢吃油腻的食物？经常吃吗？

371. Do you take meals regularly and on time?
您平时的饮食规律吗？能不能按时进餐？

372. Do you make sure that each meal is warm enough when you take it? Or are you unable to do that because conditions do not allow it? Or do you simply prefer cold food and beverages?
您平时能顿顿吃上热饭热菜吗？是吃不上热的，还是您自己喜欢吃凉的、喝凉的？

373. Besides anorexia, do you have other digestive problems, such as nausea, vomiting, belching, acid reflux (regurgitation), or abdominal distention (sensation of fullness in the abdomen)?

除了食欲不振之外，还有没有其他的消化方面的症状，比如恶心、呕吐、嗳气、吞酸、腹胀等等？

374. (If the patient has belching and acid reflux:) Have you sensed some special odor in your breath, for example, acid and foul?
（如有嗳气吞酸的症状）反上来的气体有特殊的气味吗？比如说酸臭味。

375. Do you feel stomachache or abdominal pain?
有没有胃痛或腹痛？

376. (If yes:) When you press the painful area is the pain alleviated or worsened? Did you try to warm the painful area with a hot-water bag? Did the warming help?
（如有的话）按一按、压一压能减轻还是加重？用热水袋焐焐能减轻吗？

377. Has anorexia been affecting your physical condition? Are you prone to feeling tired?
食欲不振对您的体力有影响吗？平时容易感到疲倦吗？

378. How about your bowel movements? Do you have diarrhea?
大便正常吗？有没有腹泻？

379. (If yes:) Can you describe in detail how abnormal they are? For example, do you have soft stools and

feel that they are not completely expelled from the body after a bowel movement? (Do you still have an urge to empty the rectum after you have a bowel movement?) Or do you have loose stools, in which you can find undigested food?
（如有腹泻）能具体描述一下腹泻的情况吗？比如，是不是大便不成形，而且大便后觉得没有排清爽仍想排便？还是便溏，而且便中可以发现没消化的食物残渣？

380. How many times do you have diarrhea in a day? Do you have diarrhea only once a day and early in the morning?
一天腹泻几次，或是只有每天清晨腹泻一次？

Polyphagia (Excessive Appetite)

Polyphagia refers to increased appetite or excessive hunger. It describes a situation in which one feels hungry shortly after intake of food, regardless of the size and frequency of the intake. Diabetes is considered to be one of the main causes of polyphagia, and polyphagia is one major symptom of diabetics. That is why in traditional Chinese medicine diabetes is called consumption-thirst, in which consumption refers to polyphagia.

Polyphagia is considered to be caused by rapid digestion of food promoted by excessively intensive stomach fire. Clinically, doctors need to distinguish between the syndromes of pure stomach heat and stomach heat with spleen cold (or strong stomach and weak spleen), both of which are manifested by polyphagia. However, polyphagia of the latter is often complicated by diarrhea.

Typical approaches of inquiry:

381. Can you describe your appetite on a daily basis? How many meals do you take, and how much do you eat at each meal?
请您具体描述一下您平时的饭量。一天吃几顿，每顿吃多少？

382. Are your meals particularly large? How much more do you eat than other people?
您的饭量特别大吗？与您周围的人比较，您比他们多吃多少？

383. Are you prone to snacking?
您常吃零食吗？

384. If you eat less than usual, do you feel hungry? Is the hunger unbearable?
如果让您少吃，您会觉得饥饿难忍吗？

385. Are you often thirsty? Do you tend to drink a lot of

water?
您常感到口渴吗？喝水多吗？

386. Are your stools formed, soft, or loose?
大便是成形的还是不成形甚至腹泻吗？

387. Do you tend to put on weight because of eating a lot?
您吃得这么多，体重增加得很快吗？

388. You do not look overweight at all. Have you lost some weight recently?
我看您并不胖，体重近来有没有减轻？

389. If you keep losing weight despite an increased appetite, have you ever checked your blood glucose level?
如果体重反而在减轻，您有没有检查过血糖？

Abnormal Taste in the Mouth

Abnormal taste in the mouth always accompanies other symptoms, so it is usually ignored or complained of as a minor symptom. Nevertheless, quite a number of patients still come to clinics for it only. Abnormal taste in the mouth includes tastelessness, as well as bitter, sweet, sour, salty, astringent, sticky or greasy taste in the mouth.

A feeling of tastelessness is an indication of partial or total loss of ability to detect flavor.

Typical approaches of inquiry:

390. Besides a feeling of tastelessness, do you also feel a sticky and greasy coating in your mouth?
除了口淡，口中有没有发粘发腻的感觉?

391. Has there been any change in your appetite?
您的食欲有没有受影响?

392. How about your bowel movements? Are they normal? Have you experienced constipation or diarrhea?
您的大便情况如何? 正常吗? 是便秘，还是便溏?

393. Are there any other digestive symptoms, such as abdominal distention (fullness) or nausea?
有没有其他消化道的症状，比如脘腹胀满或恶心欲吐等?

394. Do you also feel tired, with a dry mouth and throat, and short of breath?
有没有咽干口燥、气短乏力之类的伴随症状?

A bitter taste in the mouth is an indication of heat syndrome.

Typical approaches of inquiry:

395. Do you also feel dryness in your mouth and throat?
您有没有口干咽干的症状?

396. Do you often feel thirsty? Do you crave cold drinks?
是不是感到口渴? 想喝冷饮吗?

397. How about the quality of your sleep? Do you ever find it hard to get to sleep?
夜间睡眠如何? 有没有失眠的现象?

398. How about your appetite? Has there been any change in it?
食欲怎么样? 有没有受影响?

399. Do you feel dizzy or have headaches while there is a bitter taste in your mouth?
有没有同时感到头晕头痛?

400. Have you noticed any change in your temperament? For example, do you find that you have a harder time controlling your temper?
性情有什么变化吗? 比如，有没有比以前容易发怒生气?

401. Do you feel pain somewhere in your body? For example, headache or distending pain (pain with a full-

ness sensation) in the rib areas?
身上有什么疼痛的地方吗？比如说头痛或者胁肋胀痛。

402. Has there been any change in your urination? For example, has the color of your urine turned dark, or is urination painful?
小便有什么变化吗？比如说尿液色深或排尿时疼痛。

A sweet taste in the mouth is an indication of stomach and spleen problems, such as dampness-heat in the spleen and stomach or both *qi* and *yin* deficiency of the two visceral organs.

Typical approaches of inquiry:

403. Besides the sweet taste in the mouth, do you have other abnormal sensations? For example, thirst, or sticky and greasy taste?
口中除有甜味外，还有没有其他异常感觉？例如口干思饮或口中粘腻不爽。

404. How is your appetite? Is it normal?
食欲如何？正常吗？

405. (If not:) Do you have a poor appetite? Or do you always feel hungry even though you take plenty of food?
（如不正常）是不思饮食，还是多食易饥？

406. How about your bowel movements? Are they normal?

大便是否正常?

407. (If not:) Are you prone to constipation or diarrhea?
（如果不正常）是干结还是稀溏?

A sour taste in the mouth is an indication of liver fire due to liver *qi* stagnation or disharmony between the liver and the stomach. A putrid and sour taste indicates food stagnation.

Typical approaches of inquiry:

408. Besides the sour taste, do you also suffer from acid reflux (regurgitation) and belching?
您除了口中有酸味之外，还有没有吞酸嗳气之类的症状?

409. Are you aware of only a sour taste in the mouth? Does a foul taste come with it?
您的口中是只有单纯的酸味，还是混有馊腐的味道?

410. Have you noticed any change of emotion? For example, are you more agitated or easily depressed than usual?
您近来的情绪有什么变化吗? 比如说比以前急躁或心中懊恼不爽。

411. Any change of appetite? Is your appetite better or worse than before, or as good as before? Are there any occasions when you do not feel like taking any food (eating) at all?

食欲有变化吗？和以前一样，还是吃饭不香？有没有根本不想吃饭的情况？

412. Do you suffer from belching, and even belching with an acidic and foul odor from the mouth?
有没有嗳气的症状甚至嗳气酸腐？

413. Any change of bowl movements? Normal or abnormal?
大便有什么变化吗？是正常还是不正常？

414. (If abnormal:) Do you suffer from constipation or diarrhea?
（若不正常）是干结，还是溏薄？

A salty taste in the mouth is an indication of kidney deficiency. Inquiries may help distinguish between kidney-*yin* and kidney-*yang* deficiency.

Typical approaches of inquiry:

415. Besides the salty taste, do you also feel dryness in the mouth and the throat?
您的口中除有咸味外，还有没有咽干口燥之类的感觉？

416. Do you have symptoms like a sore lower back or limp knees?
您有没有腰膝酸软的症状？

417. Do you often feel coldness in your hands and feet?

Or do you feel heat in the palms of your hands and soles of your feet?
您感到手脚发凉还是手脚心发热?

418. How is your quality of sleep at night?
夜里睡眠如何?

419. Do you have to urinate during the night? How frequently?
您起夜吗? 夜间排几次尿?

A feeling of astringency in the mouth (as if eating an unripe persimmon) indicates either damage to fluid due to dryness-heat or *qi* and fire rising up in reverse.

Typical approaches of inquiry:

420. Can you describe in detail the sensation in your mouth?
您能不能具体形容一下您口中感觉到的味道?

421. Have you been under a lot of pressure at work recently? Do you often stay up late?
您最近工作忙吗? 有没有经常熬夜?

422. Are you also aware of dryness and bitterness in your mouth?
您是否同时也感到口干口苦?

A sticky and greasy sensation in the mouth, or even inability to detect the flavor of any food is an indication of spleen-dampness. Inquiries may help distinguish between cold-dampness and heat-dampness.

Typical approaches of inquiry:

423. Please describe the sensation in your mouth.
请您具体形容一下口中的感觉。

424. Can you taste the flavors of food?
您吃东西有滋味吗?

425. Is your appetite as good as before?
饭量和以前一样吗?

426. Do you always feel thirsty? Do you crave water or other beverages when you are thirsty?
您感到口渴吗? 想不想喝水?

427. How about your bowel movements and urination?
您的大小便情况怎么样?

Xerostomia (Dryness of the Mouth) and Thirst

Although dryness of the mouth is closely related to thirst, they are actually different symptoms. Xerostomia or dryness of the mouth refers to a feeling of insufficient saliva in the mouth, while thirst describes a craving for liquid. So patients with xerostomia do not necessarily need to drink water, while those with thirst have a craving to do so. Generally speaking, thirst is a symptom of exuberant fire, and a dry mouth is a symptom of insufficient body fluids. Xerostomia and thirst are two common clinical symptoms, especially in patients suffering from febrile diseases. However, in the case of febrile diseases, xerostomia and thirst can only be treated as accompanying symptoms. The following inquiries are appropriate for patients whose chief complaint is either dry mouth or thirst. Febrile patients are excluded, since their chief complaint is usually fever.

Patients with lung dryness and those with *yin* deficiency often complain of thirst. Patients with water retention that impedes upward delivery of fluids to the mouth may complain of xerostomia only, but not thirst. Drinking water produces immediate discomfort responses, such as nausea or even vomiting.

Typical approaches of inquiry:

428. Do you have a dry mouth? If so, do you have a craving to drink water or other beverages?
您感到口干吗？想不想喝水？

429. (To patients who complain of dryness of the mouth but do not have a craving for water or other beverages:) Don't you want to drink water at all or do you

feel uncomfortable after drinking?
（对于口干渴而不欲饮者）您是根本不想喝水还是喝了难受？

430. Do you vomit what you drink right away?
喝了会不会立刻吐出？

431. (To dry-mouth patients who have a craving for water:) When do you feel thirsty the most during the day?
（对于口干渴而欲饮者）您在一天什么时候感到口渴最厉害？

432. Do you feel dryness all over your body, for example, in the nose, lips and skin?
您有没有感到全身都干燥，比如鼻干、唇干、皮肤干燥等等？

433. Do you cough? Do you have mucus in your throat?
您咳嗽吗？喉咙里有痰吗？

434. Do you have a burning sensation in the palms of your hands and soles of your feet?
您有没有手脚心发热的感觉？

Halitosis (Foul Breath)

Halitosis, a condition of having breath with an unpleasant smell, is also called foul breath. It may be self-sensed or sensed by others, indicating the presence of heat in the viscera and bowels. Stomach-heat-induced foul breath is usually accompanied by thirst and desire to drink cold water or other beverages, oral ulcers, constipation and darkened urine. Food-stagnation-induced foul breath is usually accompanied by acid regurgitation, belching, and epigastric distension, and patients with such foul breath often have a history of dyspepsia. Foul breath may also be induced by phlegm-heat accumulated in the lung, and in such cases, patients may have sputum with a fetid odor and distending pain in the chest. Different types of foul breath are thus readily distinguishable.

Typical approaches of inquiry:

435. Do you like to eat hot and spicy food?
您平时喜欢吃辛辣的食物吗?

436. Did you have any experience of overeating before the onset of this condition?
您发病前是否暴饮暴食过?

437. Besides foul breath, do you have any other discomfort in the mouth, such as pain in the tongue or gums?

您除了口臭外，嘴里还有什么别的不适吗？比如舌头疼痛或牙龈疼痛。

438. Do you often need to expectorate?
您咳嗽吐痰吗？

439. What is the color of the sputum? Does it smell bad?
痰是什么颜色的？有没有臭味？

440. Is your digestion normal?
您近来消化好吗？

441. Has there been any change in your appetite?
食欲有没有变化？

442. Do you feel abdominal distension (fullness sensation in the abdomen)? Do you belch or break wind abnormally?
有没有腹胀、打嗝、放屁等异常情况？

Chapter Six
Sleep Disorders and Mental Impairments

Insomnia (Sleeplessness)

Insomnia or sleeplessness refers to inability to obtain adequate sleep. It may be manifested in different forms: difficulty in getting to sleep, tendency to wake during the night and difficulty in getting back to sleep, or tendency to sleep on and off throughout the night. In severe cases, patients may stay awake all night. A variety of factors contribute to insomnia, and the pathogenesis may involve imbalance between either *yin* and *yang* or *qi* and blood in some visceral organs, such as the liver, the gallbladder, the spleen, the stomach, and the kidney. Of all those imbalances, uneasiness of the mind (the heart) is considered to be the "ultimate" factor in insomnia. Anxiety, worry, fear and fright may all lead to insomnia when a certain level of uneasiness is reached. Clinically, inquiry may help discriminate the conditions of the viscera in terms of insufficiency or excess. In excess conditions, the common patterns include mental agitation by heart fire, liver fire, or phlegm-heat, while in deficiency conditions mental uneasiness may be due to *yin* deficiency with exuberant fire, deficiency of both the heart and the spleen, and *qi* deficiency of the heart and the gallbladder.

Typical approaches of inquiry:

443. How long have you been suffering from insomnia?
您患失眠多久了?

444. Please describe how your insomnia occurs and how serious it is. Do you find it hard to fall asleep or easy to wake up during the night and hard to return to sleep? Have you ever been "up all night"? And how often is that?
请您具体描述一下失眠的情况和程度：是入睡困难还是睡而易醒不能再睡?有没有彻夜不眠过？这样的情况常发生吗?

445. Do you often have dreamful sleep? Are you often woken early by nightmares? (To mature males only:) Have you ever had wet dreams?
睡眠中做梦多吗？常被噩梦惊醒吗？（对中青年男性）梦遗吗？

446. Do you know the cause(s) of your insomnia? For example, are you disturbed by something unpleasant, problematic, or alarming during work or life?
您自己知道失眠的原因吗？比如说，在工作上或生活上发生了气愤不快的事情、难以解决的事情或担心害怕的事情。

447. Have you noticed any changes in your emotions since you began to have problems sleeping? For example, are you getting more and more easily agitated? Or do you get angry more often? Or are you increasingly worried about anything?
您患失眠以来，心情有什么变化吗？比如说，您是不是越来越容易感到烦躁？是不是遇事容易生气，或者感到恐惧，总怕有祸事降临。

448. Have you noticed any changes in your memory because of insomnia? Do you forget things more easily?
失眠对您的记忆力有明显的影响吗？是不是容易忘事了？

449. Are you aware of any dryness or a bitter taste in your

mouth?
您感到口干口苦吗?

450. If you do not sleep well at night, do you feel tired the next day?
您夜里睡不好觉，白天感到困倦吗?

451. Do you suffer from dizziness or a headache when you wake up?
睡醒后感到头晕或头痛吗?

452. How about your appetite? Do you experience chest congestion, stomach distension (bloating or fullness sensation), acid reflux (regurgitation), or belching?
您的食欲怎么样? 有没有胸闷、胃胀、泛酸、嗳气之类的不适?

453. How about your bowel movements recently? Do you suffer from constipation or diarrhea?
您的大便情况近来怎么样? 有没有便秘，还是大便溏薄?

454. Any changes in urination? For example, do you have to get up frequently at night for urination, and have you observed that your urine has become darker?
小便有变化吗? 比如夜间尿多或者尿色变深。

455. Do you have a heat sensation in the palms of your hands and soles of your feet?
您感到手、脚心发热吗?

456. Do you have any other discomfort or symptom(s)?
您还有什么其他不适?

457. Do you often take sleeping pills?
您常服用安眠药片吗?

458. (If yes:) Are the sleeping pills effective?
(如果服用)安眠药有效吗?

Somnolence (Sleepiness or Drowsiness)

Somnolence refers to a state of being ready to fall asleep regardless of daytime or nighttime. In many cases, somnolent patients may be able to go back to sleep shortly after waking. Somnolence is different from clouding of consciousness. Unlike those who suffer from clouded consciousness and experience a chronic sensation of mental clouding, somnolent patients are mentally clear when awake.

Somnolence may be due to encumbrance of the spleen *yang* by dampness or deficiency of both the heart and the spleen. It may also be due to decline of kidney *yang* or insufficiency of kidney essence. In the case of head trauma, blood stasis in the brain may also give rise to somnolence.

Typical approaches of inquiry:

459. How many hours do you sleep every day?
您一天能睡几个小时？

460. When you get up, do you feel high-spirited or drowsy?
睡觉醒过来感到精神焕发还是仍然昏沉欲睡？

461. Can you fall asleep in the daytime? And under what circumstances? For example, can you fall asleep during a meeting or a conference, or while you are watching TV?
白天犯困吗？在什么情况下您就能睡着？比如开会、听报告、看电视等等。

462. Do you experience headaches or dizziness while you are awake?
您在清醒时有没有头晕头痛之类的症状？

463. Have you noticed any change in your memory?
记忆力有什么变化吗？

464. Are you as energetic as before at work?
工作的精力和以前一样吗？

465. Is there any change in your power of reasoning and analysis?
思考问题的能力有变化吗？

466. Do you think that you have less tolerance of coldness than others?

您比其他人怕冷吗?

467. Are your hands and feet always cold or warm?
平时手脚是凉的还是热的?

468. How are your lower back and legs? Have you experienced conditions such as soreness in the lower back and edema of the legs?
您的腰腿怎么样? 有没有腰痛或者小腿浮肿等情况?

469. Do you have a good appetite? Has there been any change in it?
胃口好吗? 饭量与病前比较有什么变化吗?

470. Has there been any change in your sense of taste? For example, have you been aware of any lack of taste or stickiness and greasiness in your mouth?
嘴里的感觉有什么变化吗? 比如说口中无味或口中粘腻。

471. (To female adults:) Have you experienced anything abnormal in your periods?
(针对中青年女性)您的月经有什么异常的情况吗?

472. Did you experience any head trauma before the onset of drowsiness (before you first suffered from drowsiness)?
发病前头部受过外伤吗?

473. Do you have any other abnormal sensations?
您自己感觉还有什么其他异常?

Amnesia (Forgetfulness)

Amnesia refers to loss of memory, which leads to forgetfulness in daily life. To be discussed here is the type of amnesia induced by the decline of the brain function, during which the memory is gradually lost. Congenital amnesia is excluded.

The heart stores the spirit and governs all the mental activities, while the kidney stores essence and communicates with the brain. The spleen governs thought and ideation. So amnesia is closely associated with conditions of the heart, the spleen and the kidney. *Qi*-blood deficiency of the heart and spleen, essence deficiency of the kidney, and disturbance of the heart by phlegm-turbidity may all lead to amnesia.

Typical approaches of inquiry:

474. When did you discover that your memory was not as acute as before?
从什么时候开始您感到记忆力不如以前了?

475. Are you losing memory very fast?
您的记忆力减退发展得快不快?

476. Do you have a hard time recalling events in the remote past, or those of the recent past, or even things you just did?
是对远期发生的事情想不起来了,还是对近期的事情甚至刚刚做过的事情容易忘记?

477. Do you sleep well at night?
您夜里睡眠好吗?

478. Do you feel energetic during the daytime?
白天精神好吗?

479. Have you felt any bout of dizziness or tinnitus recently?
近来有没有头晕耳鸣之类的症状?

480. Have you experienced other symptoms such as oppression in the chest and nausea?
近来有没有胸闷恶心之类的症状?

481. Have you noticed any change in your sex life?
您感到性生活方面有什么变化吗?

Chapter Seven
Constipation, Diarrhea and Urination Complaints

Constipation

Constipation is a morbid condition due to abnormal conveyance function of the large intestine. It is characterized by undue hardening of the feces so that unusual straining is required to achieve defecation, or by lengthening the interval between bowel movements to three or four days or more. Generally, constipation can be classified into two categories:

constipation of excess type and that of deficiency type. The former is most likely caused by either accumulated heat in the stomach and intestines that consumes the intestinal fluids, or stagnant *qi* that impedes the conveyance function of the large intestine. The latter can be encountered in any of the deficiency conditions of *qi*, blood, *yin* or *yang*, which lead to either deficiency of the intestinal fluids or reduced ability of conveyance.

Typical approaches of inquiry:

482. I know it is embarrassing to verbalize the conditions of your bowel movements, but it is important if I am to solve your problem.
我知道描述大便的情况不雅，但对于解决您的问题却至关重要。

483. How long have you been suffering from constipation?
您患便秘有多久了？

484. How frequent are your bowel movements? Once a day, once every two or three days?
几天大便一次？每天一次还是两三天一次？

485. (If the interval between bowel movements is over three days:) Is it because you do not have an urge to empty your bowels, or you have the urge but cannot do so. (You do not have any sense of rectal fullness

or you have such a sense but cannot empty your bowels.) Which is your situation?
（如果三天以上才排便一次）是根本没有便意，还是有便意但排不出来?

486. Can you explain why you have difficulty in defecation? Are your stools too dry and hard, or are they not hard but you do not have the strength to pass them out? Which is your situation?
能不能解释一下为什么排便困难? 是因为大便干燥坚硬，排不出来，还是大便不硬，却没有力量排出来?

487. Do you feel relief or fatigue after a bowel movement?
大便之后感到舒畅还是感到全身乏力?

488. If there is no bowel movement for several days, do you experience any rumbling in the stomach (bowel sound), breaking wind, abdominal distention (fullness sensation), or abdominal pain?
几天不排便时有没有肠鸣矢气，腹胀腹痛等不适?

489. Does constipation affect your appetite?
便秘对您的食欲有影响吗?

490. Are you aware of dryness in your mouth and throat?
有没有感到口干咽干?

491. Have you or people near you sensed foul breath from you?

别人能闻到您口臭或者您自己能感觉到口臭吗?

492. Do you prefer hot or cold drinks?
您喜欢喝冷饮还是热饮?

493. Are your limbs often cold? Have you ever felt coldness or pain in the stomach?
平时有没有四肢发凉，腹中也感到发冷和疼痛的现象?

494. How is the quality of your sleep? Besides constipation, do you also have problems sleeping?
您的睡眠怎么样? 除便秘之外，您的睡眠有障碍吗?

495. Do you have any other discomfort?
除了上面的问题之外，您还有什么其他不适?

Diarrhea

Diarrhea refers to abnormally frequent intestinal evacuations with more or less liquid stools. A variety of factors may cause diarrhea, including external contraction of wind, cold, summer-heat, heat or dampness, as well as internal injuries due to intake of improper food or emotional disorder. Dysentery, which is also accompanied by abnormally frequent fecal output, is mainly identified by bloody-and-purulent stools and tenesmus, and thus will not be discussed here.

Clinically, diarrhea is subdivided into two categories in accordance with its onset and duration, namely acute diarrhea and chronic diarrhea. The former term denotes diarrhea that has a sudden onset and short course, while the latter is marked by long duration or frequent recurrence. In most cases, acute diarrhea is caused by cold-dampness, dampness-heat or improper food, and chronic diarrhea is mainly due to spleen deficiency. One major cause that leads to chronic diarrhea is emotional disorder. This may induce liver *qi* stagnation, which restricts the spleen function. Another major cause is kidney *yang* deficiency, which leads to insufficient warmth of the spleen. Diarrhea of this type usually occurs early in the morning, and is sometimes called fifth watch diarrhea, or diarrhea before dawn.

Typical approaches of inquiry:

496. How long have you been suffering from diarrhea? Is it a sudden and acute case, or has it been like this for a long time?
您腹泻几天了？是新患的病还是已经患病很久了？

497. (To acute diarrhea patients:) Do you happen to know the reason for your diarrhea? Did you eat food that might have been spoiled? Did you catch a cold? Or did you overeat?

（对于急性腹泻者）您自己知道这次您腹泻的原因吗？有没有吃不干净的东西？有没有受寒？有没有暴饮暴食，吃多了？

498. Did you catch a cold, accompanied by symptoms like chills, fever and headache?
有没有受凉感冒，恶寒、发热、头痛？

499. Do you have abdominal pain?
肚子痛吗？

500. (If yes:) Is your pain alleviated when you press your abdomen or warm it with a hot-water bag?
（如有腹痛）用手按压、用热水袋焐，能使疼痛减轻吗？

501. Do your stools give off an unusual odor? Do they smell worse than usual or even give an extremely fetid smell like rotten eggs?
大便的臭味有什么异常吗？有没有特殊的臭味，比平时大便要臭？还是像臭鸡蛋那样臭味浓重还夹杂着一股腐臭的味道？

502. Do you have painful and burning sensation in the anus when you empty your bowels?
排便时肛门感到灼热疼痛吗？

503. (To chronic diarrhea patients:) Has your diarrhea been off and on, or has it lasted continuously?
（对于慢性腹泻者）您的腹泻是时好时坏，还是一直不好？

504. Is there any particular reason for each attack of diarrhea or aggravation of it? Does it have anything to do with improper food, emotions, or any other abnormal factors that you can think of? Or is there simply no reason?
每次腹泻发作或加重有什么原因吗？与饮食有关？与情绪有关？有没有其他原因，还是没有任何原因？

505. Do you have diarrhea at any particular time during the day? For example, do you have diarrhea at dawn every day and feel comfortable afterwards?
每天腹泻有没有固定时间？比如清晨天未亮时必然腹痛腹泻，泻完就舒服了。

506. Are there a lot of food dregs in the stools?
排出的大便中有很多未消化的食物吗？

507. Are you more intolerant of coldness than others? Are your hands and feet always cold or warm?
您平时比别人怕冷吗？手脚是凉的还是热的？

508. Has chronic diarrhea had any impact on your health? For example, do you have chronic fatigue or a sore lower back and limp knees?
长期腹泻对身体有什么影响吗？比如感到身体疲倦乏力，或者腰膝酸软。

Frequent Urination (Urinary Frequency)

Frequent urination or urinary frequency means voiding urine at abnormally brief intervals. Patients with such symptom may urinate for up to dozens of times a day. Frequent urination may be subdivided into deficiency and excess patterns. Among the deficiency patterns, *yang* deficiency is predominant, and is manifested as long voiding of clear urine. On the other hand, dampness-heat is always the leading cause among urinary frequency of the excess pattern. In this case, urgent and/or painful urination, as well as other discomfort during urination, are accompanying symptoms.

The body fluids are controlled by the lung, the spleen and the kidney, disorders of any of which may lead to frequent urination.

Typical approaches of inquiry:

509. You say that you have to urinate too many times a day. Can you please tell me how many?
您说每天排尿次数太多，一天要排尿多少次?

510. How long have you been suffering from frequent urination?
您有小便频数的症状多久了?

511. (To those with acute onset:) Do you have any discomfort when you urinate? Do you feel any pain?

When you have the urge to urinate, can you control the process?
（对于新近发病者）排尿时有什么不适的感觉吗？感到疼痛吗？有尿意时能憋得住吗？

512. Did you have any discomfort in your lower abdomen before you started to have the urination problem?
排尿次数增多前，您排尿时小腹处有什么不舒服吗？

513. Have you had a fever recently?
最近发过烧吗？

514. Are there any changes in the appearance of the urine? For example, has it become turbid?
尿液有什么变化吗？比如变得混浊了。

515. (In chronic cases:) Is there any change in the urine amount on each voiding? Is it (the urine amount on each voiding) less than before?
（对于发病已久者）每泡尿量与以往排尿正常时比较有变化吗？是不是减少了？

516. Have you ever lost control of your bladder?
有没有发生过憋不住尿以致失禁的情况？

517. Do you have a burning sensation in the palms of your hands and soles of your feet? Or do you feel cold in your hands and feet?
您感到手心脚心发热还是手脚发凉？

518. Are you less tolerant of coldness than before?
全身有没有比以前怕冷?

519. Do you have dizziness and tinnitus as well?
有没有同时出现头晕耳鸣的症状?

520. Is your appetite reduced? Are you less energetic than before? Have you been getting tired more easily?
食量有没有减少? 精神是不是比以前差了? 有没有感到愈来愈容易疲倦?

521. Do you often cough? Do you bring up mucus when you cough? Do you feel shortness of breath?
您平时咳嗽吗? 咯痰吗? 有没有感到气短?

Nocturia (Excessive Urination at Night)

Nocturia refers to excessive urination at night in terms of both frequency and amount. Patients with such symptom urinate at a normal level during the day time, but need to wake up for urination during the night more than two or three times, and the amount of urine discharged at night is more than one fourth of the total amount of urine discharged during a day and night. In some extreme cases, the total amount of the urine released in the night is close to or even more than that in the day.

Nocturia is an immediate consequence of disorders of the kidney and bladder. Since daytime is *yang*, and nighttime is *yin*, nighttime is considered to be a period in which the *yin* overtakes the *yang*. Nocturia is generally attributed to kidney *yang* deficiency. In some cases, however, deficiency of the spleen *yang*, which fails to replenish the kidney *yang*, may lead to *yang* deficiency of both the spleen and the kidney. And when this happens, nocturia may also ensue. The major difference in symptoms between patients with kidney *yang* deficiency and those with spleen-kidney *yang* deficiency lies in that the latter usually have low body weight, poor appetite and loose stools, in addition to the common symptoms of kidney deficiency such as sore lower back and tinnitus.

Typical approaches of inquiry:

522. When did you start to notice that you were waking at night frequently to urinate?
您从什么时候开始注意到夜尿增多?

523. During the daytime, do you dribble urine right after you urinate?
您白天小便有没有尿后余沥点滴不尽的现象?

524. Is there any change in your hearing ability?
听力有什么变化吗?

525. Do you have tinnitus?
有没有出现耳鸣的症状?

526. Have you had a good appetite in recent years? Have you lost weight?
您近年来胃口一直很好吗? 身体有没有比以前消瘦?

527. Have your stools turned loose?
大便有没有变稀?

Incontinence of Urine

Although both incontinence of urine and enuresis denote involuntary discharge of urine, there is a fundamental difference between them. While enuresis occurs only during sleep, incontinence of urine takes place even when awake. Post micturition dribble is a term that describes the involuntary discharge of residual urine after urination. In this case, the process of urination is still under the patient's control. So the concept of incontinence of urine includes neither enuresis nor dribbling after urination.

Incontinence of urine of the deficiency pattern is most commonly encountered in clinical practice. Deficiency cold of kidney *qi*, *qi* deficiency of the lung and spleen, and deficiency of liver-kidney *yin* can all disturb *qi* transformation of the bladder and disable its function in containment of urine. Incontinence of urine can also occur due to dampness-heat of the bladder, which is an excess pattern. In this case, dampness-heat runs down to the bladder and disables its functions.

Typical approaches of inquiry:

528. How long have you been suffering from involuntary discharge of urine?
您患小便失禁的毛病有多久了?

529. Did it start suddenly or gradually?
是突然发生的还是逐渐发生的?

530. Do you leak urine all the time, or only under certain circumstances, for example, when you cough or sneeze?
是随时都有尿液流出，还是在一定情况下才有尿液流出? 比如在咳嗽时或者打喷嚏时。

531. Did you catch any respiratory illness such as persistent coughing before you perceived the urination problem?
发生小便失禁之前，您有没有得过呼吸系统的疾病，长时间地咳嗽过吗?

532. Do you have a burning or stinging pain when urine comes out of the urethra (the canal that carries the urine out of the body)?

尿液流出时尿道有灼热刺痛之类的症状吗？

533. Do you urinate more frequently than before?
排尿的次数有没有增多？

534. Is the amount of urine on each voiding increased or decreased?
每次的尿量比没有小便失禁时是增多了还是减少了？

535. Do you have a sore lower back and limp legs?
有没有腰酸腿软之类的症状？

536. Do you feel colder in your hands and feet compared with the past? Or do you feel warmer? Is there a burning sensation in the palms of your hands and soles of your feet? Do you have night sweats?
您感到手脚比以前凉了还是热了？有没有手、脚心发热，夜间盗汗的情况？

537. Since you first had the urination problem, have you noticed any other changes in your health, such as your energy and appetite?
自从小便失禁以来您的身体状况有什么其他变化吗？比如体力和饮食方面。

Post-Micturition Dribble

Post-micturition dribble refers to involuntary discharge of residual urine after urination. Patients who are physically weak due to a chronic disease may have such a symptom. In those cases, kidney deficiency may lead to bladder cold, which impairs the function of *qi* transformation in the bladder, and eventually lead to post-micturition dribble. Improper food intake and fatigue may weaken the middle *qi*, resulting in a reduction in its lifting power. Without sufficient lifting power, the residual fluids may run downward, leading to post-micturition dribble. Acute post-micturition dribble, accompanied by a painful sensation and difficulty in urination, is usually due to dampness-heat in the bladder.

Typical approaches of inquiry:

538. How long have you been dribbling after urination? Did it occur recently or some time ago?

    您患有尿后点滴不尽的病症有多久了？是新近发生的还是由来已久了？

539. (In acute cases:) Besides dribbling after urination, do you have difficulty in urination and a burning sensation in the urethra?

    （对于新病患者）除了尿后点滴不尽外，有没有排尿困难和尿道灼痛？

540. Is your urine clear or cloudy?
您排出的尿液一般是清亮的还是混浊的?

541. (In chronic cases:) Do you dribble every time or only sometimes after urination?
（对于久病患者）是每次排尿后都有余沥不尽，还是有时有，有时没有?

542. Besides the dribbling, do you have a sore lower back or cold limbs?
您除了尿后点滴不尽外，有没有腰背酸软、四肢发凉等不适?

543. Is your appetite not as good as before? Do you have loose stools?
有没有食量减少，大便稀溏的症状?

Chapter Eight
Male Sexual Dysfunction

Seminal Emission

Seminal emission refers to involuntary discharge of semen without sexual intercourse. For an adult male, it is a normal physiological condition to experience seminal emission once or twice a month. Only frequent emission along with other associated symptoms is considered as a pathological state. Deficiency of kidney *qi* or exuberant fire in both the heart and the kidney are two major pathways to frequent seminal emission. The former may lead to insufficient power to contain semen, and the latter may induce a downward movement of dampness-heat to agitate the storage of the semen.

Other terms such as *nocturnal emission*, *wet dream* and *spermatorrhea* all describe different situations of frequent seminal emission. Nocturnal emission refers to involuntary discharge of semen during sleep. The term *wet dream* denotes an erotic dream accompanied by seminal emission, and is borrowed to describe the situation in which seminal emission occurs with an erotic dream. Spermatorrhea means abnormally excessive emission of semen without a dream, and is commonly referred to as an abnormal seminal emission while awake, as opposed to nocturnal emission.

Typical approaches of inquiry:

544. How often do you have a nocturnal emission on a monthly basis?
您每月遗精几次?

545. Do you feel any discomfort the following day?
遗精后身体感到有什么不适吗?

546. (If yes:) Do you feel sleepy or annoyed during the daytime?
（如遗精后感到不适）白天感到困倦，还是感到心烦?

547. Have you had a seminal emission during the daytime?
白天清醒时有精液流出过吗?

548. Can you recall whether the emission came with or without a (an erotic) dream?
夜间遗精是做梦中发生的，还是没做梦就发生了？

549. Do you sleep well at night? Do you have a hard time falling asleep or are you easily awakened from sleep?
夜间睡眠好吗？入睡困难或容易醒转吗？

550. Do you sweat abnormally?
出汗有没有异常？

551. (If yes:) Do you have night sweats? Or do you sweat even with slight physical exercise or simply for no reason, during the daytime?
（如有异常汗出）是不是夜间盗汗？还是白天自汗，稍微一活动或是没有任何原因就出汗？

552. Has there been any impact on your general health? For example, do you feel tired often? Or do you have other symptoms such as loss of memory, poor appetite or unintentional loss of weight that makes you look markedly thinner?
身体有没有明显的影响？比如精神疲惫，记忆力减退，食欲不振，体重下降，明显比以前消瘦。

553. Do you often have a feeling of dryness or bitterness in the mouth?
平时有没有口干或口苦的感觉？

554. Is there any change in your urination, such as darkening of urine or a burning sensation accompanying urination?
小便有变化吗？比如尿色加深，排尿时尿道有热感。

555. Is your external genital region always wet? Do you feel itchy as well?
阴部是不是经常潮湿？有没有瘙痒的情况？

Impotence

Impotence refers to an abnormal state of an adult male characterized by inability to copulate because of failure to have or maintain an erection. Excessive sexual life in adulthood and abnormally frequent masturbation in adolescence or premature sexual life may lead to impotence via damaging the essential *qi* and weakening the fire of the life gate. Anxiety damages the heart and the spleen, leading to deficiency of both *qi* and blood. If *qi* and blood in the thoroughfare vessel is affected, impotence may occur. Fear damages the kidney and may drive the kidney *qi* to move downward. When this persists for a period of time, impotence may occur. The liver governs the tendons and tendon-like tissues, the confluence of which frames the male copulatory organ. Disorders of the emotions may induce constraint of liver *qi*, which may impair the erectile function of the penis. If dampness-heat pours down to the genitalia, impotence may also take place.

In summary, impotence may be subdivided into different syndrome patterns such as declined fire of the life gate, deficiency of both the heart and spleen, fear-induced kidney damage, depression of liver *qi*, and down-pouring of dampness-heat.

Typical approaches of inquiry:

556. How long have you been suffering from this erectile problem?
您患阳痿多久了?

557. You have lost the ability to erect, or you can erect but the erection cannot last for long. Which is your case?
是完全不能勃起，还是能够勃起但不持久?

558. How long have you been married? When did you start to have the erectile problem?
结婚几年了? 从什么时候阳痿的?

559. Did you have the habit of masturbation when you were an adolescent?
年少时有手淫的习惯吗?

560. Before the problem started, how often did you have sex on a weekly basis?

没有阳痿之前，每周有几次性生活?

561. Did something ever frighten you in the middle of having sex?
有没有同房时因为什么突发事情而受到惊吓过?

562. Did you notice any emotional (psychological) change after you discovered your erectile problem? For example, do you feel sluggish all the time? Have you become more sensitive and easily become nervous? Have you become depressed and easily got upset or even furious?
出现阳痿后，心情有什么明显的改变吗? 比如精神萎靡不振，或者是胆怯多疑，或者是心情抑郁，烦躁易怒，等等。

563. Has there been any change in your appetite?
食欲受影响了吗?

564. Has there been any change in the quality of your night sleep?
夜间睡眠有没有受影响?

565. Are you more intolerant of a cold environment? Are your hands and feet always cold? Do you have a sore lower back and limp legs?
有没有全身怕冷，手脚发凉，腰膝酸软的现象?

566. Have you ever found your scrotum wet and smelly?
有没有发现阴囊经常潮湿臊臭的情况?

Premature Ejaculation

Premature ejaculation refers to the condition in which ejaculation of semen occurs prior to or immediately after penetration of the vagina by the penis, followed by softening of the penis, so that normal sexual intercourse cannot be completed. Causes and mechanisms for premature ejaculation vary with different circumstances. Invasion of dampness-heat, frenetic stirring of ministerial fire, loss of containment of kidney essence due to kidney *qi* deficiency, and loss of arresting power of the heart and spleen due to heart-spleen *qi* deficiency may all lead to premature ejaculation. An irritable or depressive temperament easily leads to unhappiness, the accumulation of which may turn stagnant *qi* into heat and damage the liver. The heat may pour down to the essence chamber (the place where semen is stored), resulting in premature ejaculation. Constitutional deficiency of *yin*, damage to *yin* due to febrile diseases, exhaustion or damage of genuine *yin* due to over-fatigue, or exhaustion of *yin* essence due to excessive sexual life may give rise to exuberance of the fire. The frenetic stirring of ministerial fire may agitate the essence chamber, and the heat may drive seminal fluid to flow, leading to premature ejaculation. Insufficient natural endowment, acquired physical weakness, fatigue-induced damage to kidney *qi*, or excessive sexual activities including frequent masturbation and premature sexual intercourse may lead to deficiency or exhaustion of kidney *qi*. Consequently, the essence or the seminal fluid cannot be held up within a desired period of time, resulting in premature ejaculation. Impairment of the heart blood by excessive anxiety and damage to the spleen-stomach due to improper food intake and overfatigue may induce deficiency of both the heart and the spleen, leading to decreased arresting power. Hence, seminal fluid may leak out easily.

Typical approaches of inquiry:

567. How many years have you been married?
您结婚几年了?

568. How long have you suffered from PE (premature ejaculation)?
您有早泄的问题多久了?

569. Did you have a normal sex life before you got PE? How many times per week did you have sex?
在发生早泄之前您的性生活正常吗? 每周有几次房事?

570. How is your temperament? Do you get upset easily?
您是怎么样性情的人? 平时容易生气发脾气吗?

571. Did you have any experience of self-manual stimulation of the genital organs (masturbation) when you were young?
您年少时有过手淫吗?

572. (If yes:) Did you do that occasionally or frequently?
（如有）是偶尔还是很频繁？

573. Have you been getting less energetic than before PE? Do you feel tired all the time?
出现早泄以来体力有所下降吗？是不是经常感到体倦乏力？

574. Do you have soreness in the lower back and weakness in the knees?
有没有腰膝酸软的症状？

575. Do you usually have palpitations?
平时感到心悸吗？

576. Do you often experience dizziness or tinnitus?
常头晕耳鸣吗？

577. (If tinnitus:) Is the pitch of your tinnitus high or low?
（如有耳鸣）是高频率的还是低频率的？

578. Has your sexual desire been affected? Do you have stronger or weaker sexual desire?
在性生活的要求方面有什么变化吗？欲望更强了还是淡漠了？

579. How about the quality of your sleep? Do you have a hard time falling asleep, and are you awakened easily?
睡眠怎么样？常常失眠、容易惊醒吗？

580. Is your appetite reduced? Do you have abdominal fullness or loose stools?
有没有食欲减退，腹部有胀感，大便稀溏的症状?

581. Do you often feel bitterness in the mouth or dryness in the throat?
有没有经常感到口苦咽干?

582. Is your external genital area always wet or itchy?
外阴部是不是经常潮湿瘙痒?

Oligospermia

The term *Oligospermia* used to denote reduced volume of semen ejaculated, even as few as one or two drops, during sexual intercourse. It refers to deficiency in the number of sperms in the semen, or less than 20 million sperms per milliliter of semen. It is a major cause of male infertility.

Chinese medicine does not distinguish between reduced volume of the ejaculate and deficiency of sperms in the semen. The latter is, in fact, a modern Western medical perspective towards oligospermia, which does not seem to conflict with the former. In any case, there is only one mechanism in Chinese medical theory to explain both. The kidney stores essence, so the most direct cause of oligospermia is kidney dysfunction. In fact, kidney deficiency of either *yin* (essence) or *yang* may lead to oligospermia. Deficiency of both *qi* and blood may impair transformation of the blood into essence such as sperm, and eventually lead to oligospermia.

Apart from the deficiency type as described in the aforementioned cases, oligospermia of the excess type may also be encountered frequently in clinical practice. For example, addiction to alcohol or overconsumption of greasy food may induce dampness-heat, which pours down, to bring about oligospermia.

Typical approaches of inquiry:

583. Have you had your semen examined? What is your sperm count?
您做过精液检查吗？精子计数的结果是多少？

584. How many years have you been married? Have you ever impregnated your wife?
您结婚几年了？太太怀过孕吗？

585. Do you have sexual impotence, premature ejaculation or any other sexual problem?
您有没有阳痿早泄之类的问题？

586. Do you have frequent wet dreams (nocturnal emissions)?
遗精频繁吗？

587. Do you have a sore lower back and limp knees? Are you intolerant of a cold environment? Are your hands and feet always cold?
有没有腰膝酸软？全身怕冷，手脚发凉？

588. Do you wake up to urinate frequently in the night?
夜间起来小便的次数多吗？

589. Do you often have ringing in the ears?
常感到耳鸣吗？

590. (If yes:) Is it a hissing sound or a roaring one?
（如有）细声高音频的还是粗声低音频的？

591. Do you have a burning sensation in the palms of your hands and soles of your feet? Do you have night sweats?
有没有手足心发热，夜间盗汗的现象？

592. Is your scrotum usually wet? Is there any unusual smell from it?
您的阴囊平时是不是潮湿的？有没有不好闻的气味？

593. (For a patient with a sallow complexion:) You look somewhat sallow. How long have you been like this?
（对于面色萎黄者）您的面色不好，这样有多久了？

594. Do you often have palpitations or shortness of breath?
平时感到心悸气短吗？

595. Do you drink alcohol?
您饮酒吗?

596. Do you often eat greasy food?
经常吃油腻的食物吗?

Chapter Nine
Menstrual Complaints

All the abnormalities in the length of the menstrual cycle, duration of menstrual discharge, and volume of menstrual blood, as well as any manifest discomfort occurring in association with menstrual periods are menstrual complaints.

There is a wide variety of menstrual complaints, among which advanced menstruation, infrequent menstruation, irregular menstrual cycle, hypermenorrhea, hypomenorrhea, amenorrhea, abnormal uterine bleeding, dysmenorrheal, premenstrual syndrome (menstrual headache, menstrual dizziness, menstrual mental disorder), vicarious menstruation (menstrual hematemesis and epistaxis) and menopausal syndrome are frequently encountered, and can be effectively treated with Chinese medicine.

The overall mechanism of menstrual complaints lies in dysfunction of the visceral organs and disharmony of *qi* and blood that lead to impairment of the thoroughfare and conception vessels. The etiological factors include external contraction, emotional strain, excessive sexual activity, too many childbirths, and improper diet. In addition, constitutional factors also play an important role in the pathogenesis of menstrual complaints.

While making inquiries, doctors should pay special attention to the length of the menstrual cycle, the volume of the menstrual discharge, the color and consistency of the menstrual blood, and the symptoms accompanying the periods.

Advanced Menstruation (Advanced Periods)

The term *advanced menstruation* or *advanced periods* denotes occurrence of menstruation one to two weeks ahead of due time. Menstruation that occurs in advance occasionally or only three to five days before the due time does not belong to the category of advanced periods. Clinically, there are two major types of advanced periods, namely *qi* defi ciency and blood-heat. *Qi* deficiency can be subdivided into spleen *qi* deficiency and kidney *qi* deficiency, while blood-heat can be subdivided into *yang* exuberance blood-heat, *yin* deficiency blood-heat and heat due to liver depression.

Typical approaches of inquiry:

597. How many days before the due date did your periods come recently?
您近来提前几天来例假?

598. For how many months have you been like this?
已经连续这样几个月了?

599. Is the bleeding heavy or light?
经量是增多了还是减少了?

600. Is there any change in the color of the blood?
经血的颜色有什么变化吗?

601. (If yes:) What is the color now? Is it pale red, deep red or red-purple?
(如有变化)现在是什么颜色的? 是淡红的，深红的，还是紫红的?

602. Has the change of your periods had any impact on your general health? For example, do you feel sluggish and tired? Do you have soreness in the lower back and weakness in the legs, or dizziness and tinnitu□?
经期的变化对全身有什么影响吗? 比如精神不好，四肢疲倦，或者腰酸腿软，头晕耳鸣。

603. Do you feel upset or have a sensation of oppression in the chest during menstruation?
行经期间有没有心烦胸闷的感觉?

604. Do you feel fullness, pain or tenderness in your breasts, rib areas and lower abdomen before menstruation?
经期之前有没有感到乳房、两胁和小腹部胀痛?

605. Do you sleep well at night?
夜里睡觉好吗?

606. Do you have to wake to urinate at night?
起夜吗?

607. (If yes:) How many times a night do you need to get up?
(如果起夜)要起几次?

608. Do you frequently have a dry sensation in the mouth and throat? Do you have a heat sensation in the palms of your hands and soles of your feet?
平时有没有咽干口燥、手、脚心发热的感觉?

609. Are you chronically thirsty? Do you prefer cold or hot drinks?
经常口渴吗? 喜欢喝冷饮还是热饮?

610. How about your bowel movements? Are you constipated?
大便的情况怎么样? 便秘吗?

611. How about your urination? Do you have short voidings of dark urine?
小便的情况怎么样？有没有每次量少，尿色加深的现象？

Infrequent Menstruation (Late Periods)

The term *late periods* refers to menstruation occurring more than seven days after the due date, with normal duration of menstruation. Since the frequency of menstruation is lowered, for example, once every three to five months in extreme cases, the term *late periods* may be substituted by infrequent menstruation.

The main mechanism involves disruption of the rhythmic ebb and flow of the blood due to insufficient blood level. The insufficiency may be caused by either deficiency of essence and blood or pathogenic-*qi*-induced stagnation. The former results from kidney deficiency or blood deficiency, while the latter, from blood-cold, stagnant *qi* or phlegm-dampness.

Typical approaches of inquiry:

612. How many days late do your periods come? How

frequently do they come?
您的例假错后多少天？多久来一次？

613. How long has this situation lasted?
这种情况已经有多久了？

614. Is your menstrual blood sticky (viscous) or watery? Is it reddish or dark-red in color? Are there any clots in it?
经血是粘稠的还是清稀的？颜色是淡红的还是暗红的？有没有血块？

615. Do you have lower abdominal pain?
小腹疼痛吗？

616. (If yes:) Is it a dull, bloating or hollow pain?
（如小腹疼痛）是隐隐作痛，还是胀痛，或是空痛？

617. Can it (your lower abdominal pain) be alleviated or aggravated when you press your abdomen?
小腹疼痛时按压能减轻还是加重？

618. How about warming it with a hot-water bag?
焐热水袋管用吗？

619. Do you have a larger amount of vaginal discharge than usual?
白带比以前增多了吗？

620. Is it watery or sticky (viscous)?
是清稀的还是粘稠的？

621. Do you have dizziness with blurred vision, palpitations or shortness of breath?
有没有头晕眼花，心悸气短之类的症状?

622. Have you noticed any changes in your emotional or mental conditions?
自己感觉到有精神、情绪方面的变化吗?

623. Do you have a tight feeling in the chest?
有胸闷的感觉吗?

624. Do you have a sensation of upper abdominal fullness? Do you feel nauseous?
有上腹部胀闷恶心的感觉吗?

Irregular Menstrual Cycle (Irregular Periods)

The term *irregular menstrual cycle* or *irregular periods* denotes a condition in which menstrual periods come at unpredictable times, usually over seven days ahead of or after the due date. The main mechanism of the disorder lies in the disharmony of the *qi* and blood in the thoroughfare and conception vessels followed by irregular ebb and flow of the blood level. Three syndrome patterns are commonly encountered in clinical practice: kidney deficiency, spleen deficiency and liver depression.

Typical approaches of inquiry:

625. Please describe in detail your irregular periods? Do the periods come ahead of or behind the due time for more than one week?
请您描述一下月经来潮不规律的具体情况，时而提前时而错后都在一周以上，是吗?

626. Are your periods heavier or lighter than normal?
每次来潮的经血量多还是量少?

627. How about the color?
颜色呢?

628. Are there clots in the blood?
经血中有血块吗?

629. Do you have dizziness, tinnitus, a sore lower back and limp legs?
有没有头晕耳鸣、腰酸腿软的症状?

630. Do you have upper abdominal distension (fullness sensation)? Do you have a good appetite? Have you ever not felt like eating?
上腹部感到胀满吗? 胃口好吗? 有没有食欲不振，不想吃饭?

631. During the periods, do you have distending pain (pain with a sensation of fullness) in the ribs, breasts and lower abdomen?
经期有没有胸胁乳房和下腹部胀痛的不适感觉?

632. Have you felt any emotional changes during your periods, such as depression and frequent sighing for no reason?
经期有没有精神上的变化? 比如郁闷不舒，时常想要叹气。

Hypomenorrhea (Scanty Periods)

Hypomenorrhea, also called scanty periods, refers to menstrual discharge of apparently less than normal amount or extremely sparse like a drip occurring at regular intervals, or shortened duration of the menstrual period with the bleeding lasting fewer than two days. Generally speaking, hypomenorrhea is either due to deficiency of essence-blood that leads to inadequacy of *qi* and blood in the thoroughfare and conception vessels or due to presence of congealing cold that impedes the flow of *qi* and blood in those vessels. Four patterns are commonly encountered in clinical practice – kidney deficiency, blood deficiency, blood cold and blood stasis.

Kidney deficiency in patients with hypomenorrhea may be innate or acquired, the latter possibly due to excessive sexual life or repeated abortions. Kidney deficiency then progresses to influence the thoroughfare and conception vessels, leading to hypomenorrhea. Blood deficiency may also lead to deficiency of the thoroughfare and conception vessels, so patients with blood deficiency are prone to hypomenorrhea as well. Factors that may cause blood deficiency include suffering from a severe or chronic disease, persistent fatigue, improper diet, and excessive worrying. All those factors give rise to *qi* deficiency of the spleen, damaging its function in transformation and transportation. Consequently production of blood is decreased. Patients who suffer from blood-cold syndrome may also be subject to hypomenorrhea, because the pathogenic cold hiding in the thoroughfare and conception vessels may emerge to interrupt the blood flow. Pathogenic cold in the blood is usually caught during the menstrual and postpartum periods. Furthermore, blood stasis may also appear during this period if a woman cannot control her emotions well. In fact, emotional disturbance may induce blood stasis as long as the residual blood from the menstrual or postpartum periods is not removed completely. Blood stasis obtained via this pathway may very well lead to hypomenorrhea due to sluggish blood flow. Finally, excessive uterine curettage that results in endometrium damage may also lead to hypomenorrhea.

Typical approaches of inquiry:

633. When did you start to have less bleeding during the period?
您从什么时候开始月经量减少了?

634. How many days does each period last? By how much is the blood reduced?
您现在每次行经持续几天? 经量减少了多少?

635. Is the blood pale or dark? Or is it purple?
经血的颜色是淡红的，还是暗红的，还是紫红的?

636. Are there clots in it?
经血中混有血块吗?

637. Have you had an induced abortion?
以前做过人工流产的手术吗?

638. Is there any reason that you can think of for the lighter bleeding? For example, did you catch cold during a period or right after you bore a baby? Did anything seriously unpleasant happen to you during a period?
经量减少有什么明显的原因吗? 比如是不是曾在经期或产后受寒，或者在经期发生过不愉快的事情严重影响了情绪。

639. Do you suffer from a sore lower back and limp legs, dizziness or tinnitus?
平时有腰酸腿软、头晕耳鸣的症状吗?

640. Do you often feel cold in the lower abdomen? How about the rest of your body, especially your limbs?
小腹发凉吗？身上和四肢发凉吗？

641. Do you feel any pain in the lower abdomen during your periods?
行经期间小腹疼痛吗？

642. (To a sufferer from lower abdominal pain:) What does your pain feel like? Is it dull or stinging?
（对于小腹疼痛者）怎么个疼法？隐痛还是刺痛？

643. Have you ever tried to relieve it with a hot-water bag? Was it helpful?
有没有用热水袋焐焐？能减轻吗？

Amenorrhea

Amenorrhea refers to failure to menarche by age 18, or absence of menstruation for six months for women with previous periodic menses. The former is categorized as primary, and the latter as secondary. Absence of menstruation during pregnancy or lactation, and after the menopausal period is a normal physiological activity, and does not fulfill the criteria of amenorrhea.

The overall mechanism of amenorrhea involves disharmony of *qi* and blood in the thoroughfare and conception vessels. It may be subdivided into deficiency and excess patterns. In the deficiency patterns, *qi* and blood may be so deficient that the *qi*-blood flow can hardly be formed in the thoroughfare and conception vessels. In the excess patterns, pathogenic factors may form a barrier to the flow of *qi* and blood in the thoroughfare and conception vessels. The causation of the disease is complicated by innate and acquired factors. (1) Innate physical weakness may lead to deficiency of kidney *qi*; excessive sexual activity may lead to deficiency of kidney essence; repeated deliveries or a prolonged disease may lead to deficiency of *qi* and blood in the thoroughfare and conception vessels. In any of the three above situations, the blood in the thoroughfare vessel (namely, the "sea of blood") will ebb and stay under the level necessary for the blood to run over under healthy conditions. (2) Improper diet, anxiety and overfatigue may damage spleen *qi*, leading to insufficient power of transformation and transportation of *qi* and blood which may eventually result in deficiency of *qi* and blood in the thoroughfare and conception vessels.(3) A massive hemorrhage, severe acute disease or protracted chronic disease may impair the generation of blood, leading to deficiency of *qi* and blood in the thoroughfare and conception vessels. (4) Introverted or depressive personality or excessive anger may induce *qi* stagnation and blood stasis which may eventually obstruct the flow of *qi* and blood in the thoroughfare and conception vessels. (5) Excessive intake of cold and raw food or contact with cold water during menstrual periods and childbirth may lead to invasion of pathogenic cold. The cold may reside in the thoroughfare and conception vessels, inducing blood stasis which leads to obstruction of the *qi* and blood flow. (6) Constitutional obesity with exuberant phlegm-dampness, or dysfunction of the spleen with impaired transporting function may allow phlegm-dampness to grow until it blocks the thoroughfare and conception vessels. Both deficiency of *qi* and blood in the thoroughfare vessel and obstruction in the thoroughfare and conception vessels may lead to amenorrhea via the same route: the blood cannot fill the "sea of blood," so it cannot run off.

In accordance with the above-mentioned etiological and pathogenetic factors, a variety of syndrome patterns commonly encountered in clinical practice may be summarized as follows: kidney deficiency, spleen deficiency, blood deficiency, blood stasis due to *qi* stagnation, blood stasis due to cold congealment and obstruction due to phlegm-dampness.

Typical approaches of inquiry:

644. (To patients who suffer from primary amenorrhea:) Do you have any discomfort, such as dizziness, tinnitus, soreness in the lower back and weakness in the legs?
（对原发性闭经患者）您有没有什么不舒服，比如头晕耳鸣、腰酸腿软?

645. Are you intolerant of a cold or hot environment?
您平素怕冷还是怕热?

646. Are your hands and feet always cold or warm? Do you have a burning sensation in the palms of your hands and soles of your feet? Do you feel better when you touch something cold with your palms?
手脚是经常发凉的还是热的? 手心、脚心有没有发热的感觉? 是不是摸凉的东西感觉舒服?

647. Do you have night sweats?
夜间有没有盗汗的现象?

648. Do you wake up to urinate many times a night?
起床小便的次数多吗?

649. (To patients who suffer from secondary amenorrhea:) Were your periods normal before? How long is it since you last had a period?
（对继发性闭经患者）您以前的例假正常吗? 这次有多久没来例假了?

650. Have you had a large amount of vaginal discharge? What is the color? Is it watery or viscous (sticky)?
白带多吗? 什么颜色的? 稀的还是稠的?

651. Do you have a poor appetite, abdominal fullness or loose stools?
您有没有食欲不振、脘腹胀闷、大便溏薄等不适?

652. Have you experienced dizziness with blurred vision or palpitations?
您有没有头晕眼花、心悸怔忡等不适？

653. Have you had lower abdominal pain?
小腹疼吗？

654. (If yes:) What kind of pain is it? Is the pain dull or sharp? Is it accompanied by distension (fullness sensation) or by a coldness sensation? Do you feel better or worse when you press your abdomen? Is the pain alleviated when you warm it with a hot-water bag?
（如有小腹痛）怎么个疼法？是隐隐作痛还是剧痛？是胀痛还是冷痛？用手按时，是加重还是减轻？用热水袋焐能够减轻吗？

655. Has there been any change in your emotions or temperament? For example, do you get depressed often, or do you get upset or even furious more easily?
您的性情和脾气有变化吗？比如说，精神上压抑郁闷，容易不耐烦或者生气发怒吗？

656. I have noticed that you have sighed several times while sitting here. Is it because you feel fullness or tightness in the chest and feel relief when you sigh?
我看您坐在这里叹了好几回气，您是不是胸胁发胀、发满，长出口气会感到舒服些？

Hypermenorrhea (Heavy Periods)

The term *hypermenorrhea* or *heavy periods* denotes abnormally profuse uterine bleeding occurring at regular intervals. Excessive menstrual flow is mainly due to insecurity of the thoroughfare and conception vessels, and the resulting loss of control of menstrual blood. The syndrome patterns of hypermenorrhea commonly encountered in clinical practice are *qi* deficiency, blood heat, and blood stasis. The *qi* deficiency pattern is often due to damage to spleen *qi* caused by constitutional frailty, improper diet, overfatigue, or serious or chronic illness. The blood heat pattern may start from constitutional *yang* exuberance, addiction to pungent and dryness-causing food, or emotional stress, each of which may be transferred into heat. The heat then disturbs the functions of the thoroughfare and conception vessels, leading to loss of control of the menstrual blood. The blood stasis pattern is often a consequence of *qi* stagnation caused by emotional upset or uncontrollable anger. An intrauterine device may also cause hypermenorrhea.

Typical approaches of inquiry:

657. Can you estimate the increased amount of menstrual blood by the sanitary towels or pads you used?
从您用的卫生巾来估计，您现在的经量比过去正常时增加了多少?

658. Does your menstrual period come on time? Is there any obvious advance or delay of your menstrual period?
来例假的时间还准确吗？没有明显提前或错后吗？

659. Can you think of any reason for the increase of your menstrual flow? For example, did you get upset or worried recently? Or have you consumed hot and spicy food?
经量比以前明显增多，您觉得有什么原因吗？比如最近有没有生气着急的事情，饮食方面有没有吃辛辣的东西？

660. (To a married woman:) Have you ever been fitted with a contraceptive ring? (or any intrauterine device?)
（对已婚妇女）您有没有上环（宫内节育器）？

661. Is the blood pale-red, fresh-red or dark-red in color? Is it dark-purple?
经血的颜色是淡红的，还是鲜红或深红的，或者是暗紫色的？

662. Is the blood dense or diluted?
经血是稀的还是稠的？

663. Are there any blood clots?
有没有血块？

664. Do you have abdominal pain during your periods?
例假期间肚子疼吗？

665. Do you have distension (fullness sensation) in your lower abdomen at ordinary times?
平时小肚子有没有胀痛的症状?

666. How has your health been recently? Are you as energetic as before? Have you ever felt too tired to talk?
您近来身体怎么样? 精力和以前一样吗? 有没有感到疲乏无力，懒得说话?

667. At normal times do you feel thirsty and want to drink cold water or other cold beverages? Are your stools hard and dry? And is your urine dark in color? How about during the periods?
平时有没有口渴想喝冷饮，大便干结，小便色深的情况? 行经期间呢?

Metrorrhagia and Metrostaxis (Abnormal Uterine Bleeding)

Metrorrhagia and metrostaxis refer to abnormally profuse bleeding and slight but persistent bleeding from the vagina during intermenstrual periods, respectively. Both metrorrhagia and metrostaxis follow the same mechanism, which involves the loss of control of the uterine blood due to damage to the thoroughfare and conception vessels. In clinical practice, syndrome patterns such as kidney deficiency, spleen deficiency, blood heat and blood stasis are most commonly encountered.

Kidney deficiency is usually due to premature sexual activity, repeated childbirths, and excessive sexual activities, as well as decline of kidney *qi* during menopause. In patients with kidney *yin* deficiency, exuberant internal heat due to *yin* deficiency may affect the thoroughfare and conception vessels and push the blood to flow in unwanted directions. In patients with kidney *yang* deficiency, abnormal uterine bleeding occurs due to loss of the kidney's storage power, impairing the control of the *qi* and blood in the thoroughfare and conception vessels.

Spleen *qi* damaging factors, such as anxiety, improper diet and fatigue, may lead to spleen deficiency. When the spleen loses control over the blood flow, bleeding from the vagina may occur at times other than menstrual periods.

Patients with blood heat may also be prone to metrorhagia or metrostaxis. The blood heat in those patients may be attributed to constitutional exuberance of *yang*, fire transformed from liver depression due to emotional disorders, external pathogens or exuberant internal heat due to excessive intake of hot and spicy food. All those factors may induce exuberant internal heat or fire, and damage the thoroughfare and conception vessels, pushing the blood to flow in unwanted directions.

Finally, blood stasis due to emotion-induced internal injury may lead to obstruction of the thoroughfare and conception vessels, forcing the blood to bypass the vessels.

Typical approaches of inquiry:

668. When did you have your last period? It is not the due time now, is it?
您上次是什么时候来的例假？现在不该是经期，对吗？

669. Is there any obvious reason behind the accidental vaginal bleeding?
这次突然阴道出血，有什么明显的原因吗？

670. Is the blood pale-red, bright-red, dark-red or dark-purple? Are there any clots in it?
血色是淡红的，鲜红的，暗红的，还是紫暗的？夹杂血块吗？

671. Is the blood watery or viscous (sticky)?
血的质地是稀的还是稠的？

672. Do you have lower abdominal pain?
小腹疼不疼？

673. (If yes:) Do you feel better or worse when you press the painful area?
（如果疼痛）用手按压能减轻还是加重？

674. Do you have dizziness, tinnitus, a sore lower back

and limp knees, or a burning sensation in the palms of your hands and soles of your feet?
有没有头晕耳鸣，腰膝酸软，手足心热的症状?

675. Do you have such symptoms as intolerance of coldness in general, with cold hands and feet in particular?
有没有全身怕冷，手脚发凉的症状?

676. Do you often feel tired, and have a poor appetite?
有没有身体疲倦，不想吃饭的症状?

677. Do you often feel thirsty, and crave a cold drink?
有没有口渴，想喝冷饮的症状?

678. Are your bowel movements normal? (If not:) Are your stools dry and hard or loose?
大便正常吗? （如不正常）是干结还是稀溏?

Dysmenorrhea (Painful Periods)

Painful periods or dysmenorrhea refers to the symptom in which lower abdominal pain occurs just prior to, during or right after menstruation. There are two major mechanisms that may induce pain during or around periods: One is obstruction in the flow of *qi* and blood. A Chinese medical maxim is, "Wherever there is obstruction, there is pain." The other is insufficient supply of *qi* and blood. Another proverb is, "Wherever there is undernourishment, there is pain."

The syndrome patterns commonly encountered in the cases of dysmenorrhea include kidney *qi* deficiency, *qi* and blood deficiency, *qi* stagnation and blood stasis, cold congealment and blood stasis, and dampness-heat accumulation.

Kidney deficiency may be innate. It may also be acquired due to excessive sexual activity or frequent childbirths, or following a protracted disease. *Qi*-and-blood deficiency is due to constitutional frailty, or following a severe or chronic disease with consumption of *qi* and blood, or due to weakening of the stomach and spleen with consequent inadequacy for the formation of *qi* and blood. In all those syndrome patterns the painful periods are induced by undernourishment.

In the following syndrome patterns, painful periods are induced by obstruction. Anger hurts the liver, and makes the liver *qi* stagnate. The stagnant *qi* can further lead to blood stasis. Stagnation of *qi* and blood in the uterine vessels eventually gives rise to pain. Contraction of pathogenic cold or taking cold and raw food during a menstrual or postpartum period may facilitate invasion of the thoroughfare and conception vessels by cold. The cold that resides in the thoroughfare and conception vessels causes *qi* and blood to congeal in the uterus, and thus pain. Constitutional damp-heat or damp-heat contracted during a menstrual or postpartum period may lead to *qi*-blood congestion of the uterine vessels, and thus also pain.

Typical approaches of inquiry:

679. How long have you been suffering from painful periods?
您痛经多久了?

680. Is there any reason that you can think of for the painful periods? For example, any illness, catching a cold after childbirth, anger, taking too much cold or uncooked food during a menstrual period?
您的痛经有什么原因吗? 比如生过什么病以后出现痛经，产后受凉，愤怒生气，经期吃了很多生冷的东西，等等。

681. Can you describe your lower abdominal pain? Is it dull or sharp? Do you also have a burning sensation or a cold sensation in the painful area?
来例假时小腹怎么个痛法? 隐痛还是剧痛? 灼痛还是冷痛?

682. Do you feel better when you press your lower abdomen? Or do you feel worse?
按压小腹是使疼痛减轻还是加重?

683. Do you feel better when you warm your lower abdomen with a hot-water bag?
用热水袋焐能使小腹疼痛减轻吗?

684. Do you have pain in the lower abdomen only, or does it travel to the rear?
痛经只限于小腹疼痛，还是连腰骶部都感到疼痛？

685. Do you also have pain and distension in the chest and breasts?
胸胁和乳房是不是也感到胀痛？

686. Is the amount of your periods increased or decreased compared with that of the past?
月经血量与过去不痛经时比较是增多了，还是减少了？

687. How does the blood look? Is it paler or darker? More watery or more viscous?
经血的颜色和质量呢？变淡了还是发暗了？变稀了还是变稠了？

688. Are there any blood clots in it? Are there a lot?
经血中有血块吗？血块多吗？

689. Do you have a normal vaginal discharge? Is the amount increased? Is it watery or viscous? Is it whitish or yellowish?
平常白带多吗？稀的还是稠的？白色的还是黄色的？

690. Do you have dizziness and tinnitus, or a sore lower back and limp knees?
平时有没有头晕耳鸣、腰膝酸软的症状？

691. Do you have palpitations and insomnia (difficulty falling asleep)? Or do you feel sluggish?
有没有心悸失眠，或者疲倦乏力？

692. Are you more intolerant of coldness than others? Are your hands and feet always cold?
比别人怕冷吗？平时手脚是凉的吗？

Premenstrual Breast Distension

Premenstrual breast distension refers to distention and tenderness of the breasts or itchy and painful sensation of the nipples starting to occur three to seven days before or during menstrual periods. It is a symptom of premenstrual tension syndrome. The disease mechanism mainly involves stagnation of the liver *qi* with abnormal *qi* movement in the thoroughfare and conception vessels. In some cases, the liver *qi* stagnation may be complicated by kidney *qi* deficiency or by spleen deficiency with dampness obstruction. In clinical practice, in order to distinguish different syndrome patterns, doctors always need to comprehend the characters of the menstrual periods and the general health conditions of the patients.

Typical approaches of inquiry:

693. You say that you feel fullness and tenderness in your breasts before your periods. How long does this symptom last? Is the distension or pain serious?
您说您每次来例假之前都感到乳房胀痛，这有多久了？胀痛得厉害吗？

694. Does the pain stop after the period is over?
例假来后就不痛了，是吗？

695. Have you checked your breasts by touching them each time you have fullness? Are they firm to touch or soft? Any lump in a breast?
每次发作时您自己摸过乳房吗？是胀硬的还是柔软的？里面有块状的东西吗？

696. How about your periods? Do they come ahead of the due time or after? Is the bleeding heavier or lighter? Is the blood darker or lighter in color?
月经的情况怎么样？是提前还是错后？量多还是量少？色深还是色浅？

697. Do you have lower abdominal pain during your periods?
来例假时小腹疼吗？

698. (If there is pain:) What does the pain feel like? Dull, distending (bloating) or cold pain?
（如有小腹痛）怎么个疼法？隐痛？胀痛？冷痛？

699. At what age did you start to have periods?
您是十几岁开始来例假的?

700. Do you usually have a large vaginal discharge? Is it white or yellowish, watery or viscous (sticky)?
平时白带多吗? 白色的还是黄色的? 稀薄的还是粘稠的?

701. Does a feeling of fullness in your breasts make you upset?
乳房胀痛让您心烦吗?

702. Does it affect you appetite as well?
有没有影响您的食欲?

Menstrual Headache

Menstrual headache refers to the headache that occurs along with menstrual periods. It belongs to the category of premenstrual tension syndrome. Different pathways may lead to menstrual headache. On the one hand, deficiency of both *qi* and blood as well as that of *yin*-essence may be aggravated during menstrual periods, leading to undernourishment in the brain, and hence headache; on the other, pathogenic factors like phlegm or static blood may move reversely upward along with the *qi* flow of the thoroughfare vessel at time of the period, consequently disturbing the brain and leading to headache. Therefore, menstrual headache can be either excessive or deficient in nature.

Typical approaches of inquiry:

703. You say that you have a headache along with your periods. How long has this situation lasted?
您说每当月经来潮时就犯头痛病。这种情况有多久了？

704. Do you have a headache every time before a period starts, or after it starts?
是每次月经来潮前就开始头痛，还是月经来潮后才感到头痛？

705. Do you have any other discomfort along with the headache, such as dizziness and blurred vision, palpitations, shortness of breath, drowsiness, or fullness or oppression in the head?
头痛伴有其他不适吗？比如头晕眼花，心悸气短，或头内昏昏沉沉，发胀发闷。

706. Do you experience any emotional change during your periods? Do you get upset more easily?
每次到了经期，性情有变化吗？是否比平时容易烦躁、发脾气？

707. Is the bleeding heavy? Is the blood pale-red, bright-

red, or dark-purple in color? Are there clots in the blood?
月经量多吗？经血的颜色是淡红的，鲜红的，还是紫暗的？有没有血块夹杂在里面？

708. Do you have lower abdominal pain during your periods?
经期小腹疼痛吗？

709. (If yes:) Do you feel better or is it more painful when you press your lower abdomen?
（如疼痛）用手按压时，疼痛是减轻还是加重？

710. Are there any other symptoms along with your headache? Do you also feel sluggish, or do you have a sore lower back and limp legs, a burning sensation in the palms of your hands and soles of your feet, oppression in the chest, or nausea?
有没有其他伴随的症状？比如神疲体倦、腰酸腿软、手脚心热、胸闷泛恶？

Menstrual Dizziness

Menstrual dizziness refers to a periodic symptom in which dizziness, usually accompanied by blurred vision, occurs along with menstrual periods.

The disease mechanism involves either insufficient blood supply in the meridians or upward invasion by phlegm-turbidity. The former may lead to undernourishment of the brain, and the latter may becloud the brain during menstrual periods. In either case, dizziness ensues.

In clinical practice, deficiency of both *qi* and blood, deficiency of *yin* with exuberant *yang*, and phlegm-dampness obstruction are the most commonly encountered syndrome patterns.

Typical approaches of inquiry:

711. Do you have dizziness whenever you have a period? How long has this condition lasted?
您是不是每逢经期就感到眩晕？这种情况有多久了？

712. What kind of dizziness do you have? For example, do you feel that your head is whirling and the environment spinning or do you feel drowsy with blurred vision?
怎么个晕法，能描述一下吗？比如天旋地转，还是昏昏沉沉，看东西有些模糊？

713. Was there any reason for the start of your dizziness? For example, did you start to have dizziness after a severe illness, or after an unpleasant event?
一开始出现这种症状有原因吗？比如说生了一场大病之后、发生了不愉快的事情之后，等等。

714. Do you have lower abdominal pain during your periods?
来例假时下腹部疼吗?

715. Are your periods heavy or scanty?
月经量是多是少?

716. Is the blood dark or light in color? Is it thin (diluted) or viscous (sticky)?
经血的颜色是淡还是深? 质地是稀还是稠?

717. Do you have oppression in the chest and nausea?
来例假时有没有胸闷想要呕吐的感觉?

718. Do you feel tired often? Do you get upset easily?
平时感到疲倦乏力吗? 容易着急生气吗?

719. Do you have a sore lower back and limp legs, a dry mouth or dry throat?
平时有没有腰酸腿软，口燥咽干的感觉?

720. Do you have excessive vaginal discharge? Is it white or yellow in color?
平时白带多吗? 是白色的还是黄色的?

Menstrual Mental Disorder

Menstrual mental disorder refers to the symptoms of abnormal emotional changes occurring periodically in accordance with menstrual cycles, such as irritability with propensity to outbreaks of anger, sadness with weeping, depression with self-murmuring, and anxiety with restlessness. These symptoms appear during menstrual periods, but disappear completely when a period is over. These symptoms belong to the category of premenstrual syndrome in Western medicine.

The main mechanism of the illness involves phlegm-fire, stagnant heat or deficiency of heart blood. During menstrual periods women are bound to have changes in their physiological conditions. In those with a phlegm-exuberant constitution, the phlegm can be transformed into phlegm-fire which disturbs the heart (spirit) under the influence of physiological changes during the periods. In those with a depressive predisposition or stagnant liver *qi* after a bout of anger, the *qi* stagnation may turn into heat, which can also disturb the heart (spirit) during the periods. In those who are timid in nature, constant worries hurt the spleen, leading to insufficient power of transformation and transportation. Consequently, the supply of blood to the heart is deficient during the periods. So it is incumbent on doctors to be aware of the constitutional or mental condition of a patient, especially any history of emotional strain.

Typical approaches of inquiry:

721. (To a patient's family member:) Does she behave strangely whenever her period comes? How long has she been like that?
（询问病人的家人）病人每值经期就发生精神情志的异常吗？这有多久了？

722. How about her behavior before and after the periods? Is it normal?
平时精神正常吗？有没有异常的表现？

723. Was there any event that triggered her illness?
发病前精神上受过什么刺激吗？

724. What are the major symptoms she shows during the periods? Does she feel sad and weep for no reason? Or does she get upset and lose control easily? Or is she restless with anxiety and talking wildly?
经期出现的精神症状主要有哪些表现？是无缘无故地悲伤哭泣，还是烦躁易怒，不能自制？还是狂躁不安，语无伦次？

725. Do the symptoms disappear more or less, or completely, after the period?
月经过后这些症状能明显减轻或完全消失吗？

726. (To the patient:) Have your periods moved ahead of or after the due time?
（询问病人）经期一般是提前还是错后？

727. Is there any change in the volume of menstrual blood?
月经量有变化吗?

Menstrual Hematemesis and Epistaxis (Vicarious Menstruation)

Menstrual hematemesis and epistaxis denotes periodic hematemesis (vomiting of blood) and epistaxis (nosebleed) occurring before or during menstrual periods, accompanied by decreased volume of menstrual flow or even absence of menstruation. It is also called vicarious menstruation. Blood heat with reversed movement of *qi* is responsible for the condition. Blood *qi* in the thoroughfare vessel which has already turned exuberant during the menstruation period may be agitated in the presence of blood-heat and lose control. When the exuberant blood *qi* moves reversely upward, nosebleed or vomiting of blood may occur. So the menstrual blood is actually released through the mouth and the nose, the amount of which determines the outcome of the menstrual abnormality, i.e. reduced menstrual flow or absence of menstruation.

Vicarious menstruation can be divided into deficiency and excess patterns. The deficiency pattern usually occurs in women with a *yin*-deficient constitution or those with *yin* deficiency due to a chronic disease that consumes the essence and blood. In either case, *yin* deficiency leads to exuberant internal heat that warms the blood and reverses the *qi* movement. The excess pattern is encountered in those who suffer from liver fire after an emotional upset, which results in reversely upward movement of *qi* and fire.

Typical approaches of inquiry:

728. How many times have you vomited blood (or had a nosebleed) before or during periods?
在经期前或经期发生吐血（或衄血）几次了?

729. Do your periods come on time?
月经还正常来潮吗?

730. Do you vomit a large amount of blood? (Does your nose bleed a lot?) Was the blood bright-red or dark-red in color?
吐出来的（鼻子流出来的）血，量多吗?是鲜红的还是深红的?

731. Do you have a burning sensation in the palms of your hands and soles of your feet? Or do you feel dryness in your mouth and thirsty?
有没有手脚心发热、口干口渴的感觉?

732. Do you feel fullness and tenderness on both sides of your chest?

有没有两胁胀痛的感觉?

733. Have you noticed any change of temperament? Are you feeling more irritable, or are you getting upset more easily?
性情方面有变化吗? 比如变得急躁不耐烦或容易生气发脾气?

734. Do you feel bitterness and dryness in your mouth? Are you constipated? Have you found your urine turning dark with short voidings recently?
有没有口苦咽干、大便秘结、小便短赤的现象?

Menopausal Syndrome (Climacteric Syndrome)

Menopausal syndrome or climacteric syndrome refers to the symptoms occurring around and during menopause, including hot flushes, sweating, irritability, tinnitus, palpitations, insomnia, amnesia, dizziness and irregular menstruation. These symptoms are associated with the physiological changes happening around and during menopause. In women at the age of menopause, the kidney *qi* starts declining. Predisposition towards exuberance or decline of *yin* or *yang* is susceptible to imbalance of *yin* and *yang*, and hence the syndrome. So kidney deficiency is the fundamental causal factor of menopausal syndrome, which can be subdivided into kidney *yin* deficiency, kidney *yang* deficiency, and deficiency of both kidney *yin* and kidney *yang*.

Typical approaches of inquiry:

735. You say that you are at the age of menopause, and have experienced discomfort related to it. Please update me on the conditions of your periods for the past few months: Have your periods come on time? Have your periods become heavy or scanty? Or did your periods stop several months ago?
您认为可能是更年期，现在有很多不舒服，请先说一下近几个月的月经情况：经期准不准？经量多了还是少了？还是已经有几个月没来例假了？

736. Do you feel waves of chilliness or hot flushes?
身上感到一阵阵发冷还是烘热？

737. Do you sweat for no reason?
无缘无故地出汗吗？

738. Are you more intolerant of heat or cold than before?
您比以前怕冷还是比以前怕热？

739. Do you feel chilly and hot alternately?
有没有一会儿怕冷一会儿怕热的情况？

740. Do you have a burning sensation in the palms of your hands and soles of your feet?
有没有手心、脚心发热的感觉?

741. Can you sleep well at night? Have you experienced sleeplessness recently?
夜间睡觉好吗? 近来有没有失眠?

742. Are there any changes in your emotions? Do you get upset easily? Can you control your emotions? Do you cry easily?
情绪方面有什么变化吗? 有没有感到烦躁，容易生气，或者控制不住自己，容易哭泣?

743. Have you found any changes in your mental state? Do you feel sluggish and even reluctant to talk with others?
精神方面有什么变化吗? 有没有感到萎靡不振，连话都懒得说?

744. Are you as energetic as before? Do you have a sore lower back and limp legs?
体力和以前一样吗? 有没有腰酸腿软之类的症状?

Chapter Ten
Gravid and Postpartum Complaints

Morning Sickness (Vomiting during Pregnancy)

Morning sickness refers to nausea and vomiting during pregnancy, and, in extreme cases, vomiting immediately after intake of any food. Morning sickness occurs typically in the morning especially during the early months of pregnancy.

In this condition the *qi* of the thoroughfare vessel moves reversely upward, leading to disharmony of stomach *qi*. As a result, stomach *qi* moves reversely upward as well, and so nausea and vomiting ensue.

During pregnancy, the blood in the thoroughfare and conception vessels becomes exceptionally abundant in order to supply nutrients to the fetus. The *qi* of the thoroughfare and conception vessels is thus stronger than usual because it governs an unusual amount of blood flow. In those who normally have weakened stomach *qi*, the stronger *qi* flow in the thoroughfare vessel may force the stomach *qi* to move upward in a reverse manner.

In some other cases, irritable temperament may generate heat due to liver *qi* depression. Pregnancy may reduce the blood supply to the liver because more blood stays in the thoroughfare and conception vessels. Subsequently, deficiency of the liver blood may help to turn the heat into fire. Thus the strong thoroughfare *qi* may bring the liver fire reversely upward to the stomach, resulting in nausea and vomiting.

In individuals with spleen *yang* deficiency, phlegm is retained inside. The thoroughfare *qi* during pregnancy may bring the phlegm reversely upward, also leading to nausea and vomiting.

So, in clinical practice, stomach deficiency, liver-heat and phlegm-dampness are the most commonly encountered syndrome patterns.

Typical approaches of inquiry:

745. Is there any obvious reason for your nausea and

vomiting, such as eating spoiled food?
您的恶心呕吐有什么明显的原因吗？比如，吃了不干净的东西。

746. Do you feel nauseous or vomit whenever you eat? Or do you do so even without eating anything?
您是吃了东西就恶心呕吐，还是不吃东西也想吐？

747. Do you vomit out the food that you take each time, or simply some mucus?
每次吐出来的都是吃下去的食物，还是只吐些痰涎？

748. How long has it been since your last period? (How long have you been pregnant?)
您的例假有多久没来了？（怀孕多久了？）

749. (To women of childbearing age whose periods do not come on time:) According to your pulse conditions, you seem to be pregnant. Did you have any stomach problem before? Are you apt to feel nauseous and vomit?
（育龄妇女，月经未如期而至者）从脉象来看您有喜了。您过去有胃病吗？有容易恶心呕吐的毛病吗？

750. Do you get upset easily?
您容易生气着急吗？

751. Do you feel dryness in your mouth now?
您现在感到口干吗？

752. Do you have a bitter sensation in your mouth?
嘴里有没有苦味?

753. Do you have a craving to drink water? Cold or hot water?
想喝水吗? 想喝凉水还是热水?

754. Where do you feel the discomfort most? In your stomach, chest or rib areas?
您身上哪里最难受? 胃部? 胸部? 两胁?

755. How is your general health? Has it been affected? Do you tire easily? Do you have dizziness, palpitations or shortness of breath?
全身情况受影响了吗? 有没有感到疲倦乏力，或者头晕眼花，或者心悸气短?

Threatened Miscarriage (Restless Fetus)

In Chinese medicine, threatened miscarriage is also called "restless fetus," which refers to a condition in which a pregnant woman experiences lower back soreness and abdominal pain with a bearing-down feeling and small amount of vaginal bleeding. If the bearing-down abdominal pain and vaginal bleeding become manifest, miscarriage often ensues. Therefore, it is reasonable to take restless fetus as an early sign of miscarriage. The major mechanism of threatened miscarriage is insecurity of the fetus due to the disorder of *qi* and blood in the thoroughfare and conception vessels. The causes are multifarious. They include: (1) kidney deficiency due to insufficient natural endowment or sexual indulgence after conception; (2) *qi* deficiency due to weak constitution, improper diet, overfatigue or contraction of a severe disease that injures spleen *qi*; (3) blood deficiency due to constitutional weakness, chronic disease or severe morning sickness; (4) blood heat due to a *yang*-exuberant constitution, liver depression with heat transformation, indulgence in pungent and dryness-causing food or affection of pathogenic heat; and (5) trauma due to knocks, falls, wrenching or lifting heavy things.

Typical approaches of inquiry:

756. How many months have you been pregnant? When was your last period?
您怀孕几个月了？最后一次例假是什么时候？

757. When did you start to have a sore lower back, abdominal pain and stirring fetus?
什么时候开始感到腰酸腹痛，胎动下坠的？

758. Do you have vaginal bleeding? Are you bleeding a lot?

阴道出血了吗？出血多不多？

759. What is the color of the blood? Is it pink, crimson or bright-red?
出的血是什么颜色的：淡红的？深红的？鲜红的？

760. Have you suffered any trauma? Did you fall recently? Or did you lift anything heavy and get hurt?
您最近受过伤吗？跌过跤吗？拿过重东西吗？

761. Do you suffer from dizziness and tinnitus?
您感到头晕耳鸣吗？

762. Can you sleep well?
您睡眠好吗？

763. Have you felt so sluggish or short of breath that you do not even want to talk to others?
您感到倦怠气短，连话都懒得说吗？

764. Do you feel thirsty and have an urge to drink cold beverages?
您感到口渴，想喝冷饮吗？

Recurrent Pregnancy Loss (RPL)

Recurrent pregnancy loss refers to the occurrence of three or more consecutive abortions or miscarriages. There are two causes of RPL, one of which is insecurity of fetus *qi* due to impairment of the thoroughfare and conception vessels, the other the deformity of the fetus due to malformation. In clinical practice, kidney deficiency pattern and *qi*-blood deficiency pattern are encountered most commonly. Kidney *qi* deficiency is most likely due to innate physical weakness or excessive sexual activity after pregnancy. When kidney *qi* is deficient, the thoroughfare and conception vessels lack security, which may lead to insufficient binding of the fetus to the maternal body. Factors causing *qi*-blood deficiency include physical weakness, damage to the spleen due to improper food intake, fatigue, or a severe or prolonged disease. Deficiency of *qi* and blood may decrease the ability of the maternal body to hold the fetus.

Typical approaches of inquiry:

765. How many times have you had abortions?
您流产几次了？

766. Was there any particular reason for each abortion?
每次流产有什么明显的原因吗？

767. Did you control your sex life during each pregnancy?
每次怀孕后有没有控制房事?

768. Are you in good health? Do you often experience dizziness, blurred vision or fatigue?
平时身体好吗? 有没有头晕眼花，疲倦乏力的症状?

769. Do you have palpitations and shortness of breath?
感到心悸气短吗?

770. Are you in a good mental state? Have you ever felt sluggish?
平时精神好吗? 有没有萎靡不振的现象?

771. Do you have a sore lower back and limp legs?
感到腰酸腿软吗?

Infertility

Infertility refers to the failure to become pregnant after living two years or more with a male who is normal in reproductive function and with regular unprotected sexual intercourse, or failure to conceive following a previous pregnancy for over two years. Infertility is mainly due to kidney *qi* deficiency which is associated with disharmony of the *qi* and blood in the thoroughfare and conception vessels. Clinically, the syndrome patterns of kidney deficiency, liver stagnation, phlegm-dampness and blood stasis are most commonly encountered in infertility cases.

Typical approaches of inquiry:

772. How many years have you been married?
您结婚几年了?

773. Do you live together with your husband?
和您的先生一直住在一起吗?

774. Has your husband had a urological examination? Does he have any reproductive problem?
您先生去泌尿科检查过吗? 他没有问题吧?

775. What kind of contraceptive measures have you taken?
你们采取过什么避孕措施吗?

776. Do your periods come on time?
您的例假准时吗?

777. Are the color and the volume of the menstrual blood normal?
月经的血量和经血的颜色有什么异常吗?

778. Are there clots in the blood?
经血中有血块吗?

779. (If yes:) Are there many?
（如有）血块多吗？

780. Do you have a lot of vaginal discharge? Is it watery or sticky?
白带多吗？稀薄的还是粘稠的？

781. Do you have abdominal pain whenever your periods are due?
每次来例假之前小腹疼痛吗？

782. (If yes:) What does the pain feel like? Is it dull, bloating or sharp?
（如疼痛）怎么个痛法：隐痛？胀痛？还是剧痛？

783. Do you have swelling or tenderness in your breasts when the perod is due? Do you have any discomfort in the hypochondriac regions (rib areas), or any fullness and pain in your lower abdomen?
每次例假前有没有乳房胀痛、两胁不适或小腹胀痛的感觉？

784. Do you have other symptoms such as dizziness, tinnitus, dry mouth, dry throat, palpitations or difficulty falling asleep?
您有没有头晕耳鸣、口燥咽干、心悸失眠之类的症状？

Lochiorrhea (Persistent Abnormal Lochia Discharge)

Lochia is the discharge from the uterus and vagina following delivery. In healthy individuals, lochia is completely expelled from the body within approximately 20 days after delivery. If the vaginal discharge persists for more than three weeks, the condition is considered abnormal, and is called lochiorrhea. (In fact, the term *lochiorrhea* has a dual meaning: Besides persistent abnormal lochia discharge, it also refers to abnormally profuse discharge of lochia. The two conditions are closely related and indistinguishable.) Insecurity of the thoroughfare and conception vessels, which may be induced by *qi* deficiency, blood-heat or blood stasis, is responsible for lochiorrhea.

Typical approaches of inquiry:

785. You have mentioned that you still have uterine and vaginal discharge now. How many days have passed since the delivery?
您说恶露迄今不止，现在是产后多少天了？

786. Is the amount of the lochia large?
现在恶露量多吗？

787. What color is it? Is it reddish, deep-red, or dark-red

with blood clots?
是什么颜色的：淡红？深红？暗红有块？

788. Is the lochia smelly?
恶露有臭味吗？

789. Are you so tired that you don't feel like doing anything?
您感到疲倦乏力，懒得动弹吗？

790. Do you have a dry mouth or dry throat? Do you have an urge to drink water? Hot or cold?
您感到口燥咽干吗？想喝水吗？想喝凉的还是热的？

791. Do you have lower abdominal pain?
小腹疼痛吗？

792. (If yes:) Do you feel better or worse when you press your lower abdomen?
（如有疼痛）用手按压能使疼痛减轻还是加重？

Hypogalactia

Hypogalactia refers to decreased or no secretion of breast milk in mothers during the lactation period. There are two causes of hypogalactia: insufficient transformation and transportation of milk, and stagnation of the milk flow. Correspondingly, hypogalactia is often subdivided into *qi*-blood deficiency pattern and liver *qi* stagnation pattern.

Constitutional weakness plus hemorrhage during delivery or spleen-stomach weakness that leads to impaired formation of *qi* and blood may result in hypogalactia. Depressive personality or postpartum emotional injury that makes the liver *qi* stagnate induces depression and stagnation of *qi* movement within the body. When the outflow of the milk is affected, hypogalactia also occurs.

Typical approaches of inquiry:

793. How many days have passed since you gave birth?
您现在是产后第几天了？

794. Have you experienced a shortage or absence of milk since then?
一直没有乳汁或乳汁很少吗？

795. (In case of a shortage of milk:) Is the milk watery or sticky (viscous)?
（如有少许乳汁）乳汁是清稀的还是浓稠的？

796. Do you have fullness and tenderness in one or both breasts, or no such sensations?
乳房胀满疼痛吗？还是根本没有胀满的感觉？

797. Did you experience swelling and hardening in your breasts after childbirth, or are they as soft as before?
乳房肿胀发硬吗？还是与产前同样柔软？

Galactorrhea (Spontaneous Flow of Milk)

Galactorrhea refers to spontaneous flow of milk from the nipple in the lactation period, without suckling of the baby. Spontaneous secretion of milk does not necessarily indicate a pathological state. Women who are strong in constitution with plump breasts and abundant milk storage and those who have just stopped breast feeding may also experience spontaneous secretion of milk.

The main reason for galactorrhea is loss of constraining power of the breast due to weakness of stomach *qi* and agitation of milk flow driven by stagnant heat in the liver meridian. Hemorrhage during delivery and the resulting loss of *qi*, as well as improper food intake, may damage the spleen and stomach. Consequently, the stomach *qi* becomes too weak to withhold the milk flow. Long-term depression after delivery may turn into heat. Anger may induce liver fire. Both liver heat and fire may over-stimulate the *qi* flow in the liver meridian. The *qi* then causes milk to leak out continuously.

Typical approaches of inquiry:

798. When did you bear your baby?
您是什么时候分娩的?

799. Do you breast-feed your baby yourself? (If yes:) Is

your baby breast-fed only, or fed with powdered milk solutions in addition to breast-feeding?
是您自己给婴儿喂奶吗？（如果是）婴儿只喝您的奶还是有时也给他（她）喂奶粉?

800. Is there quite an amount of milk that is leaked out?
自行流出的奶汁量多吗?

801. Is it watery or sticky (viscous)?
是稀的还是稠的?

802. Do you have a sensation of fullness, hardening or pain in your breasts?
乳房发胀发硬和疼痛吗?

803. Have you noticed any change in your emotions recently? For example, do you get upset easily?
近来性情有什么变化吗? 比如烦躁，容易生气。

804. Do you feel bitterness in the mouth or dryness in the throat? Do you also have a sensation of fullness in the chest and rib areas?
您感到口苦咽干，胸胁胀满吗?

805. Do you have constipation? Is your urine darker than before?
有没有大便秘结和小便色深的现象?

Chapter Eleven
Pediatric Complaints

Hyperkinetic Disorder in Children (Attention Deficit Hyperactivity Disorder; ADHD)

Hyperkinetic disorder, also called attention deficit hyperactivity disorder (ADHD), is a behavioral abnormality characterized by hyperactivity, inattention and impulsiveness. It commonly occurs among school-age children, resulting in poor school performance. In most cases, ADHD is due to insufficiency of natural endowment. However, postnatal physical weakness and incomplete recovery from certain diseases may also be important factors. The main mechanism involves disharmony of *yin* and *yang*, *yin* deficiency with exuberant *yang*, or upward floating of asthenic *yang*. In clinical practice, heart-kidney deficiency, kidney deficiency with hyperactive liver, and heart-spleen deficiency are the most commonly encountered syndrome patterns. Doctors need to differentiate the children with hyperkinetic disorder from those who are simply energetic or naughty. "Naughty children" may also exhibit occasional inattention and get addicted to little tricks in class. However, they are able to exhibit normal school performance and refrain from improper behavior after correction from teachers.

Typical approaches of inquiry:

806. (To the parents:) How old is your child? What grade is he (she) in?
（问家长）您的孩子多大了？现在在上几年级？

807. You say that your child cannot focus on listening but constantly plays little tricks in class. Does he (she) stop doing that after correction by his (her) teacher?
您说您的孩子上课不能专心听课，喜欢做小动作，老师制止后能够停止吗？

808. Does your child have trouble sitting still during meals, while at school or doing homework? Is he (she) always fidgeting and squirming?
您的孩子吃饭、上课和在家里做作业时坐得住吗？总是在座位上动来动去不能安静吗？

809. How is his (her) school performance? Can he (she) cope with his (her) homework?
您的孩子的学习成绩怎么样？能够完成作业吗？

810. How is his (her) memory? Is there any obvious difference when compared to those of other children?
他（她）的记忆力怎么样？与其他小孩比较有明显的不同吗？

811. How is his (her) temperament? Does he (she) get upset easily?
他（她）的脾气怎么样？脾气暴躁，容易激动吗？

812. Does he (she) often wet the bed?
他（她）经常尿床吗？

813. Does he (she) have night sweats?
他（她）有夜间睡觉出汗的毛病吗？

814. How is his (her) diet? Does he (she) have a good appetite? Does he (she) prefer one type of food over others?
他（她）平时的饮食情况怎么样？吃饭香吗？有没有偏食的情况？

815. (To the child:) Do you find it difficult to follow the teacher's instructions?
（问患儿）你觉得学习难不难？

816. Do you find school interesting or boring?

你愿意上学吗?

817. Do you feel tired in class?
你觉得上课累不累?

818. Do you have vivid dreams while you sleep?
你夜里睡觉时做梦多吗?

Parorexia (Pica)

Parorexia or pica refers to disordered appetite with a craving for unusual foods or substances, such as uncooked rice, mud or paper. It may occur among children who are infested with parasites and those who suffer from malnutrition or mental disorders.

Typical approaches of inquiry:

819. (To the parents:) What kind of unusual things or foods does your child like to eat?
（问家长）您的孩子都喜欢吃哪些异物?

820. Do you tell him (her) that those things are not edible? Does he (she) listen to you, and do as you tell him (her)?
您有没有告诉他（她）这些东西不能吃? 他（她）听吗?

821. How long has he (she) been doing this?
他（她）有这个毛病多久了?

822. Does it affect his (her) normal meals?
对日常饮食有影响吗?

823. Did he (she) vomit or expel in stools any parasites like roundworms?
他（她）吐过或随大便排出过蛔虫之类的寄生虫吗?

824. Have you found anything abnormal in his (her) psychological make-up?
孩子的精神和情绪有没有异常的情况?

Enuresis (Bed-Wetting)

Enuresis or bed-wetting refers to the involuntary passage of urine during sleep at night. Enuresis is normal in infants because their urinary control ability has not yet been established. Nor is it abnormal that a school-age child occasionally urinates in bed during a sound sleep. However, children beyond the age of 3 who still wet the bed every night are considered to be enuretics.

Enuresis is often encountered in syndrome patterns of kidney *qi* insecurity, spleen-lung *qi* deficiency, and stagnant heat in the liver meridian.

Typical approaches of inquiry:

825. (To the parents:) What grade is your child in? How is his (her) school performance?
（询问患儿家长）您的孩子上几年级了？学习成绩怎么样？

826. Is your child liable to perspire? Is it easy for him (her) to catch a cold?
平时容易出汗吗？容易感冒吗？

827. Does he (she) eat more than other children of the same age, or less?
饭量与同龄孩子比较是多是少？

828. How about his (her) temperament? Is he (she) a grumpy child?
孩子的脾气好吗？性情急躁吗？

829. Does he (she) talk in his (her) sleep?
孩子夜里睡眠时说梦话吗？

830. (If yes:) Very often or occasionally?
(如果说梦话)经常说还是偶尔说？

831. Does he (she) often grind his (her) teeth during sleep?
睡眠中常有磨牙的情况吗？

Chapter Twelve
Other Complaints

Fatigue

Fatigue refers to weariness due to bodily or mental exertion. It is a symptom that ubiquitously appears in various acute and chronic diseases. Only patients with fatigue as their chief complaint are of concern here.

Generally speaking, fatigue is mainly attributed to deficiency of *qi* and/or encumbrance by dampness. In the height of summer, the heat that consumes *qi* and fluids often makes one listless and fatigued. Hard labor and improper diet that cause dysfunction of the spleen may lead to retention of dampness. Turbid dampness impedes the normal movement of *yang qi*, resulting in tiredness and lack of energy. Those with inborn weakness or inadequate recuperation after a serious illness also complain of fatigue owing to deficiency of *qi* and blood.

Typical approaches of inquiry:

832. How long have you been suffering from fatigue?
您感到身体疲乏有多久了?

833. (To those who complain of fatigue during the height of summer:) Have you installed air-conditioners at home and at work? What is the approximate room temperature?
（盛夏暑日新发者）您家里和上班的地方安空调了吗? 室温一般在多少度上下?

834. (To chronic fatigue patients:) Can you describe your work briefly? For example, how many hours do you work daily? How often do you work overtime? (How many days a week do you work overtime?)
（长期感到疲乏者）请您简要地向我描述一下您的工作情况，比如一天工作几小时? 每周平均加几天班?

835. Do you participate in physical activity on a regular basis?
您平时进行体育锻炼吗?

836. Can you describe your diet?
请您说说您的饮食情况。

837. What illnesses, if any, have you suffered from in the past?
请您详细介绍一下您患过的疾病。

838. Have you had a physical examination in a hospital recently?
您最近有没有到医院去做过体检?

839. (If yes:) Were there any abnormal indications?
（如做过）发现什么异常没有?

Obesity

Obesity, a condition characterized by excessive bodily fat, may be induced by overeating, lack of physical activity, genetics, etc. Obese patients usually suffer from dizziness, fatigue, listlessness, reluctance to speak and shortness of breath. Obesity may easily be assessed in terms of height and weight. Whenever the body weight is more than 20% over the standard, the condition is designated as obesity. In clinical practice, obesity of the phlegm-dampness pattern and that of the *qi*-deficiency pattern are most frequently encountered.

Typical approaches of inquiry:

840. Judging by your height, your standard weight should be around XX kilograms. Your current weight is xx% over the standard. Can you tell me what you think the reason is? Is it the overeating of greasy and sweet food or lack of physical activity?
按照您的身高，标准体重应该是xx公斤，您现在的体重已超出标准体重xx％以上。您平日饮食中油腻太多，喜欢吃甜食，还是运动太少？

841. How is your appetite?
您的胃口怎么样？

842. Do you have a bigger or smaller appetite than others?
与周围的人相比食量较大还是较小？

843. What is your daily diet?
您平日常吃哪些食物？

844. Do you control your diet?
您控制食量吗？

845. Do you like carbonated beverages?
喜欢喝碳酸饮料吗？

846. (If yes:) What kind of carbonated beverage do you drink? And how much do you drink every day?
（如喜喝）具体喝什么？每天喝多少？

847. Are you engaged in sedentary work or hard physical work?
您的工作性质是整天坐着不动的还是很消耗体力的?

848. Do you take regular physical exercise?
有没有定时的健身锻炼?

849. Do you often have accumulated mucus in your throat?
您平时喉咙里有痰吗?

850. Are you more intolerant of coldness or heat than others?
您和别人比较，是怕冷还是怕热?

851. Are you susceptible to sweating?
容易出汗吗?

852. Have you ever had edema in the legs or ankles?
下肢和脚踝出现过浮肿吗?

Pitting Edema

Pitting edema refers to generalized or localized edema in which pitting results in indentation in the edematous tissues which disappears only slowly. The overall mechanism for edema is disorders of fluid metabolism, which involve the lung, spleen and kidney. The lung governs and regulates water passages. Wind invasion may disable the purifying function of the lung, which leads to blockage of the water passages. This kind of edema appears especially in the eyelids, head and facial areas. Long-term residence in a damp place, or exposure to water such as standing in the rain without protection and walking with bare feet in water may allow dampness to penetrate the body. Overeating or addiction to uncooked and cold food may also give opportunities for dampness to invade the body. The dampness may disturb the spleen, leading to the loss of the ability to transform and transport water-fluid. The stagnant water-fluid is then accumulated and spread under the skin, resulting in edema. Edema of this kind usually appears in the limbs.

The aforementioned edemata are of excess pattern. If edema of excess pattern is not treated properly and in time, the spleen *yang* may be damaged, resulting in edema that is recurrent and difficult to cure. Further development of spleen *yang* deficiency may lead to deficiency of kidney *yang*. The edema persists, with progressive aggravation. Edema of *qi*-blood deficiency pattern is a disorder of the water-fluid metabolism caused by reduced metabolic ability of the spleen and the stomach, or by lack of nutrient supply to the viscera and bowels due to prolonged duration of a disease. There are major differences between edema of *qi*-blood deficiency pattern and that of spleen-kidney *yang* deficiency pattern in clinical manifestations. In the former case, symptoms of *qi* deficiency such as shortness of breath and fatigue, and those of blood deficiency such as pale and sallow complexion, palpitations and dizziness are readily noticeable, while *yang* deficiency symptoms such as intolerance of cold and cold limbs can hardly be observed.

Typical approaches of inquiry:

853. How long have you been suffering from edema?
您患浮肿多久了?

854. Did its onset take place suddenly or gradually?
是突然发生的还是逐渐发生的?

855. Which part of the body did the edema start with?
浮肿是从身体哪个部位开始的?

856. Was there anything special that you think may have caused the edema, such as fever and sore throat from a cold, or being drenched by rain, or overeating cold or uncooked food?
出现浮肿之前有什么明显的诱因吗?比如感冒发烧,咽喉疼痛,或者被雨水淋湿,或者生冷的东西吃多了。

857. Which part of the body is the most swollen? Your face, lower back and abdomen, or lower limbs?
您现在身体哪个部位浮肿最明显?面部?腰腹?下肢?

858. Does the edema make you feel any discomfort, such as a sensation of heaviness in the body and limbs?
浮肿让您感到有什么不适吗？比如身体沉重或肢体沉重。

859. Is there any change in the volume of your urine? Is it the same as before or has it been reduced since the onset of edema?
尿量有变化吗？发现浮肿之后尿量和以前一样还是比以前减少？

860. Besides edema, do you feel any other discomfort? For example, do you have palpitations or shortness of breath?
您除了浮肿之外还有什么不适？有没有心悸气短之类的症状？

861. Has there been any change in your appetite or digestion? Do you eat as well as before?
饮食和消化受影响了吗？食量有没有减少？

862. Are your stools hard and dry, soft, or loose?
大便是干是稀？

863. Are you more intolerant of coldness since you started to suffer from edema? Are you more intolerant of coldness than others?
病后比以前怕冷吗？您比一般人怕冷吗？

Jaundice

Jaundice refers to a condition that is manifested by yellow discoloration of the eyes and skin as well as darkening of the urine, and is frequently encountered in liver and gallbladder ailments. Yellow discoloration of the eye whites (i.e. sclera) is the most significant criterion for the identification of jaundice.

If the discoloration is a bright-yellow color, it is called *yang* jaundice. In most cases, *yang* jaundice is brought on by dampness-heat or warm toxin, and is characterized by acuteness in occurrence, severity in symptoms and shortness in disease course.

On the other hand, jaundice marked by a dull-yellow color belongs to the *yin* pattern, which may be caused by cold-dampness, blood stasis or blood deficiency due to spleen deficiency. *Yin* jaundice is a chronic morbid condition characterized by somewhat indistinct symptoms as well as long disease duration. Syndrome differentiation of jaundice patients mainly relies upon physical signs, but inquiries are also helpful.

Typical approaches of inquiry:

864. How long has it been since you noticed a yellowish color in your eyes? Did you notice it yourself or did someone else call your attention to it?

您发现眼珠发黄有多久了？是您自己先发现的还是别人先发现的？

865. (To patients with acute jaundice:) Do you have a fever?
（对于黄疸病期短者）您发烧了没有？

866. Have you taken your body temperature? What was the highest temperature?
测过体温吗？最高多少度？

867. How is your appetite, good, not very good or poor?
胃口怎么样？胃口好，不很好，还是很不好？

868. Are you tolerant of greasy food?
您现在还有胃口吃油腻的食物吗？

869. Have you felt nauseous? Have you vomited?
有没有恶心？呕吐过吗？

870. Have you suffered bleeding from the nose or gums?
有没有出过鼻血或牙龈出血？

871. (To patients with chronic jaundice:) What symptoms do you have? And what are the major ones?
（对于病期长者）您自己觉得有哪些不舒服的地方？主要是怎么样的不舒服？

872. Do you feel any pain in your rib areas?
胁肋部疼痛吗？

873. Has there been any change of your urine color? Is it

darker?
尿的颜色有没有变化？黄色加深了吗？

874. Has your appetite decreased sharply since you started to suffer from these symptoms? How big is the change in your appetite?
您患病以来食欲减退得明显吗？现在的饭量和病前比较差了多少？

875. Have you ever drunk alcoholic beverages? What kind of alcohol did you drink, and how much every day?
您过去喝酒吗？喝什么酒？每天喝多少？

Inquiries into Past Medical History, Family History, Personal Life History, etc.

For past medical history:

876. Please tell me about any hospitalizations and surgeries you have undergone.
请告诉我您过去生病住院或做过手术吗?

877. What illnesses have you had in the past? Any injuries?
您过去生过什么病? 受过伤吗?

878. Do you have any allergies?
您对什么过敏吗?

For family history:

879. Has anyone else in your family ever had problems like yours?
您的家族中有没有人得过与您一样的疾病?

880. Please tell me about any illnesses that may run in your family, for example, diabetes, cancer or stroke?
请告诉我您的家族中有没有多发的疾病，比如糖尿病、癌症、卒中?

For personal life history:

881. Do you smoke and/or drink?
您抽烟喝酒吗?

882. (If the patient smokes:) How long have you been smoking?
（如病人抽烟）您抽烟有多久了?

883. How many cigarettes do you smoke every day?
每天平均抽多少支?

884. (If the patient drinks:) How long have you been drinking?
（如病人喝酒）您喝酒有多久了?

885. What kind of alcoholic beverages do you drink?
您平时喝什么酒?

886. How much do you drink ordinarily?
每天大概喝多少?

887. Do you drink tea habitually?
您有喝茶的习惯吗?

888. Do you eat greasy food frequently?
您经常吃油腻的食物吗?

889. Do you eat fruit and vegetables every day?
您每天吃蔬菜水果吗?

890. When do you get up every day?
您平日几点起床?

891. When do you usually go to bed?
您通常几点睡觉?

892. Do you participate in physical exercises regularly?
您常进行体育锻炼吗?

For inspecting the patient's tongue and checking the patient's pulse:

893. Please open your mouth, and let me check your tongue.
请张开嘴，让我看一下舌头。

894. Please curl your tongue upward, and let me examine the underside of it.
请把舌头向上卷起，我看看舌头底面。

895. Please stick out your tongue.
请把舌头伸出来。

896. Now I would like to check your pulse. Please put your hand on the cushion with the palm facing upward.
现在给您号脉，请把手放在脉枕上，手心向上。

Farewell:

897. I hope you get well soon.
祝您早日痊愈。

898. I wish you a speedy recovery.
祝您早日恢复健康。

899. I hope you will be back to your normal self soon.
希望您不久就能恢复。

900. See you next week.
下星期再见。

INDEX

图书在版编目（CIP）数据
中医问诊900句：英汉对照 / 谢方，谢竹藩著.
— 北京：外文出版社, 2016
ISBN 978-7-119-09553-0
Ⅰ. ①英… Ⅱ. ①谢… ②谢… Ⅲ. ①问诊 – 英语 – 口语
Ⅳ. ①H319.9
中国版本图书馆CIP数据核字（2015）第150076号

策划指导：胡开敏
英文改稿：Paul White
责任编辑：范淑娟
印刷监制：冯　浩

中医问诊900句
谢　方　谢竹藩　著

出 版 人：徐　步
出版发行：
外文出版社有限责任公司（中国北京西城区百万庄大街24号）
邮政编码：100037　　网址：http://www.flp.com.cn
电　　话：0086-10-68320579（总编室）
　　　　　0086-10-68995852（发行部）
　　　　　0086-10-68327750（版权部）
印　　刷：北京天宇万达印刷有限公司
开　　本：787mm × 1092mm　1/32
印　　张：7.75
2016年1月 第1版　2016年1月 第1次印刷
（英汉）
ISBN 978-7-119-09553-0
05800
（平）

目录
CONTENTS

第三辑 碎锦拾遗

第一辑　观潮悟道

直待凌云始道高

唐朝杜荀鹤有一首《小松》很是耐人寻味："自小刺头深草里，而今渐觉出蓬蒿。 时人不识凌云木，直待凌云始道高。"长松入云，傲霜凌雪，当然会被人们赞美歌颂。但长松并不是生来就身高千尺，也是要经历种子发芽，自小及壮的。当其破土而出，掩于草丛之际，与小草无异。渐渐地，它便要与蓬蒿齐高，最后，必将凌空入云，直冲霄汉。这时人们才意识到它的与众不同。然而，当它混迹于小草，淹没于灌丛时，谁能知道它的凌云之志，未来将展现绝世之姿呢?

松柏如此，人亦无异。有些人和我们一样出身平凡，同步入学，共历时艰。在同一赛道起步，初时不过尔尔，日久天长，他们就一茬一茬地超越众人，崭露头角，最后一骑绝尘，不可企及。他们曾经经过我们身边，甚至和我们并肩走了很长一段时间，在我们不经意间，他们渐行渐快，渐行渐远，直到不见踪影。而我们仍然迈着固有的步伐，不紧不慢地跟着。之前和我们并行的时候，我们并不觉得他们有什么特殊之处，若干年之后，发现彼此居然有了天壤之别，乃至于看到他们脱胎换

骨，我们无论如何都不敢相信，曾与如此英杰共过事甚至饮过酒。

是的，大师往往就在身边，只是大多数人发现不了，或者发现了也不愿意承认。当他泯然于众之时，没有人会对他高看一眼，只有当他独自一人立于悬崖之巅的时候，众人才会开始对他热情仰望，赞美不绝。正如松没于草，不为人知，及至凌云，众人无不道高。

开窍

人生起气来可以七窍生烟，喝了剧毒会七窍流血，能通烟过血，说明七窍是通的。一旦有哪窍不通，说明身体可能出了问题。《红楼梦》第五十七回云：“彼时贾母又命将祛邪守灵丹及开窍通神散各样上方秘制诸药，按方饮服。”显然贾母身体有恙，须服开窍通神散，冲开堵塞的窍门。可见身体正常的情况下，人们身上的窍门都是开通的。

然而思想上的窍门恰恰相反，一般都是关着的，有些人甚至关了一辈子，从来没有开通过。有些人费了九牛二虎之力，才开了一丝缝隙。只有少数人找准了路数，打开了窍门。开没开窍门，表现是完全不一样的，没开时愚不可及尚不自知，开通后智不可及且心知肚明。智者虽然混迹愚者之中，却如立于空中，以高于常人的视角俯瞰人间，一丝一毫皆历历在目。所以我们在纷繁复杂的生活中常见有人会心一笑，意态从容，更多的人则是茫然无知，神情慌乱。因为没开窍，故百思不得其解；因为开了窍，故万事了然于心。人们常说人生通达了，其实就是思想窍门终于开了。

要畅通窍门，首先必须大量阅读，增加文化底蕴，汇聚思想力量。初时也许不能撼动窍门分毫，但日积月累之后，待到形成一股强大内力之时，并敌一向，自可无坚不摧，届时窍门大开，世界焕然一新。

要畅通窍门，还须多多经历。最好是失败多于成功，逆境多于顺境，坎坷多于坦途。因为得时常易迷失，失时才能保持清醒。痛定思痛之后，思想会日益深刻，境界会日益阔远，凝聚的力量逐渐雄浑激荡，将决堤拍岸，不可阻遏，窍门封闭得再紧，也终将被冲裂。

思想开窍是生活的高级状态，是人生的无上境界，只有那些极具智慧的人才能做到。

用力不同

人生的不同阶段，着力该有所区别才对。年轻时要有冲力。在蓁莽荒秽、山河阻隔的地方开拓出一条属于自己的道路来，须当披荆斩棘，筚路蓝缕。这时候最需要的是一股冲劲，以不惧万难之心，排山倒海之势，一鼓作气，勇往直前。此时最忌讳的是心存畏惧，犹豫不决，因为一停顿，力便有所消减，重新凝聚就不是那么容易了，力竭势衰，曾不能穿鲁缟，何况穿云裂石。只要不顾一切地奋力前冲，那些看起来不可逾越的障碍都将踏于脚下，似乎无路之处定会柳暗花明。冲劲越足，越多的毫无可能将转化为理所当然。

人到中年，比拼的是耐力。年轻时身强力壮，精气充沛，初生牛犊不怕虎，可以大胆地闯，无畏地试，大不了重新再来，东山再起，力气有的是，时间一大把。但正如暴风不终朝，骤雨不终日，随着岁月流逝，青春不再，势沉力猛之态自然要逐渐减弱，这时比拼的再也不是气壮山河的冲劲，而是绵绵不绝的耐力。谁的力持久，谁的路就绵长。有些人，年轻时倒是冲劲十足，到了中年，不曾蓄力，不懂生力，一下子后继乏力，很快就沉沦下去。而有些人深懂借力，长于借力，力量源源不断，故能将事业进行到底。

进入老年，讲究的是定力。所谓定力，便是心中已有谋划，未来已有安排，耳中所闻，眼中所见，决计不能撼动分毫。灯红酒绿，苍凉寂寞，历经万千情境，内心早已不起任何波澜。大多数人其实都是处于一种情绪变化、目标漂移的状态，今天获得一信息而彻夜难眠，明天损失一小利又坐立不安，茫然失措，永无宁日。只有少数人能经得住生活的折磨、名利的诱惑，做到依然故我。

年轻时横枪跃马席卷千军，中年时渊渟岳峙绵亘不绝，老年时心若止水如如不动，这才是不同人生阶段的正确用力方式。

豪雄

说到豪雄，在我们脑海里或许会闪现横枪跃马的将军形象，也可能会闪现叱咤风云的政治家形象，或者是功夫卓绝的侠客形象。但宋朝的理学家程颢定义的豪雄，却与此截然不同。他有一首诗《秋日偶成》云：

闲来无事不从容，睡觉东窗日已红。
万物静观皆自得，四时佳兴与人同。
道通天地有形外，思入风云变态中。
富贵不淫贫贱乐，男儿到此是豪雄。

他认为，真正的豪雄，是任何时候都意态从容，心中不羁不牵的，一觉可以睡到自然醒。他眼中的万物都各得其所，动静相宜。他心中的趣向与四时景象高度契合，两两相得。天地间有形无形之物寓含的道，与他悟得的道是连贯相通的。他的思绪幺远，在风云变幻之中。富贵相招，他不会有半点改变。贫贱相迫，他依然乐在其中。

乍一看，诗中溢美的豪雄，似乎毫无驰骋疆场纵横四海的英雄豪杰气概。但仔细琢磨，能做到程颢所言者，岂止是豪雄，简直是圣人。显然，在程颢看来，豪雄不是指英勇无敌豪气干云，有着一副威风凛凛的架势，而是指思接千载心游万仞，有着一种和煦从容的姿态。他也许并不高大伟岸，气势如虹，但他一定内心充盈，畅通无碍。看上去他渊渟岳峙静如处子，精神却吞吐天地，与日月同光。

以程颢的界定，我们放眼古今，真的很难找到几个真正的豪雄。在国力强盛经济发达的今天，人们理想状态是不计贫富、意态从容，思及万物道生于心，可生活中接触的人仍有慌慌张张思虑重重，对四季、对自然少有关心。雄姿固然是缺少的，豪气就更难感受到。偶见一些超凡出众者，也远不及程颢所指。无疑，程颢把豪雄的标准定得太高了。

安度一生

一个人要安全地走完一生实在不是一件容易的事，更无庸说顺利地走完一生。当然此处所指的一生不是指短暂的一生，几岁十几岁就夭折，或者二三十岁就英年早逝，算不上完整的一生。按照古人的说法，至少要活过五十岁，才算是正常的一辈子。

战争、天灾、饥荒这些大的时代背景摊上一个，这个人的一生就将千疮百孔。绝症、车祸、意外听起来似乎是小概率事件，可身边每年都有发生。躲过各种死神的追捕，才能勉强地活下来。从历史的长河中有选择性地截取一个五十年，可能都发生过许多不平凡的事情。如果随意截取，就会碰到大大小小的自然灾害或人为事件。大唐盛世、北宋初年、文宣之治、康乾盛世这些时代，或许能找到一段相对平静的岁月，但纵观上下五千年，安全度过五十年谈何容易。

就个体而言，突然死于地震海啸、病毒水火、车祸空难者大有人在。经过历史自然以及命运的残酷筛选，一大批人都将被无情淘汰，只有一部分人能够活下来，而活下来才有资格谈活得如何。所以安全活过五十年本身就是一种胜利，就值得举手相庆，因为比历史上的绝大多数人都更加幸运。特别是中华人民共和国成立七十多年来，可谓历史鼎盛的时代，生存早已不是问题，人们谋求的是如何更好地发展。从生活质量上说，古人与今人不可同日而语。

宦海沉浮、商场风云、生活磨难、情感挫折，这些都是人生的平常经历，比起战争灾害简直不值一提。平安地度过人生，是一个人的大运程；至于顺不顺利，不过是一个人的小确幸，只要平安，无论怎样，都是美好的人生。

安享当下

小时候我们有梦想，长大了我们有期待，这是催促我们积极进取的动力，但也是搅乱我们心绪的祸源。因为总想着未来，所以我们常常忽略现在。如果当前的情形不如意，我们自然会迫切地寄望未来；若当前一切顺利，我们也无暇尽享其妙，而更想要居安思危未雨绸缪，因而永不知足，也就永无宁日。

正确的人生展开方式，其实应该是奋发向上，享有当下，不期未来。任何时候，人都应该积极有为而不是消极等待，耕耘时不必老想着收获，应该将时下的事情扎实做好，然后坦然接受现有的一切欢乐或者痛苦。不要总是过分寄望于未来，在虚无缥缈中花心思耗时间，人生在希望中度过，听起来很不错，但掠过满是烟火气的当下，剩下的只是无尽的等待而已。就在此时，我们可以去山寺外赏花，长河边折柳，静夜中望月，哪怕掩袖叹息，迎风流泪，长歌当哭，那也是一种真实，值得我们全身心投入。

如果有个鸡蛋，尽可以想办法去孵化成小鸡，但不要陷入蛋生鸡鸡生蛋，鸡、蛋无穷匮的虚幻想象当中，因一个鸡蛋而成为富翁的未来，虽然理论上有这种可能，但没有期待性。再如，当着科长就老老实实地在这个平台上把事情做到极致，不要去设想当到处长会如何美妙，否则整个人生除了两三次晋升的喜悦外，其余都是漫长的等待和无尽的烦恼。当着讲师就循序渐进地把课讲好，享受学生们的赞美或者接受他们的质疑，不要一味设想当了教授荣获盛名之后的境况，等到那时再欢喜也不迟。

不思未来不代表不思进取，而是不作无谓的想象，想象或许能获取力量，但更多会带来欲壑难填的烦忧，生动的现实就在触手可及之处，为什么还要去透支不可预测的未来?

人到中年

车好如奔驰者，刚开的时候也不见得就很顺手，开个几万公里以后，人与车之间，各个部件之间磨合得日益默契，这时才会感觉平顺畅达，如行云流水一般。待行驶四五十万公里之后，车的所有部件皆已陈旧，跑起来耗油费力，这时就得赶紧想办法处置。否则，不仅开起来不痛快，甚至有性命之忧。

新买的皮鞋，刚穿时肯定不是很舒适，甚至容易起泡成茧，穿上一两个月后慢慢就适应了，合脚了，走起路来轻便自如，毫无滞碍。一两年之后，皮革开始老化，这里起毛那里开裂，不仅有碍观瞻，还会影响行动，必须果断地进行断舍离。

刚出炉的茅台，虽品质上乘，却辛辣激烈。有人珍藏了几十年，期以稀为贵。其实这时酒气早已蒸发得所剩无几了，就酒本身的品质而言，到了嘴里可能已不是固有滋味。储存八年十年的酒，最是温柔敦厚。喝起来必是芳香满鼻，口舌生津。

人也一样，年轻的时候比较青涩，不仅别人接触起来觉得气辛味苦，就是自己也时常觉得生疏莽撞。年纪大了，又过于油滑，毫无期冀中的不问东西，少了一份华丽，也就失了一种生气。人到中年，恰到好处，正如磨合好的车、穿顺脚的鞋、放香醇的酒。成熟稳重，经万事而不乱；从容淡定，处百变而不惊。与人相处，如沐春风。临流默坐，快然自足！

人到中年，是花开正艳的时候，是嫩叶深绿的时候，是秋高气爽的时候，是江入大海的时候，饱满浑厚、雍容自在，舒之弥四海，卷之不盈怀。

磨难

磨难在经历的时候是磨难，经历过后就是故事。正如《西游记》中唐僧师徒经过九九八十一难，每一难对唐僧来说都有性命之忧，经受时无时无刻不胆战心惊，魂飞魄散，可一一记录下来就成了一个个精彩的降妖伏魔故事，我们听起来无不觉得跌宕起伏，生动有趣，可我们有谁去设想过唐僧彼时的心境和感受呢?

生活中其实也有许多的磨难，也许在某个阳光灿烂的午后出现，或者在某个月明星稀的夜晚来临，小者让我们忧心，大者让我们恐惧，谁都不愿在明媚的日子突闻一声惊雷，在平静的大海中偶遇一阵台风，可命运有时偏要安排苦难相随，想避都避不开。那些生长在战争年代的人，免不了要穿越枪林弹雨，被迫流离失所，经历千百劫难，冒着生命危险。走不出来，便遭遇了事故；走出来了，便带着一身的故事。回忆起来，虽然惊心动魄，但毕竟已成往事，足以让自己夸耀一世。

生活中的磨难，其实是帮助我们成长最好的钙片，让我们身板强壮起来，骨头坚硬起来，心理成熟起来，不再因为风吹草动而心惊肉跳，不再把一声呼哨当作雷霆之音。正是磨难让我们的人生变得完整，变得丰赡。一些君主生于深宫，长于妇人之手，菽麦不分，五谷不辨，即使拥有天下，终究胆怯心虚，力有未逮，江山必难永固。而那些身经百战，在刀光剑影中走来的开国之君，往往就信心十足，不惮风霜雪雨，生死都不在话下，其他还有何惧?

磨难，顾名思义就是磨得痛苦，难得无解。碰到了自非儿戏，轻者脱层皮，重者或许丢了半条命。在你决定选择走什么样的人生道路时，就已经注定你要经受什么样的磨难。当然你也可以选择躺平，毕生碌碌无为，但风雨后的彩虹，你注定是看不到了。

存乎一心

如果注定是一只青蛙，我宁愿待在井底。一孔之天虽小，于我已足矣。且在井水深处，独自放声，高低起伏由我，不必左顾右盼，惶惑难安。鸣之嘹亮喑哑，亦无须在意，反正都是孤芳自赏。兴之所至，纵横水面，雀跃井壁。意兴阑珊时，便卧于水草丛中，静思遐想，在不知不觉中入眠。外面的世界有多大，风物有多少？不得而知，亦无意得知，我知道，只要跃出井沿，天空会陡然辽阔，自己却会瞬间渺小，在陌生的空间，找不到熟悉的水草，难免会怅然若失，与其在繁华的世界惴惴不安，不如在寂静的天地一念不起。

当然，如果身具鲲鹏的潜质，我一定会奋力飞向天空，绝云气，负青天，展翅翱翔。绝不会做那抢榆枋而止、腾跃于蓬蒿之间的燕雀。长空中固然有风雨，大地上必然有暗箭，但既然选择了天空，就意味着永不停息地飞翔，而且是无人陪伴的天涯孤旅。越过千山万水，穿过层云叠嶂，只影但向高远处而去。

是鹰击长空还是蛰伏井底，取决于对自身的价值判断，翅膀不硬，就不必作长空之想，敢于戏水，就去大海中遨游！自认为一只井底之蛙，自自在在于方寸之间腾挪跳跃，安安静静地度过一生，似乎并无什么不妥。而自认为是一只图远的鲲鹏，尽可以在搏击长空中获得乐趣，在俯视人间时胸胆开张。宏大或微小，显扬或幽隐，各有各的妙处，一切皆存乎一心。

人生的搏斗

我们一辈子都在搏斗。少年时期，我们与书本搏斗。学知识学文化，一直都在上课学习之中，书本是我们最大的“敌人”，每天都要与它拼杀一番，恨不得把它撕碎吞进肚子里。可就是那么百十本书，耗去了我们十几年时光。有人拼赢了，成为大学生。有人高考失利了，与大学失之交臂。相同的是，都用尽了美好的少年时代。

青壮年时期，我们与人事搏斗。但凡有人的地方，就有利益之争、地位之争。事实上，我们一直处于一种竞争的状态，以获得某种优越的身份，好在社会上有个立足之地。毕竟，我们不是生活在桃花源，“黄发垂髫并怡然自乐”只是一种理想境界。现实之中，人们一定是要分个彼此的。所以明争暗斗不过是家常便饭。为什么人们觉得疲劳孤独，因为生活的本质就是拼搏。竞争哪有不劳累的？对手之间又有多少温情可讲？任何时候，都处于一种备战之态，而且始终是一个人在奋斗，肩负着压力，忍受着寂寞，经历着苦难，这就是我们整个青壮年时代的真实写照。

老年时期，我们要与病魔搏斗。退休以后，曾经复杂的人事突然烟消云散，即使还保留着旺盛的战斗力，也找不见昔日的敌手。而此时，病魔却盯上了我们，主动发起了进攻，逼迫我们奋起反抗，这场战役一直要打到人生结束，而且注定是越打越激烈，最后必将以我们的失败而告终。但是，是毫无还手之力地被击溃，还是英勇顽强地抵抗至力尽，最后像个英雄一般地倒下，完全取决于我们的观念和意志。

我以为，少年时与书本的搏斗是必须的，但惜时的同时也要惜力；青壮年时与人事搏斗，不必过于较真，谈笑之间风云流散；如此老年时与病魔搏斗便游刃有余，即使打上几次遭遇战，也还是消耗得起的。

思行万里

因为要参加一个活动，乘车穿越了整个城市，在路上耗费了几个小时。路要左转右拐，甚至有时必须“舍近求远”。车流如水，汇集成河，裹挟其中，只能顺势而行。一栋栋建筑占据了大部分城市空间，在一个个被切割的单元边奋力突围，我突然感觉这座城市并不属于我们，城市的主体是那些高耸入云的摩天大楼，我们只是填充在街区和道路上的材料，渺小如沙粒。而恰恰是我们自己，在原本空旷平整、长满花草树木的地方，种植了钢铁森林，然后每天在里面跌跌撞撞地游走，消耗着青春岁月。我们一边怨声载道，责怪着交通堵塞，空气污秽；一边又乐此不疲，混迹于嘈杂闹市、拥挤广场。是所谓痛并快乐着。

相对于驾车阻塞难行，我更愿意畅思纵横四海。思绪是不会受阻塞的，只要胸怀够开阔，灵魂够纯净。且不说穿越城市，就是穿越国家，穿越历史，也不过倏忽之间。那种在朝代之间变幻，在山水之间转换的感觉畅快淋漓，绝无堵车绕路的烦闷之气。所以非不得已，我实在是不愿意身动，陷在支离破碎的城市空间不能自拔。我宁愿心动，沉浸在一个远古的江南小镇不思进取。

其实，我们完全可以选择放弃狭小的生存环境，奔向更加广阔的自由天地。可为什么大家还是愿意被堵被塞被局限，是习惯使然，还是无力挣脱？是身有所欲，还是思有未逮？

尊严

活着，每个人都有尊严。至于宝不宝贵，要视其处境而定。生活都成了问题，不乞讨则无以为生，这时尊严便不值什么钱了，只要能混口吃的，下跪哀求再委屈也得认命。没有尊严附身，就像没有穿衣地奔走，回到了动物原形。监狱里往往只唤其号，不呼其名，因为这里只是一个群体，不存在各具特色的个体，尊严被剥夺了，你就不是你，而只是一个活着的生命，大家都一样，名字也就失去意义了，编号的用处不过是为了不至于混淆。古代进监狱，犯人无论是达官还是显贵，首先都要被折辱一番，有时候还要被打上几十甚至上百杀威棒，不仅打伤打残你的身体，还要打掉你的威风气焰，实际上就是让你尊严扫地，逢人抬不起头，做一个没有羞耻心的行尸走肉。

有时候，对尊严也无需过于看重。越是强调尊严，越难放下身段。而行走于江湖，生存于社会，时时处处都要抛开尊严，弯腰俯首，态度任何时候都比能力重要，始终保持着矜持与傲然，倒是拥有了十足的尊严，却很可能一事无成，即使你满身才华。当然，尊严至上者也不在少数，他们宁愿放弃飞翔的机会、登顶的可能，也丝毫不愿侮辱自己的尊严，稍许削减自己的精神。

那些被羞辱到极点，或者曾经全部丢失过尊严的人，有时更容易悟道，更容易有成就。经历牢狱之灾后，反而更加通达豁然，懂得了人生的价值和意义。像李煜、苏轼、元好问等，莫不如此。经历过毫无尊严的日子，他们更能体会尊严的重要性，更会看轻看淡荣华富贵和权势名利。

尊严是人的精神内核，但人与人的尊严观却截然不同，在有些人眼中，尊严一钱不值，丢了就丢了。而在另一些人眼中，尊严有时胜过生命，丢了，无论如何都要找回来。

不过如此

苏轼曾有诗《观潮》云："庐山烟雨浙江潮，未至千般恨不消。到得还来别无事，庐山烟雨浙江潮。"大致是说，庐山烟雨和浙江海潮是两大著名景致，没去观赏将终生遗憾。但是真的到现场一看，也没什么特别之处，不过是区区庐山烟雨普通浙江海潮罢了。景未亲临，总觉美如仙境，无与伦比，特别是经人描绘传说，更有一睹方休的欲望。及至亲眼目睹，似乎与想象之景梦中之境相去甚远，盛名之下其实难副，不免生起失望之意：原来一切不过如此。事情也是一样，未曾亲历，总会将其想象得神秘酷炫，多姿多彩，恨不得身临其境，全程参与。但若真的置身其中，不过都是日常点滴，细枝末节，并不曲折离奇、高潮迭起。

未涉官场之人，看到官员们备受尊崇，威风凛凛，羡慕至极，发誓一定要跻身官场，一尝滋味。及其如愿，案牍劳形，万事烦心，责任重大。此时方意识到，官员似乎并没有想象中的好当。

没做过富翁，以为富人的生活都是豪华奢侈，一掷千金，坐着豪车，住着别墅，整日无所事事，不是听音乐喝红酒，就是给美丽女人送花送钻戒。于是千方百计要发家致富。富了之后，才知道富人有富人的烦恼，一样要操心事业，一样要谋划未来，一样要协调关系，一样要搏击风浪，一个不小心，可能早晚之间就变成穷光蛋。富过后才明白，富翁原来也不像人们看到的那般潇洒自如。

美丽如庐山烟雨，壮观如浙江海潮，未见时特别想见，见了后也不过如此。得意如官员，潇洒如富翁，没做成时特别艳羡，做成后滋味也无甚特别。人生就是如此，见过经过，万事万物皆普通平常。

一如既往

把最后一页日历撕完，一年又在手下翻过。也就是说，生命又减去了一岁。这时人们往往会有些急切，有些怅然，也有些期待。在一年的尽头，人们都喜欢进行盘点，看看自己到底在经济上，在职位上，在情感上，在知识上，在身体上有多少进益，又有多少减损。是得不偿失，还是得多失少，梳理清晰总比揣着一笔糊涂账好，至少在接下来的日子，可以扬长避短，更富成效。

我已经很久不作过往回顾与未来展望了。我不喜欢把一生的时光切割成一段一段，每当一段流逝，便要反复哀叹，动情吟咏。我是以整生为时限来计量得失成败的，所以年的新旧变更于我，只是时序有所推移而已，并无心理上的影响。换句话说，我不再以年龄衡量我的老少，也不会以一年的光景好坏定输赢。要看就看远一点，以一生为期，那时才值得回忆和总结。

所以我像往常一样循序渐进地落实着固有的计划，这些绸缪因为没有短期目的性，显得散漫而平淡，如果以年作为评价时间，也不会出现超凡出众之果。但若绵延数十年，一定会显现石破天惊之功。旧的一年过去，我没有什么感伤，新的一年来临，我也没有什么期待。只是像往常一样，检查了一下行装，在早就选好的道路上继续缓步前行而已。

我收到了许多温馨的祝福、善意的提醒，他们其实夸大了时光更迭的警示作用，这个新旧交叉的刹那转瞬即逝，过后一切都会照旧。如果观念没有更新，就是天天将“新”字写在脚底，也还是会走老路。我感到庆幸的是，我已经无需通过岁月的惊心而回头，而是一路心情愉悦地循着曙光去探胜。

难熬时段

过去在农村，最难过的是夏天的双抢时间，一个月内必须收割好稻子插好秧。而这个月正处于南方最酷热的时候，特别是每天下午两点左右，田里的水几乎要沸腾，路上的石板烫得让人不敢迈步，走进烈日草地里，偷闲片刻是乘凉。那是最难熬的时刻，每天挺过这一时段，剩下的就不在话下。

后来时常通宵加班赶文稿，凌晨两三点钟是个坎，特别疲劳困顿，每次都要拧脸刺股，咬牙坚持，过了瞌睡点，便渐渐清醒兴奋了。近日与朋友闲聊，他劝我尝试着跑跑马拉松，一听说要跑几十公里，我当即表示不敢问津，他说其实长跑最累的就是跑到五六公里的时候，过后便越跑越舒畅。看来做任何一件需要毅力和耐心的事情，都有最难熬的节点，挺不住就将前功尽弃，挺住了就会一马平川。

人生也是如此，要完成既定的事业，总有一个难熬的时段。我想我也许已经身临这个节点，读书到了悟与未悟之间，创作到了成与未成之间，一切嘈杂之音汹汹而来，一切引诱之力源源不断，令人顿步不前，心旌摇动。熬过去考较的不仅是定力，还有智慧。视而不见五色，听而不闻五音，像天上的云飘过湖面而不留影，像空中的风穿过森林而不留迹。大千世界，我在；芸芸众生，我与。但我不想稍作停留，必须下定决心，一往无前，才能越过那个最难熬的时段。

成事的条件

王国维《人间词话》云：“古今之成大事业、大学问者，必经过三种境界。‘昨夜西风凋碧树。独上高楼，望尽天涯路’，此第一境也；‘衣带渐宽终不悔，为伊消得人憔悴’，此第二境也；‘众里寻他千百度，蓦然回首，那人却在，灯火阑珊处’，此第三境也。”这三种境界用今天的大白话讲，就是独行、坚持、到达。独行是寂寞的，坚持是难忍的，到达是伴随光明的。王国维所言三个境界在观点上并无创新之处，只是在表达上分别用了晏殊《蝶恋花》、柳永《蝶恋花》、辛弃疾《青玉案》中的名句连缀而成，所以显得新颖别致，故而脍炙人口。

成大事业大学问，我以为须得具备四个条件：洞穿的智慧、断舍的勇气、不辍的坚持以及格物的天赋。纷繁人世，恰似云雾缭绕的苍茫大海，须要有一双慧眼，如灯塔的航灯一般，穿透层层夜幕，看清暗礁冰山，寻找正确的人生航向。所有虚伪的世故、美丽的谎言、狡黠的心机，在慧眼的洞穿之下，纷披如败草落叶。

我们生存于人世，正如结网于社会，千丝万缕百般缠绕，胁迫利诱，裹挟推搡，有些时候身不由己，有些时候流连忘返。必须有坚定意志、淡泊之心，才能捋得清斩得断脱得身，从此顿开枷锁，轻松自如，扬长而去。去时当独自默然而行，远离热闹人群。被曲解被轻视甚至被羞辱，是必历之常态，而孤灯伴影寂寞相随，几乎是终生标配。无韧性无恒心，当然无以至千里。

而重中之重，在于格物。《礼记·大学》云："致知在格物，物格而后知至。"格物能力有多强，决定了至知将达到什么程度。有些人毕生努力，却业绩平平。有些人不鸣则已，一鸣惊人。对人情世态、万事万物的认识理解，常人经过历练而深刻，天才却先天具足通透达观之性。糊里糊涂懵懵懂懂地虚度一生者也不在少数。

大凡成就大事业大学问者，考其一生，多具备此四种优越品质，四种品质或无不突显，或此强彼弱，但皆不可或缺。

孤帆远去

历史的长河一泻五千年，到了此时此处，已是潮平两岸阔了。泛舟于柳边月下，赏景垂钓，悠然自得，从此不必再担心激流漩涡暗礁险滩了。在水光山色的大图画中，是乘巨轮还是驾扁舟，是停于水之中央，还是驶入莲花深处，都没有本质的区别。风雨是难免的，冷暖是必经的，那只是生活中的点缀，不足以动摇心神，惊人魂魄。

正因为无往不适，无往不快，我宁愿荡起小舟一叶，任凭生活的细浪推动前行。我知道，再怎么漂流，也遇不到飞瀑急湍、猛浪怒涛，既然没有沉没的危险，就不妨从流漂荡，任意东西。河中有河中的深邃，沿岸有沿岸的旖旎。居于中心，我自有威及四方的力量；游于边沿，我自有信马由缰的萧散。生活的船儿载我直行就任凭它直行，沿洄就任凭它沿洄，直行就观赏崭新的美景，沿洄则重新观赏一次乃至多次美景，于我只是一路经行，一路观赏，除此别无所求，所以快点慢点，直行迂回都无关紧要。那些一意要到达目的地的人才会讲究速度，讲究路线。

我也曾经着力划动双桨，掌控着我的生活之舟，如脱弦之箭，朝着既定的方向，飞奔未来。可到头来，并没有让我心情舒畅，相反，倒令我愁肠百结。于是我松手放开双桨，将小舟还给生活本身，任由它带着我漂泊遨游。生活并未辜负我的信任，冥冥之中，它给我作下的安排，竟完全符合我的心意。生活之舟漂流的路线也许并不完美，但真切而自然，与我的天性禀赋十分契合。我知道，我的生活之舟漂移过程中，有人试图强行改变它的方向，甚至迟滞它的流动，但一切都徒劳无功。它左右逢源，纵一苇之所如，飘然而去，最后孤帆远影，消失在茫茫水面。

造谣中伤阴谋诡计织就的箭雨

造谣中伤阴谋诡计织就的箭雨，横向竖向斜向从不同的方向密集射来，穿行其中，中招是必然的。特别是年轻时血热气盛，喜欢分众而出，猛打猛冲，而且不穿铠甲，正如三国时期的莽汉许褚，动辄赤膊上阵，最后常带着一身羽箭重伤而归。但那时血气方刚，无所畏惧，受伤容易，恢复亦快。

后来学会了防御之术，挥舞盾牌，横挡竖磕，将来箭纷纷击落在地，虽然有时仍会被冷箭射中，毕竟能躲过大多危险，避免了无谓的损伤。而且，随着抵御功夫的精进，平常力道的暗箭根本造不成什么威胁。但此时也不过是兵来将挡水来土掩，只要不受伤害，已经算是极大的成功了，还是毫无还手之力的。

智高一筹后，不再用盾牌死挡硬接箭雨，而是琢磨着扎好草人，效仿孔明草船借箭的法子，依托雨雾烟尘的掩护，深入虎穴，鼓噪而进，主动吸引明箭暗箭万箭齐发，向自己射来，最好是一支不剩。在此之前，但只着力把草人设计好，摆放好，而自己置身其中，无论箭自何方射来，都不至于到达身上。那些箭枝只要一射入草人之中，便无声无息无影无踪。只待闲暇时，慢慢将草人身上的箭枝一一拔出，捆好装袋入库，需要时，可以倾囊相射，以其人之道，还治其人之身。

若真正练成了雄厚内功，便不再惧怕箭雨了。根本无需躲避。正面布好的箭阵，猝不及防的冷箭，一概张襟受之。谈笑之间，身形微震，便将飞箭碎为齑粉。不仅自身损伤不了分毫，还让射箭者见之胆寒，从此再也不敢偷施冷箭，否则，哪天弹回自己身上，便要自作自受了。

在这漫天箭雨的人间走完一生，我们不知要身中多少毒箭，防是没法防得住的，即使防备再周全，百密尚有一疏，受伤是难免的。比较好的办法要么是练就金钟罩铁布衫，强弓硬弩也无法伤及；要么是练就无上内力，箭不及身，就已被混元之气震落于地。

做个有争议的人

孔子曾作过一个判断："乡愿，德之贼也。"用现代的语言表达，就是一个人人都说好的人，一定是个德行有问题的人。只有逢人说人话，逢鬼说鬼话的人才会赢得所有人的赞扬。换句话说，一个人人认可的人必是一个毫无原则毫无态度的伪君子真小人。生活中，无论是政界商界还是学界，都有不少这样的"老好人"，如果在投票举手表决定乾坤的简单甄拔选优机制中，他们一定会青云直上。

当然人人都反感厌恶的人也好不到哪里去，只是他们的丑陋拙劣都显露无遗，人们一接触便能迅速地感受判别，防范起来比较简易。而"乡愿"往往以敦厚老实的假面目示人，不知不觉中，人们不仅自己受其蒙骗，还将为成就其名而张目，成为他们跳远的垫石、登高的踏板。人人尽道其恶，或人人尽溢其美，皆非善类。普通的人都是多数人肯定，少数人非议，而真正优秀者往往是富有争议的人。富有争议，说明他们身上有着吸引他人注意的特质。一个毫无传奇色彩，不具非凡才能的人，是很难让人关注并生发兴趣的。一般来说，引起他人争议者必是与众不同者，要么能力超群，要么学识超群，要么智慧超群。超群就自然有人由衷钦服，真诚赞美。面对超出自己一大截的强者，大多数人还是愿意坦承自己学不如人、技不如人、艺不如人、识不如人。但也有不少人，心中永远将自己摆在第一位，不管别人有多强大，都要找到人家的短板，说三道四，死活不肯承认他们的长处优势。所以即使是鲁迅这种大师级的人物，虽然一生铿锵有力全身傲骨铮铮，仍然常被人讽刺挖苦，攻击诋毁，用以成就他们的私名。

争议，有时难免唾沫横飞，污水横流。这让饱受争议又喜好清静的人少不得要掩鼻塞耳，洗心净意。但能引起争议者又岂是凡人！既然非凡，就要承受非凡之议、非凡之辱，相较于做个人人言好的“乡愿”，真不如做个毁誉参半的争议人物好，至少可以放浪形骸，畅快平生。

时位移人

清代周容曾写过一篇文章《芋老人传》，非常生动深刻。文中讲到一个书生进城赶考，途中在一个老人家里避雨，其时又冷又饿，老人为他煮了一碗芋头，书生吃后觉得乃是人间最美味的佳肴。后来书生考中进士，官至相国，穿的都是绫罗绸缎，吃的都是山珍海味。可再珍稀贵重的食品在他觉来，都远不及当年那碗芋头那么香甜可口。于是他令人将那个老人请到家里，专门为他烹煮芋头，可他吃后觉得也是口味一般，与赶考时吃的芋头味道相去甚远。他百思不得其解，老人却一语道破。他说，芋头还是那碗芋头，可今时不同往日，你当年不过是个穷书生，而且遇到阴风冷雨，饥寒交加，如今已是堂堂相国，餐餐可谓食不厌精，脍不厌细。时位一变，人的很多方面包括味觉、情绪就会跟着产生变化，此谓“时位之移人也”。相国听完不禁恍然大悟，由衷敬服老人的奇谈高论。

随着时位的变化，人们的心态、思绪、情感、眼光甚至口味都将发生变化，但胸怀、识见、智慧却不一定有所长进。正如那位相国，已经位极人臣，决断天下了，却始终弄不明白一碗芋头滋味变化的道理。某些人自年轻时即进入官场，累迁至贵爵高位、一方诸侯。什么人间尤物、金玉珠宝、绝世美味都经历过见识过玩味过品尝过，按说，他们最有可能悟得天地大道人生至理，与过去的自己相比，将发生脱胎换骨的变化。可惜的是，他们的确前后判若两人，却只是情感愈来愈虚伪了，物欲愈来愈膨胀了，享受愈来愈奢华了，处事愈来愈世故了，而锐气却愈来愈钝化了，眼光愈来愈短浅了，胸怀愈来愈狭隘了，思想愈来愈陈旧了。不变的是智慧，以前约等于零，现今仍然约等于零。

于我而言，随着年龄的增长，时已巨变，而位则岿然不动。因为待人之情如旧，处世之法如旧，遇到时位已变的故交旧友，自然显得不合时宜。至于观点理念，自诩尚能月新年异，而遇到时位虽变而心智如旧的故交旧友，竟觉相顾无言以对。因为见面彼此尴尬别扭，渐渐就疏于来往，久了，遂有遗世独立之感。芋老人言时位之移人者，所感最深。

朋友

一般来说，随着生活的深入持久，家中的物品必是越积越多，到最后满房满屋，不得不进行断舍离。平素里，我们采购物品常常痛快淋漓，然置之家中却无所用，扔了又舍不得。与朋友之间常馈赠礼品，送人时自是从商场、网上购买新品相送，人送的则带回家中，多半用处也不大，丢了又不忍心。如此一来，进多出少，日积月累，家中藏物便不可胜数。其实一个家庭，除了锅碗瓢盆、柴米油盐、桌椅板凳、衣帽鞋袜等必备物品，许多东西一年甚至数年都用不了一次。比如书房中的书籍，有些恐怕一辈子都不会再翻动，但真要舍弃，总觉得怪可惜的。衣柜里的衣服，有些已经挂了几年甚至十几年，想着哪天还可以穿上一两次，事实上直到老去，基本上不会再碰了。其他物品也多是如此，长年不动者恐占一半以上。但收拾起来，却觉得件件都还有用，几乎没有什么是可以毫不痛心地断舍的。

通讯录和朋友圈里的朋友也是一样，在社会上走得越远越久，结识的朋友肯定是越来越多的，毕竟被我们拉黑的人只是极少数。早期我们认识的无非家人亲戚、同学战友、老乡同事。但在职场久了，每聚一次餐，每开一次会，每参加一次活动，甚至出一次差，我们可能都会跟陌生的人加上微信，变成“圈”中朋友。但大多数人一年到头都难得见上一面，或者彼此问候一声。虽然不怎么联系，可我们心里总想着某一天会用得着，所以一直不肯删除。就像那些在家中某个角落躺了十几年的针头线脑，不愿轻易抛弃。然而，日常我们保持热线联系的不过几十人，甚至只有十几人。尤其是那些不爱应酬，不好热闹，多一事不如少一事，喜欢昼伏夜行隐身民间山野的人，更没几个在线朋友。就算是朋友遍天下的人，一旦蹉跌失势，可能也没几个人慨然相助。

夜里想喝酒解愁，竟找不到合适的人。

家中物品多了，不仅占据空间，还有碍观瞻。

所以时不时需要作个全面清理。身边朋友多了，牵涉的时间精力必然增多，更有甚者，带来的负面消耗也会递增。心理上也要隔三差五地作个分类，下决心进行了断。对于那些一次性的朋友，要像对待一次性口罩之类的物品一样，坚决断绝来往。对待有些阶段性的朋友，要像对待陈旧破败物品一样，懂得随时置换更新。经过不断的调整检测优化，一直陪伴共同前行的朋友可能会越来越少，但一定会越来越精。

壮心不已

年轻就是好，有无限的可能。今天还是个懵懂少年，明天也许就能洞穿人间。今天还是个浪荡游子，明天也许就会折节读书。说走就走，该言即言，无惧权贵，不畏艰险，内外透着胆气，浑身充满力量。他人不敢小觑，自己也满怀希望。年轻时，特别喜欢李白的一首诗《上李邕》：

大鹏一日同风起，扶摇直上九万里。
假令风歇时下来，犹能簸却沧溟水。
时人见我恒殊调，闻余大言皆冷笑。
宣父犹能畏后生，丈夫未可轻年少。

写这首诗时，李白正当年轻气盛，踌躇满志。他云游四方，遍干诸侯。来到巴蜀地区，拜谒时任渝州刺史的李邕。在李邕的宴席上，李白不拘俗礼，高谈阔论，旁若无人。他的畅言无碍，引起了李邕等人的极度不悦。李白意兴阑珊，辞别李邕时写下了这首意气风发的诗篇。诗中表达了自己的远大志向，将自己比作乘风翱翔的大鹏，欲一飞冲天，直上九万里重霄。不想却遭到莺燕之类的嘲讽冷笑。连孔子这样的圣人都说过“后生可畏”，大丈夫岂能轻慢有志少年。有朝一日定让你们看看我展翅高飞的姿态。

李白是个少有大志的人，欲“申管、晏之谈，谋帝王之术。奋其智能，愿为辅弼，使寰区大定，海县清一”。他的目标是要成为皇帝的左膀右臂，治理天下，平定寰区。区区一个渝州刺史，哪里在他的眼中。虽然后来李白未能实现襟抱，但年轻时的那股气势却是锐不可当的。

记得自己少年意气，也曾目中无人。见了县长觉得不过如此，见了经理觉得浅陋粗俗，见了教授觉得彼可取而代之。心中正是李白的那话“大鹏一日同风起，扶摇直上九万里”，待我搏击长空，你们都将渺小如蚁。可是岁月不居，时光如流，今未扬名，明未建功，蹉跎半生，一仍如旧。不免意衰气减，茫然若失。

斗转星移，流年似水。新年再读李白《上李邕》，幸仍有闻鼙鼓而执金戈之心。王维《老将行》中老将犹壮志未已：“莫嫌旧日云中守，犹堪一战取功勋。”我是否也要“试拂铁衣如雪色，聊持宝剑动星文”？毕竟当代中国，江山壮丽，人民豪迈，前程远大。

六度

身有“六度”之人，才堪称完美。六度是指态度、温度、风度，厚度、高度、深度。前三度为处事法则，后三度为涵养境界。有态度的人都是果决的人。很多人为了躲避风险推卸责任，多表现得首鼠两端，不敢做决断，定是非，缺乏担当精神和承受之力。那些敢拍板能成事的人，必定都有态度有主意，正是他们引领着社会的潮流和历史的方向。

有温度的人都是富有情感的人。即便是钢铁巨人，如果没有温度，那也是冷血动物。很多统帅将军杀伐果断，毫无怜悯同情之心，以牺牲他人鲜血染红顶缨，正所谓一将功成万骨枯。有温度的人却不同，即使身居要津，富可敌国，也总让人温暖如春，亲切和煦。

有风度的人都是轻名利的人。风度即从容潇洒，磊落飘逸，与外在容貌无关。心若有所寄，体若有所待，形之以外，则局促惶恐，起伏跌宕，难以自安。若身不系物，心不托名，则体态轻盈，神色自若，风度自出。

厚度体现一个人的学识积累，所积愈浑厚，挥洒愈自如。正如练武之人，基本功好了，打什么套路都显得力道十足，姿态优美。行走于薄冰之上，一踩便碎，安能翩翩起舞？必须脚底扎实了、稳固了，才能施展幅度更大、难度更高的动作。

高度体现一个人的格局。登高眺望，凌顶纵览，要能将世间人事尽收眼底，不仅要具有小鲁之气概，更要有小天下之志向。有些人天生鼠目寸光，小肚鸡肠，即使站得再高也看不清事，离得再近也识不透人，是格局遮断了他们的视线，限制了他们的想象。

深度体现了一个人的境界。肤浅的人就像鹅毛浮于水面，永远不知水底的世界，他们目力所及，思虑所触，皆是浅表。能横向到边纵向到底的人，就像知道谜底的猜谜人、知道结局的观影人，他所表现出来的镇定从容，令那些不知就里一惊一乍的人难以望其项背。正是因为透彻，所以才高远。

六度附身，不是圣人，便是神人，恐怕只有孔子孟子老子庄子等才能有如此神通吧。

历史这面镜子

“以史为镜，可以知兴替；以人为镜。可以明得失。”圣人明君自能成为后世典范，但凶残狠恶之人，同样为后人提供了作奸犯科的“榜样”。学史，能汲取善者之仁义修正自身，亦能承其恶者之阴毒而贻害同类。

汉末之董卓，借清君侧之名，尽起西凉之军，趁乱据有京城，拥兵自重，挟天子以令诸侯。董卓死后，兵祸又起，汉庭再度风雨飘摇，曹操趁乱劫取天子及大臣，并安顿于自己的地盘许昌，从而掌控了朝廷，也开始挟天子以令诸侯。完全仿照董卓当年的路数行事。只是曹操比董卓更加狡黠干练，更加多谋善变，始终牢牢把握了主动权，直到汉朝灭亡，曹氏父子对朝廷内外大事处置得当，游刃有余。如果说董卓是面镜子的话，曹操就依照这面镜子重塑了自己，并将悖逆进行得更加彻底。

及至诸侯尽灭，三国鼎立时代正式开启，挟天子以令诸侯的战略就彻底失去了意义。曹丕继位魏王之后，汉朝就没有存在的必要了。曹丕想废了汉献帝，但又不想落个篡夺帝位的历史骂名，于是派人逼迫汉献帝禅让皇位。禅让指的是将皇位让给有德行才干的人，曹丕既想得到大位，还要得到美名，是典型的鱼与熊掌亦想兼得。汉献帝在无奈之下，只好痛哭流涕地让位，曹丕继位之时，竟然还厚颜无耻地说道：“尧舜之事，今日方知。”众所周知，上古时期，尧曾禅让于舜，舜后来禅让于禹，尧舜禹都是以德行服膺于天下的，曹丕何德何能，居然也自比尧舜。

天道好还，曹丕不知自己的言行不久便被司马炎完全照搬。曹氏集团在经过高平陵事变后，迅速衰微，司马懿一朝重权在握，尽诛曹氏一门居高拥兵者。后魏主曹髦被弑，曹奂继位后，不过是个傀儡，司马炎索性废弃了曹奂，程序一如曹丕之法，由曹奂禅让给司马炎，曹丕由此而成为司马炎最好的一面镜子。

为什么我们经常感慨：历史总是惊人的相似。其实这并非偶然，因为前事不忘，后事之师。依着葫芦画瓢，照着表率行事，何难之有，谁人不会?

治水三法

治水，是贯穿古今的一项重大国计民生工程。治水之法虽云繁复，归根到底无非三种：堵、疏、导。治水史上有两对著名的父子，一对是虞舜时期的鲧禹父子，一对是战国时期的李冰二郎父子，他们分别尝试了堵疏导三种治水方法。鲧用的是最简单最原始的方法，所谓兵来将挡水来土掩，鲧直接以土木砂石对洪水加以拦截，以一种人类与自然相对抗的方式进行决战。然而落后的人力终是无法胜天的，鲧成了末路英雄，以悲剧性的结局完成了伟大的试错。

禹承父志，当然不愿走父亲用性命证明是错误的路子。他不仅不堵水，还大力开凿畅通堵塞洪水的渠道，让洪水更加快捷便利地驰骋交通，任由洪水“扬长而去”，奔流到海。于是他成功地找到了治水妙汁——疏。但李冰父子修建的都江堰，完全改变了自然与人类的力量悬殊对比。他们因时因地制宜，深淘滩低作堰，按照自己的规划意图，将江水导向预定的河道。灌溉、饮用皆从人愿。孙子兵法云：“为兵之计，在顺详敌之意，千里一向，并敌杀将。”李冰父子正是用了这一妙法，既不与江水“硬杠”，亦不任其肆意而去，而是导引分流，为我所用，充分体现了人类高超的智慧。

其实，治舆与治水道理是一样的。《国语·周语上》云：“防民之口，甚于防川，川壅而溃，伤人必多，民亦如之。是故为川者，决之使导；为民者，宣之使言。”堵得越狠，爆发得越猛，完全放任自流，也会泛滥成灾。一定要有目的有步骤地加以引导，使舆论朝着有益于家国事业的方向分流。情绪亦如此，吞声久了，心中生恨，伤及自身。一味地发泄，自己倒是放空了，却将负面能量转移给了他人。要善于调节引导，将其化解于自然之中，泯灭于天地之间。

堵疏导三法，虽理念不同，方式相左，但应用起来完全可以融会贯通，有时三法并举，更收奇效。

春之变

冬去春来，万物复苏。人们心中的郁结也开始瓦解冰消了。冬天虽有纯洁的白雪，童话的世界，但更有冷风刺骨、寒鸦哀鸣。而春天，只给人美好想象无限希望，故而谁都盼着春天早日到来，似乎春光明媚了，罪恶就少了，病毒就灭了，战争就停了。最少，会油然而生出这种冀望。春天一到，总好似体内有粒种子开始萌芽，有股力量随时都要爆发，双脚插入泥土，仿佛就能长出枝叶，绽放万千繁花。

所以春天来了，首先起变化的是人的感觉，好像冰封了一个季节的活力开始四射了，冷却了的热情开始四溢了，少年人怀春，壮年人怀梦，老年人怀望。这种心理上情感上的美妙蜕变，只可意会，难以言传。总之是满怀希望充满力量。

其实春天的仙气一吹，万物都发生了变化，不仅是人的心态。映入眼帘的颜色，开始花式呈现，红的黄的绿的紫的，五彩缤纷，姹紫嫣红，一改冬天纯白或枯黄的单调。这些多彩的颜色，不论山坡平地、墙角楼顶、室内户外，随处可见，可任意饱览。大地长出的色彩，鲜艳本纯粹，最是让人赏心悦目。

春天的颜色一时多了起来，声音也变得热闹不已。冬天的寂然被鸟儿们打破了。谢灵运的“池塘生春草，园柳变鸣禽”，可谓体悟高妙。确实，甫一开春，鸟儿的鸣叫声就欢快起来，莺啼燕语，雁叫鹊喜，蜂飞蝶舞，蛙鸣虫唧，分明是一个生机勃勃的世界。听着自然的交响，难免沉醉不知归路。

春天还像个热爱装扮的姑娘，轻轻飘过，风中的味道就变了，香气扑鼻，暖意袭人。杜甫云：“春风花草香”，林升言：“暖风熏得游人醉”，皆是春游后之真情实感。四季之中，唯春天最是香甜，否则为何蜂蝶要采花酿蜜？春天也最温暖，微风轻拂，人就惬意慵懒，恨不得倚草枕树而眠。

春天来的时候，是舞动腰肢婀娜而来的，天地万物的姿态也随之柔软起来，杨柳垂下万条丝绦，枯树长出片片新绿，山添了妩媚，水多了轻柔。便是一身侠骨，至此也要多上几分柔情。多情细腻如秦观者，见了这春天的柔媚，自然便要叹：“西城杨柳弄春柔，动离忧，泪难收。”都是春之柔情惹的祸。

春天来了，万物皆变。我没理由一成不变。只要一味变好，且随春作千万变。

第二辑　诗海钩沉

败于合围的项羽

秦失其鹿，天下共逐之。刘邦和项羽都是逐鹿人，也是最后生死对决的逐鹿人，只是结果有些出乎意料：一代英雄项羽自杀，而一介平民刘邦夺得天下。项羽出身世家，乃名将之后，家族在楚地享有崇高的声誉。其人力能扛鼎，勇冠三军。巨鹿之战中，尽显神威，一举击溃秦军主力，召见诸侯时，众人入辕门，无不膝行而前，莫敢仰视。彭城之战，以三万兵马杀得五十六万汉军血流成河，死伤无数，刘邦望风逃窜，差点就被活捉。项羽一生，几乎没打过败仗，唯一一次失败就是垓下之战，最后四面楚歌，自刎乌江。

反观刘邦，不过是个泗水亭长，乡镇中的混混，如果不是被大势裹挟，恐怕当个县令都不敢奢望。在起义洪流席卷天下之时，由于机缘巧合，刘邦居然成为一方诸侯，灭秦后又被项羽封为汉中王，慢慢积攒了与项羽分庭抗礼的力量。后拜韩信为大将，联合各路诸侯，以雷霆一击，终于将项羽这个强硬的对手彻底击垮，从此江山姓了刘。

一个是力拔山兮气盖世的英雄豪杰，一个是文不能治国武不能安

邦的地痞流氓，后者却成了终极赢家。让人百思不得其解。司马迁认为问题出在项羽自己身上，说他："自矜功伐，奋其私智，而不师古，谓霸王之业，欲以力征经营天下。"确实，项羽太过相信个人的力量，以为凭着自己的非凡武艺，取天下易如反掌。事实上，他确曾仗着勇猛无敌，取得过无数次大捷。但正因如此，所有的谋士武将在他眼中都无关紧要，可有可无。既然找不到存在感，又发挥不了任何作用，原本打算在他手下谋取功名的人才，纷纷离他而去。虽然刘邦也不是什么好人，但一来只有他具有与项羽抗衡的实力，二来他愿给别人封地封侯，共享胜利成果。所以，刘邦的力量越来越强大，而项羽却成了孤家寡人，不败都没有天理了。

一个人的才华过于超群，朋友伙伴会少一些，如果又不善于藏拙，更容易遭到众人联合打击围剿，难逃失败的命运。正如项羽一样，虽然他自身的毛病是致败的因素，但众人的自私与嫉恨，更是让他毁灭的关键。

折梅赠春

三国时，江东有个名将叫陆凯。有一年他带兵南征，在梅岭见到漫山的梅花开放，他打马经过，落梅如雪片片飞。他觉得美妙异常，不由想起了一个北方的朋友，于是他采下一枝梅花，回到驿站，恰有驿使北去，他悉心地包好那枝梅花，托驿使带给他身在长安的朋友范晔，并赋诗一首相寄："折花逢驿使，寄与陇头人。江南无所有，聊赠一枝春。"

江南乃富庶之地，绫罗绸缎，稀世珍宝，陆凯家里肯定不缺，要送点贵重的物品给远方的朋友，于他绝非难事。然而送什么也比不上送花，而且是凌寒独自开的梅花。看起来似乎不值一钱，实际上却豪赠了一春。高妙之人，彼此赠金送银，那就俗了。梅花本就是高洁耿介的象征，意味着两人的情谊深厚纯粹，不沾丝毫世尘。

古人的高情雅致有时真的让令人赞叹，我们虽也欣赏鲜花奇草，也赞叹梅的冷傲孤高，但见了桃林梅岭，只会想到拍个视频照片，发发朋友圈，决计不会想到要为朋友寄上一枝，更没有吟诗作赋的兴致和能力。论起情谊，论起才学，论起雅兴，我们恐怕都要输给古人，生活的情趣自然更是相去甚远了。

诗人陆凯是江东名将陆逊之孙，出身名门，不仅善于作战，文化素养也是极高的。他的朋友范晔定是个妙人，可惜史书上缺少关于此人的资料。有趣的是，南北朝时期也有陆凯和范晔，而且两人也是好朋友。范晔时在南朝宋为官，才华横溢，曾编撰了著名的《后汉书》。陆凯为北魏朝臣，文武双全。故有人认为《赠范晔诗》为此陆凯所写，花也是他所折。但写诗者显然是南方人，陆凯却是北魏人；所寄者身在北方，而范晔却一直待在南方。显然，南北朝时期的陆凯、范晔与诗及梅并无瓜葛，但却声名更盛。折梅赋诗的三国陆凯，无疑是个名士，从他赠春的气度看，绝对是个胸怀阔远之人。他在北方的朋友范晔虽无记载，但彼此同气相求，想必也差不到哪里去。

绝望地前行

从诗艺的维度上说，生于当代中国的诗人是不幸的，因为诗在唐宋已达到了巅峰，余下的元明清诗人也实现了完美的拾遗补漏。就像一座大宅院，室内早就挤满了人，堂内也加不了塞，院内偶尔的一两个席位，也被那些雄强者给占了去，余者拼命向前，也只能远观而不能近前。在这个诗的国度里，以诗人自居，需要极大的勇气，正如站在华山之巅，面对着东邪西毒南帝北丐说你是个剑客。

若要说狂傲，没人狂傲得过李白，朝廷召见，他毫不掩饰地表示：“仰天大笑出门去，我辈岂是蓬蒿人。”要说沉郁，又有谁能与杜甫比肩：“无边落木萧萧下，不尽长江滚滚来。”王维笔下“大漠孤烟直，长河落日圆”的雄浑，陈子昂内心“前不见古人，后不见来者”的苍凉，王瀚道出“醉卧沙场君莫笑，古来征战几人回”的悲壮，恐怕也无人能及。送别场面中，王维的“劝君更尽一杯酒，西出阳关无故人”王勃的“无为在歧路，儿女共沾巾”，已到不可超越的高度。情感世界里，李商隐的“身无彩凤双飞翼，心有灵犀一点通”，元稹的“曾经沧海难为水，除却巫山不是云”，有谁还赋得出比此更深的情？人生感悟上，白居易的“同是天涯沦落人，相逢何必曾相识”，王之涣的“欲穷千里目，更上一层楼”，都已深入骨髓。怀古咏史时，刘禹锡的“人世几回伤往事，山形依旧枕寒流”，张若虚的“人生代代无穷已，江月年年望相似”，都让人感伤得无以复加。

站在新时代的诗坛，仰望这一座座山峰，让人感到自豪，也让人感到绝望。赵翼的《论诗》虽然很豪迈，“李杜诗篇万口传，至今已觉不新鲜。江山代有才人出，各领风骚数百年”，终究只能作为自我安慰之用。当然，一切必须向前看，往上攀，难不成因绝望就无为？

梅花与苔花

王安石吟诵《梅花》的那刻，当是最为寂寞孤独之时：“墙角数枝梅，凌寒独自开。遥知不是雪，为有暗香来。”否则，他也不会那么细致敏感，在无人注意的角落，发现与己处境相似的一丛梅花。抗雪凌寒，傲然独放，既有慷慨悲壮之气，又富高洁绵邈之情，确乎感人至深，动人魂魄。其时，王安石正在勇敢地推动前所未有的改革，却遗憾地遭遇排山倒海的阻力，而且很大一部分阻力来自王公贵族、亲朋好友，他内心的孤寂与苍凉可想而知。见到那几枝灿然开放的梅花，他仿佛觉得那就是他自己，被狠狠地逼到了墙角，遭受风雪严寒的无情摧残。可是风雪中的梅花并不生出丝毫的畏惧，仍然完美地绽放，传递着幽香，在僻静处造出一番风景来，雪做了它的背景，寒成了它的反衬。想来王安石定是从那数枝梅花身上，获得了深刻的感悟，攫取了无穷的力量。他吟赏的梅花，无疑具有英雄的气质和禀赋。

而袁枚所激赏的苔花，显然是个平凡者的形象：“白日不到处，青春恰自来。苔花如米小，也学牡丹开。”身处偏远地区，阳光不到，雨露难沾，但是春天来了，热爱美好的天性还是要勃然喷发。是枝就必然要散叶，是花就当然要开放。虽然不能像牡丹一样花开时节动京城，得到众人的惊羡和妙赏，但也一定要借助无限春光，绽放全部生机，哪怕像米粒一样大小，像滴水一般微不足道，好歹没有辜负春天的关照，没有辜负生命的期许。

像梅花那般傲霜凌雪，高怀远韵，需要的不仅是勇气，还有力量。而像苔花那般欣然开放，不求动人，只要顺应天机，自然而然就行。做不了梅花，做朵苔花还不成么？

千年望族

说到中国的千年望族，钱氏家族一定是名列前茅的。大家硕儒，名将重臣，历朝历代层出不穷。钱氏发达，始自唐末钱镠。钱镠出身低微，起于行伍，因屡立战功而不断得到拔擢。最后割据一方，建立吴越国。因为地域狭小，无力纵横四海。在天下大乱五代十国交替并行之际，他一直尊中原为正朔，并始终保持高度警惕，全力保境安民，大力发展经济。在他的治理运筹下，吴越之地少遇干戈，国富民足。苏轼赞曰："是以其民至于老死不识兵革，四时嬉游歌鼓之声相闻，至于今不废，其有德于斯民甚厚。"

钱镠一辈子活了八十一岁，头脑极其清醒，并保持至终，从来没有昏聩骄纵过，这在历代国君中是非常罕见的。《吴越备史》说他："倜傥有大度，志气雄杰，机谋沉远，善用长槊大弩，又能书写，甚得体要。有知人之鉴，及通图纬之学，每处众中，而形神有余。"文天祥夸他："武足以安民定乱，文足以佐理经邦，实有大臣贤者之风。"可见，钱镠是个文武双全的人。他攻越州，据浙西，讨董昌，平内乱，建吴越，武功赫赫。同时，他气度恢宏，善于用人，爱民如子，治政有方，把吴越十三州管理得井井有条。

尤为难得的是，他颇有自知之明，知道自己偏居一隅，难继正统，是以保持谦虚谨慎之姿态，谁得中原，他都俯首称臣纳贡，维系好与大国之间的关系，是以中原数度易主，他与吴越国却稳如泰山。北宋相继平灭诸国后，他的后继者钱弘俶依照他的处世理念，顺应时势，“纳土归宋”。百姓免却干戈流离之苦，钱氏家族也得到宋太宗的大力分封。拥有控弦之士十万，却主动放弃对抗，这是需要胸怀和远见的，可钱弘俶深懂钱镠遗训，没有发动无谓的战争，东南富庶之地有幸免于兵祸。南唐后主李煜则不然，既无力抵抗，又不甘于投降，结果举军匆匆迎敌，一触即溃。百姓遭殃，自己更是成了俘虏，受尽屈辱，最终还是难逃一死。相对而言，李煜显得很不明智。当然，国破家亡，反而成就了作为词人的李煜，从此中国文学史上，李煜的名字熠熠生辉。

钱氏家族虽然失国，却保有了富贵显赫。自此世代相传，人才辈出，成为绵延千年的名门望族，这一切，皆源自唐末的钱镠，他才是当之无愧的伟大人物。

花开缓归

清朝王士祯曾云："钱武肃王目不知书，然其寄夫人书云：'陌上花开，可缓缓归矣。'——不过数言，而姿致无限，虽复文人操笔，无以过之。"这里有段掌故，讲的是五代吴越国王钱镠之事。钱镠乃行伍出身，虽常穿行刀光剑影之中，却侠骨柔情，对其夫人吴妃极富深情。每到春来，吴妃便要回到临安老家去住上一阵子。有一年，吴妃住得稍长了些时日，身在杭州的钱镠十分想念，于是修书一封，派人送与妻子，只"陌上花开，可缓缓归矣"数字，吴妃阅后当即感动得泪下数行。乡里闻知，一时传为佳话。

"陌上花开，可缓缓归矣"，意思是说，田间陌上的花已开遍了，你可以一边赏着花，一边慢慢归来了。心中的思念明明是深切的、急迫的，表达却是温馨的、从容的。将军的气度、文人的温婉，二者兼备，既慷慨又感人。难怪王士祯说其艳称千古，文人难为。即便现在我们读起来，也还是觉得温暖可人，被其中蕴含的真情深深打动。比起那些绵绵情话，这简短的两句不知要高明多少倍。所以情真意切处，实在不需要宏富的篇章以及华丽的语言。

这段温情故事，后来被人编成山歌，取名《陌上花》，含思宛转，凄切动人，在乡间广为传唱。一百年后，苏轼就任杭州通判，听到此曲，觉得其词鄙野，因感于钱镠故事，专门为之写下《陌上花三首》，词句精美，其一犹胜：

陌上花开蝴蝶飞，江山犹是昔人非。

遗民几度垂垂老，游女长歌缓缓归。

以苏轼纵横之才情，写起诗文来当然妙笔生花，其叹往摹今自是别有一番风味，然而毕竟是接续演绎，比起原版的“陌上花开，可缓缓归矣”，总觉得味道差了少许。

回归真我

1839年，有个著名的诗人因为厌倦了官场，决然辞官归故里，到家乡的书院开始了讲学生涯。这人名叫龚自珍，时年48岁，本来在官场还有很长一段路可走，上升的空间很大，可他腻了倦了，余生只想做学问搞创作，于是抛弃了别人无比羡慕的官职，做回了一介平民。因为要安排书院讲学，安顿妻儿家小，他两次往返京城。整整一年，他都是人在旅途，不仅饱览了山河，也阅尽了人间。

这一年中，龚自珍几乎每天都写一首诗，他学习唐朝的李贺，看到想到什么，立即用纸条记录下来，回家一整理，就是一首完整的好诗了。用这种方式，他共创作了315首诗，并编辑成册，因为这年是己亥年，龚自珍命其名曰《己亥杂诗》。其中的第5首《己亥杂诗·浩荡离愁白日斜》和第125首《己亥杂诗·九州生气恃风雷》艺术成就最高，也最为后人所称道：

浩荡离愁白日斜，吟鞭东指即天涯。

落红不是无情物，化作春泥更护花。

九州生气恃风雷，万马齐喑究可哀。

我劝天公重抖擞，不拘一格降人材。

龚自珍一生共写了600多首诗，其中己亥年写的诗就占了一半，而且多是精品，令人叹为观止。究其原因，恐怕跟他辞官归隐有着密切的关联。以前在官场，他不敢说也无心写，浪费了大好时光，虽然积累深厚，但终究没有得空很好地表达出来。一旦去意已决，他的创作热情就开始爆发，创作灵感便如万斛源泉，不择地而出。而且敢讲真话，敢赋深情。因为再也无意官场，是以他也不用投鼠忌器，海阔天空，但只快意翱翔。

身体上获得了自由，思想上获得了解放，从此恰如蛟龙入海，猛虎归林，龚自珍出走半生，终于找到了那条属于自己的人生之路。

天才少年

王勃被誉为“天才少年”，还真不是浪得虚名。一篇《滕王阁序》冠绝古今，唐高宗曾赞其为“千古绝唱”。其才华不仅当世称善，千载之后，亦为众人所倾慕。历朝历代对其赞不绝口。《旧唐书》说他：“六岁解属文，构思无滞，词情英迈，与兄才藻相类，父友杜易简常称之曰：此王氏三株树也。”与他同列“初唐四杰”之一的杨炯盛赞他：“九岁读颜氏《汉书》，撰《指瑕》十卷。十岁包综六经，成乎期月，悬然天得，自符音训。时师百年之学，旬日兼之，昔人千载之机，立谈可见。”明朝胡应麟曰：“王勃兴象宛然，气骨苍然，实首启盛、中妙境，五言绝亦抒写悲凉，洗尽流调，究其才力，自是唐人开山祖。”伟大领袖毛主席也夸他：“这个人高才博学，为文光昌流丽。”

王勃年纪轻轻即名满天下，并非偶然。一方面他天才逞纵，另一方面他勤奋好学。六岁即能诗，九岁便撰写学术著作《指瑕》，十岁便饱览六经。可见他用功之深。当然，这跟他家学渊源息息相关。上溯祖宗八代，他的先辈没有一人不著书立说。特别是他的祖父王通，更是隋朝儒学大师，桃李满天下。生于官宦世家，所以王勃自幼便深受熏陶，饱读诗书。可惜天妒英才，倘若容他再活二十年，唐朝的诗歌版图一定会改写。就算是李白杜甫，也须让他三分。

王勃占尽了人生所有的优越，好家庭，高天赋，勤读书，所以苍天不让人间见他白头。有时候，人生还是有些缺憾的好。

闲情还是闲愁

宋朝词人贺铸有首著名的《青玉案》：

“凌波不过横塘路，但目送、芳尘去。锦瑟华年谁与度？月台花榭，琐窗朱户，只有春知处。

碧云冉冉蘅皋暮，彩笔新题断肠句。试问闲愁都几许？一川烟草，满城风絮，梅子黄时雨。”

这首词是贺铸的代表作之一，写得委婉精美，深情绵邈，广受赞誉，流传千古。南宋周紫芝《竹坡话》赞云：“贺方回尝作《青玉案》词，有‘梅子黄时雨’之句，人皆服其工，士大夫谓之贺梅子。”因这首词，贺铸被称为“贺梅子”。

该词居然有两个版本，有三个地方表达不同，有两处只是写景上略有差异，几可忽略不计。最关键的区别在于最后一段：

“试问闲情都几许？一川烟草，满城风絮，梅子黄时雨。”

其实就是一字之差。后者是“闲情”，前者是“闲愁”，但就是这一字之别，意义便完全不一样。如果是抒发“闲情”，那诗人应该是轻松自然、毫无牵挂的，眼中的景必是清静淡雅的，笔下的情应该是恬然安适的。比如：试问闲情都几许？一溪白云，满耳鸟鸣，春风拂时柳。可是作者描绘的形象却是烟草、风絮，还有梅雨，这分明是一种“闲愁”。看到如烟的川草、漫天的飞絮、连绵的梅雨，谁能不莫名地生起淡淡的愁意呢？以此而论，此版本当是贺铸真章。

贺铸其人，素有豪爽之气、侠客之风、狂士之态，胸怀大志，却一生沉于下僚。能诗文，尤工于词。其词内容、风格独特多样，兼有豪放、婉约二派之长，其清丽哀婉者，近于秦观、晏几道；其悲壮激昂者，又近于苏轼、辛弃疾。《青玉案》一词，盖属婉约一类。考贺铸一生际遇，所谓“闲愁”者，非闲愁也，乃真愁也。

令人敬佩的辛弃疾

词到苏轼手上，恰如河入长江，变得开阔幽深，变化倏忽，不可名状。原来那种文人的狭义私情一扫而空，天地万物人情世事皆入笔端，辽阔深远，气势如虹，开豪放一派之先河，此后之词方可渐与唐诗并论。到了辛弃疾手上，更加涛澜汹涌，奔腾澎湃，词之雄强壮烈一面进一步凸显。此时词与诗之表达范围并无很大区别。王国维云：“（词）能言诗之所能言，而不能尽言诗之所能言。”“诗之境阔，词之情长”是指相较诗而言，词之整体特点如此，在苏轼、辛弃疾的词里，无所不能表达，境既阔，情亦长，二者兼备。

而且辛弃疾毕生只作词，不写诗，从不将词作为“诗余”对待，而是一心一意将词的功用发挥到极致，其词几乎首首精美，篇篇绝伦。故被誉为“词中之龙”。其中《破阵子·为陈同甫赋壮词以寄之》《青玉案·元夕》《永遇乐·京口北固亭怀古》《水龙吟·登建康赏心亭》《摸鱼儿·更能消几番风雨》《菩萨蛮·书江西造口壁》等皆千古名篇，脍炙人口。美言警句尤多，想象力十分丰富。其千古名句有“青山遮不住，毕竟东流去”“了却君王天下事，赢得生前身后名”“众里寻他千百度，蓦然回首，那人却在，灯火阑珊处”“休去倚危栏，斜阳正在，烟柳断肠处”“我见青山多妩媚，料青山见我应如是”“却将万字平戎策，换得东家种树书”，等等，实在是数不胜数。

这些名篇名句我都很喜欢，但我尤为推崇他《水调歌头·和马叔度游月波楼》中的几句：“唤起一天明月，照我满怀冰雪，浩荡百川流。”意思是：呼唤满天皎洁的月光，照见冰雪般透明的情怀，我们胸襟宽广浩荡，似百川融汇奔流。多么光明磊落，多么气度恢宏！上马击贼，下马读书，千军万马中他是英雄，浩繁卷帙中他是文豪，这样的辛弃疾，除了敬佩，我依然还是敬佩。

适得其反

北宋还是有不少与其他朝代不一样的地方，既无外戚揽权，亦无宦官干政，而且高度重视文人，不杀士大夫，算是一个比较文明的朝代。但自从中期开始，直到灭亡，党争却是愈演愈烈，最终直接葬送了天下。新党与旧党，一个是改革派，一个是保守派，互相纠缠算计，争斗不休。一方上台，必将另一方罢官贬谪，清除殆尽。双方轮流坐庄，皇帝也没办法完全掌控局面，终于将王朝拖向覆灭的深渊。

最后一轮得势的是新党，他们一上台，便十分凶狠，对旧党进行全面清算。不仅罢官免职，更在朝廷竖立元祐党人碑，碑上刻了三百零九个人的名字，大名鼎鼎的苏轼就排在首位。这些人永远不得录用，他们的后代也永世不得为官，不得与皇亲贵族通婚成亲。党人碑不仅京城要立，每个地方都要立，目的在于昭告天下，让人们都知道这些人的“劣迹”，这分明就是要一脚踩得对手永世不得翻身。

可令他们意料不到的是，立碑没多久，金人就兵临城下，攻占了北宋的都城，北宋和新旧党一起完蛋了。国都亡了，党争恩怨自然一笔勾销，大家都是逃命要紧，谁还顾得及什么石碑？之前立碑刻名旨在羞辱那些人，没曾想反而把这些人的名声宣传扩大了，因为石碑的故事流传下来，他们也常常被人们提起。那些宵小如果知道会是这种结果，恐怕无论如何都不会为他们竖碑刻名的。

小人虽然常常居心叵测，主观上构陷，背地里放箭，但碰到真正通透达观的人，不仅损害不了他分毫，而且很可能成就他。元祐党人碑就是一个典型案例，有些石碑上留名的人物在当时也许未必很著名，经此一闹，反而声名赫赫，流传千古。

猿吟鹤唳

苏轼曾有诗《次韵僧潜见赠》云："猿吟鹤唳本无意，不知下有行人行。"指的是猿吟树林鹤唳长空乃自然本性，不会顾及低处是否有行人路过。换句话说，不管低处行人有没有意见，猿都要吟，鹤都要唳，这是自然而然的事。实际上这是苏轼自己的真实写照。苏轼是个疾恶如仇、性格耿直之人。他自言生性急躁，遇有不惬意之事，便觉"如蝇在食，吐之方快"。所以王安石熙宁变法，他屡次上书直陈其弊，得罪了改革派。以司马光为首的保守派上台后，全面清理改革派，他又对改革派表示同情。所以，两边都不讨好。但正因为他秉持正义，不偏不倚，高贵的人品赢得了千古赞誉。

他真正地体现了猿吟鹤唳之性，根本不在乎别人作何感想，只要自认为正确，就完全可以做到"虽千万人，吾往矣"。至于后果，且待痛快地表达完再说。事实上，凭着他的聪明智慧，他未尝不知站在当权者对立面的后果，可是他仍然坚持己见，不吐不快，这既说明他的忠诚勇敢，也体现出一个文人的风骨。接下来的遭遇正如他所料，贬谪是最起码的打击，好在他是个乐天派，对不愉快的事转眼就忘却，而在可观之物中找出可观之处，所以能真正做到无往而不乐，这要得益于他超然物外的旷达豁然。

对于“不知下有行人行”，苏轼付出了沉重的代价，但终归是有惊无险。相较于所失，他得到的实在不可以价值计。要是他是个瞻前顾后唯唯诺诺的投机者，也许能在新党旧党之间左右逢源，毕竟两派的领袖都非常欣赏他，甚至只要他保持缄默，他的仕途都将一帆风顺。可是如此一来，就不可能有千百年来一直令人敬佩喜爱的苏轼。

人生就是这样，有时只管如猿吟鹤唳，不管下面是否有行人，这样做大概率会失之东隅，但也许会收之桑榆。

四大美女考

古之四大美女，号称有“沉鱼落雁闭月羞花”之貌，她们分别是西施、王昭君、貂蝉、杨玉环。这几个人历史上是否都存在且不论，就美貌而言，亦多有穿凿附会之处。四大美女中，有三人是作为工具被利用的，只有杨玉环没有成为馈赠礼品或者杀人利刃。她集三千宠爱于一身，几乎可以说赢得了君王的爱情，这在皇帝身上是一种极为珍贵的奢侈品，虽然在马嵬坡她年纪轻轻就香消玉殒，但生前她享尽了富贵荣耀和专宠爱怜，人生短暂却价值非凡，也算是未枉费来世上一遭。事实上，她在遇见唐玄宗之前已是有夫之妇，是被唐玄宗硬夺为己有的，皇帝从此不早朝，怠惰政事，变得日益昏聩，只愿和杨玉环天天赏花弄月，听歌观舞，而且长相厮守竟然丝毫不腻，未曾移情别恋，可见杨玉环容貌之美魅力之大。

西施和貂蝉都是美人计中的神兵利器。西施被越王勾践送给吴王夫差后，很快就获得专宠深爱，吴王对她言听计从，百般信任，为她竟不惜要了功臣良将伍子胥的命，最后落得个国灭身死的下场。西施要是没有超人的容貌和致命的诱惑，见惯了吴越美女的吴王夫差能如此失去理智吗?

貂蝉能够让醉心荣华富贵的吕布反戈并击杀董卓，让有望称帝的董卓无顾极有可能夺得的江山，她的容貌一定是让人见了就想据为己有不容他让的。要不然，情同父子且富有半个天下的董卓、吕布二人为何反目成仇生死相搏?

王昭君其实是四人中最为悲惨的一个，她是被赠予异族的礼品，也是和亲靖边的工具。她的外表必然是漂亮的，否则匈奴单于看不上，也有损于汉朝大国形象。但她肯定不是后宫中最美丽的女孩，否则汉元帝不可能会拱手相让。那时的匈奴并不十分强大，汉朝也并不十分虚弱。如果王昭君真的美得不可方物，汉元帝一眼便迷住了的话，随便找个借口便可将其留下，匈奴人也奈何不了汉朝。什么毛延寿画像受贿，故意将其画丑，及至汉元帝发现不好收回成命，只能眼望着心上人离去云云，都是文人编造的爱情故事罢了。试想，吴王夫差可以为了西施不顾国家存亡，董卓吕布可以为了貂蝉翻脸不认人，唐玄宗可以为了杨玉环不理朝政，难道汉元帝为了王昭君对匈奴人耍个赖不合情理吗?之所以没有强挽硬留，实在是王昭君还没有美到让汉元帝不管不顾的地步，也就是说，汉元帝身边一定不乏容貌胜过至少不亚于王昭君的人。

历史太悠久了，必有演绎的成分，观其大略就好，不必细究。

暴而不昏的杨广

隋炀帝杨广是史上著名的暴君昏君。说他暴君，自是名副其实，他好打好杀，爱征爱伐，视人命如草芥，不仅大量士卒民众死于征战修筑，就是功臣良将他也是杀剐随意。连自己的兄弟姐妹甚至侄子外甥都不肯放过，几乎杀戮殆尽。以暴君名之，一点都不冤枉他。说他昏君，还是值得商榷的，事实上，他一直都清醒明了，即便是天下大乱之时，他也毫不糊涂，只是无能为力，无法挽狂澜于既倒罢了。年轻时，他甚至是神明英武、多才多艺的。夺得皇位后，他才肆无忌惮，慢慢堕落荒淫，变得凶残暴戾的。

说起历史上才华横溢的帝王君主，我们首先会想到南唐后主李煜、宋徽宗赵佶，其实隋炀帝杨广的才华似乎不逊色于他们，而且杨广是文武双全。在隋灭陈之战中，杨广是三军统帅，指挥着千军万马。在其后的东征西讨中，他也屡次御驾亲征，建立了不少功勋。不唯如此，用现在的话说，杨广还是个高颜值的大帅哥，且是英气勃发一类，史书称其“美姿仪，少聪慧”。

杨广少时天资聪颖，勤奋好学，故能为诗，善属文。其《悲秋》《春江花月夜》置之梁祖、简文诸集中而不能辨。又有“寒鸦飞数点，流水绕孤村”数语，曾为秦观取入词中，成为绝妙好词。王夫之评杨广《泛龙舟》曰：“神采天成，此雷塘骨少年犹有英气。”可见其诗文成就之高。单论文才，隋唐诗坛绝对应有杨广一席之地。

可惜杨广当上皇帝以后，热衷杀伐，滥用民力，穷奢极欲，变成了一个人人痛恨的暴君。祖君彦云其“磬南山之竹，书罪无穷；决东海之波，流恶难尽”。《书》曰：“天作孽，犹可违，自作孽，不可逭。”杨广的倒行逆施，终于导致天下大乱，义军蜂起，未几，隋朝便崩溃覆灭，他自己也落得个身戮国灭为天下笑的悲惨结局。

当初，隋炀帝也想做个卓然史册、雄踞宇内的千古一帝，只是揽取了至高无上而又毫无节制的权力后，日渐走向了残酷暴虐的深渊。有人感叹道：隋炀不幸为天子，安石可怜作相公。若使二人穷到老，一为名士一文雄。确实，如果隋炀帝当年未夺其兄太子之位，一定会成为一个令人景仰的诗家圣手。奈何权欲误人，惜哉杨广！

化身千亿

柳宗元远贬柳州，久居蛮荒之地，对故乡十分思念。有一年秋天，朋友浩初上人远道前来探望他，两人出城登山游玩，柳宗元想起亲朋故旧和家乡的风物人情，感慨地写下《与浩初上人同看山寄京华亲故》："海畔尖山似剑铓，秋来处处割愁肠。若为化得身千亿，散上峰头望故乡。"大概柳州一带多为喀斯特地貌，山形都十分尖锐，看起来像把把利剑，而柳宗元谪居柳州，愁肠百结。愁肠对利剑，自有一番痛楚。在此境遇下，更是思念故乡。恨不能化为千万个自己，站满所有的山头，一起眺望着远方的故乡。诗中无限愁苦，无限深情，令人读后不禁泪为之流，肠为之断。

想来陆游必是读过柳宗元的这首思乡诗，而且一定烂熟于心。有诗《梅花绝句二首其一》为证："闻道梅花坼晓风，雪堆遍满四山中。何方可化身千亿，一树梅花一放翁。"显然，陆游也想幻化出千万个自己，只不过陆游不是要每个自己都去思乡，去断肠。而是希望在每株梅花前立一放翁，尽情欣赏高洁美妙的梅花。陆游可真是贪心不足，他深知自己一人无法一一妙赏漫山之梅花，于是想到柳宗元那句“若为化得身千亿”，冀盼能够瞬间变出千万个自己，一次看尽满山梅。

但放眼古往今来，诗中文里，能变化出无数个自己来的，恐怕只有孙悟空了，他可以拔出一把毫毛，吹一口气，变出成千上万个孙悟空，抵挡妖魔鬼怪，而其真身却站立于云端，悠然欣赏着自己的化身一一将那些魑魅魍魉击为齑粉。

我也像柳宗元和陆游一样，经常梦想着能变幻出千万个化身。不过我既不用来思乡，因为故乡虽遥，却一日可达；也不会用来赏梅，应为良辰美景太多，不必心系一处。我要用无数个化身来应付无数个我不愿出现而又不得不出现的场景，而我的元神则如孙悟空一样，驾祥云飘游于空中，赏析人间一切生动的情景。

元白

元稹与白居易合称“元白”，我以为不仅是因为两人的诗歌艺术成就都达到了极高的艺术境界，在唐朝乃至后世皆具有崇高的声誉；更是缘于两人的情谊真挚深厚，旷久持远之故。他们为我们留下的不只是千秋万世名，还有生死相依情。

元白二人同年考中进士，起初都在秘书省做官，后来各有辗转升迁，时有分合聚散，但无论天涯海角，两人书信从未断绝，而且情谊日渐见厚，元稹曾有诗《得乐天书》动情地说道：“远信入门先有泪，妻惊女哭问何如。寻常不省曾如此，应是江州司马书！”收到贬谪江州的白居易来信，元稹涕泪横流，妻惊女哭。白居易则在《梦微之》中无限感叹：“晨起临风一惆怅，通州湓水断相闻。不知忆我因何事，昨夜三更梦见君。”道路阻隔，各自在偏僻之处为官，只好寄情于梦了。一个“是夕远思君，思君瘦如削”，一个“梦中握君手，问君意何如”，这类互诉衷肠的诗句，在两人的书信中比比皆是，不知道的还以为是一对恋人之间的刻骨相思呢！

鲁迅曾书赠瞿秋白曰："人生得一知己足矣，斯世当同怀视之。"元白之间，当是如此知己情怀了，彼此珍惜，终生牵挂，甚至阴阳两隔，仍然念念不能忘，终霄劳梦想。元稹去世得早，失去知己的白居易备感寂寞忧伤，经常作诗怀念老友，愈老尤甚。他的一首《梦微之》最能表达彼时心境：

夜来携手梦同游，晨起盈巾泪莫收。

漳浦老身三度病，咸阳宿草八回秋。

君埋泉下泥销骨，我寄人间雪满头。

阿卫韩郎相次去，夜台茫昧得知不？

又是梦中携手同游！两人生离时常常梦中相见，死别后更得借助梦境重逢。奈何此时一个已埋骨泉下，化为朽壤；另一个则白雪满头，风烛残年了。

时至今日，溯源这段情谊，不免作千年一叹。元白之间，可谓惺惺相惜，可谓不离不弃，可谓至死不渝。这便是所谓的高山流水遇知音吧。他们曾联袂寄身人间，今则并肩光照简册。

对牛弹琴

汉牟融编撰的《理惑论》载：“公明仪为牛弹清角之操，伏食如故。非牛不闻，不合其耳矣。转为蚊虻之声，孤犊之鸣，即掉尾奋耳，蹀躞而听。”这是一则很有趣的故事，也是很典型的中国式寓言。公明仪是个音乐高手，尤善弹琴。也许是厌倦了人们的赞美夸奖，一次他突发奇想，面对着一头正在吃草的牛弹起了琴，琴曲典雅高致，公明仪弹得也十分用心，可是牛却无动于衷。公明仪并不死心，换了不同的曲调，可牛终是毫无反应。最后公明仪以琴声模仿蚊虻之声以及落单牛犊的哀鸣之声，这下牛竖起耳朵，甩着尾巴，显然听得非常认真。公明仪很是沮丧，那么清雅的琴曲，牛竟不懂欣赏；而简单的模仿声，牛却有所回应。后人将对牛弹琴喻为对愚笨者讲道理，白费口舌。

其实人牛殊类，牛听不懂人弹琴再正常不过，人不也不通牛叫之意吗？公明仪实在是闲得无聊，大概他觉得自己的琴艺高超绝伦，足以惊天地泣鬼神，感动一头牛当然不在话下。没想到，牛根本不作理会，这让公明仪颇为不爽，估计他心里不知骂了多少遍牛的愚蠢无知。牛固然是愚笨的，然而明知其愚笨还要对它弹琴，似乎比它也聪明不到哪里去。

生活之中，不知有多少人自诩为公明仪，觉得自己博学多才，高人一筹，逢人便要讲道理，授知识，传经验。如果别人不理解或者不反馈，便要大骂其人笨蛋白痴。无形之中，却暴露了自己的浅薄孟浪。一个真正有智慧的人，不会轻易对人吐露心思，解释行为，阐明洞见，必须是面对同频的人，才会发出同音，所谓同气相求同声相应是也。对着笨牛弹琴，对着傻瓜念经，这种累了无功还拉低段位的荒唐事，他们是决计不会干的。

心有灵犀者一点就通，无须过多解释，正如俞伯牙和钟子期，彼此互通互达，神照意会，乃是一对妙人。一方喋喋不休，一方懵然无知，正如公明仪与牛，彼此不知所云，维度各异，不仅闻者笨，说者亦蠢。

耆英会约

宋神宗即位之后，颇思有一番作为，与力主变法的王安石一拍即合，大刀阔斧推动朝野的改革创新，结果引起一大批朝臣的极力反对，这些人多是元老级的重臣。但宋神宗与王安石置之不理，依然高歌猛进。曾经当过宰相的富弼也是反对改革的主力成员，时已年迈退休，归居于洛阳。他效仿唐白居易的“香山九老会”，把文彦博等部分退居在洛阳的老臣聚集起来，成立了“洛阳耆英会”，耆英者，德高望重之老者也。会员共有十三人，每个人轮流坐庄，宴请大家。当时虽然在位但基本处于赋闲状态的司马光，也被邀请加入，因为他也是极力抵制王安石推行新法的。

一伙同一阵线的老者聚会，谈来谈去无非是如何阻止王安石变法，也许闲来也赋诗作文。但这种带着较强政治目的性的聚会，不像金谷集会、竹林集会、兰亭集会那般注重雅趣，能出些佳作上品。洛阳耆英会似乎并没留下什么令人振奋的诗文，倒是他们协商订立并由司马光执笔拟就的《会约》颇有深意，今天读起来仍觉新颖别致：

一、序齿不序官；

二、为具务简素；

三、朝夕食不过五味，菜果脯醢之类，共不过二十器；

四、酒巡无算，深浅自斟，主人不劝，客亦不辞；

五、逐巡无下酒时，作菜羹不禁；

六、召客共用一简，客注可否于字下，不别作简；

七、会日早赴，不待速；

八、右有违约者，每事罚一巨觥。

会约共八条，非常具体细致。逻辑关系大概是，所发聚会通知不是分发，而是只备一纸，依次相送，每人在通知书上注明是否出席。按时开席，不等不催。就座时按年龄长幼而非官阶大小安排席位。餐具简朴干净不尚奢华。主菜仅限五个，果脯小吃不超过二十小碟。如果光盘而大家又意犹未尽，可以加菜。喝酒自便，不劝不禁。违约者罚酒一大杯。这种聚会就非常轻松自如，没有任何负担了。

什么时候开始的聚会就大有不同了。宴请首先得找个豪华知名的地方，重要嘉宾到了才能开席，点菜必是多得吃不完，喝起酒来也是如醉如梦。特别重要的是席次安排，那是一种身份的体现，绝不能出现任何差池。有时同样一批人聚会，职位常变席位常调整，极易让人生出世事变幻人情冷暖的感慨。洛阳耆英会按年龄定位的办法，倒是一劳永逸地解决了座次难排的问题，可为今天宴请者鉴。

松生于灌木

松生于灌木丛中，一年两年，三年五年，也许不见其异。松与灌木两者一并生长，同荣共辱，谁也不比谁强。时间久了，已习惯于彼此的平凡，争高于数米之内，竞茂于孤山之上。风波只在茶杯里，差距不过五十一百步，故虽有长短盈亏，总体尚在同一维度。

忽一日，松开始冒尖上窜，横空出世，鹤立于灌木丛中。灌木们始而惊讶：这棵与我们一样匍匐在地的小树，竟能在旬日间越众而出，一枝独秀，把我们轻松踩在脚下。继而愤恨：为何大家同处一方水土，同在一片天空，平时并未见其天赋异禀，运命非常，缘何突然就高我们一头，而且似乎上行趋势不可阻遏。未几，松高入云，直指长空。黛色参天二千尺，霜皮溜雨四十围，根深叶茂，张枝成荫，巍然屹立，聚鹤停云。灌木只能抬头仰望，敬服于地，以松自豪，庆幸自己与其同生一方沃土，有过一段共同经历，今方得以受益沾溉，与大材为邻。灌木们有所不知，当年松虽与他们一起破土抽芽，缓慢长高，却暗暗深扎根须，汲取大地营养，同时尽展枝叶，吸收日月精华。无论白天黑夜，风中雨

里，松从未停止过聚集力量。今看似一朝凌空，实则为经年蓄势之果。但这又何足为外人道？松从来无语，但只破空。

生活何尝不是如此？杰出的英才早年肯定也是混迹于常人之中，慢慢增长才干，点滴积蓄力量，待诗书满怀，定将如万斛泉源，不择地而出。刚开始时，身边故旧老友并不以为然，甚至常常出言相讥，设绊相阻，然而当其学术才华已渊深无涯涘，博洽无伦比，众人将转而一致交口称赞，顶礼膜拜，称之为圣，誉之为神。

处处惠施

对于好吃的零食，小孩子们大多是很吝啬的，让他们无偿地拿出来分享，嘴皮说破，恐怕也赚不出其十一。他们必是死死捂紧口袋，始终警惕地关注着你的一言一行，生怕你动粗用强。有时看到他们的那副认真神态，我们忍不住要打心里发笑。其实我们跟他们也没什么两样，遇到一点蝇头小利，特别是自己职权范围内生发出来的，那是一定要千方百计予以锁定，决计不容他人染指的。别人如果觊觎，一定要制造麻烦设置障碍，甚至恐吓威胁，让其知难而退。

战国时，惠施在魏国为相，庄子前去探望他。鉴于庄子响亮的“国际”声名，有人提醒惠施说：“庄子来魏，名义上是来看你，实则是想取你而代之。”惠施很是担忧，派人搜捕了庄子三天三夜。庄子主动前去见他，说：“南方有一种鸟叫鹓，从南海起飞，飞到北海去，非梧桐不栖，非竹果不吃，非甘泉不饮。地上有只猫头鹰拾到一只腐臭的老鼠，鹓鶵正好从其上面飞过，猫头鹰以为鹓鶵要来跟自己争食，紧张地抬头注视着鹓鶵的一举一动，并发出‘吓’的一声怒吼，欲以此来恐吓驱除鹓鶵。现在你也要为你的魏国来‘吓’我吗？”庄子的话说得再明白不过，有些东西在你心里或许是美味佳肴，在我眼中不过是陈芝麻烂谷子，我才不稀罕呢！换句话说，我庄子是个立志高远凌空翱翔的人，天下都不在话下，何况区区的一国相位。我哪能跟你这种俗人一般见识，眼中只有位子，胸中只有好处，一叶障目不见泰山。

然而庄子是超人类的，他必然也是孤独的，像他这种襟抱的人恐怕几千年也才出几个。惠施之流才是多数且正常的，放眼历史和当今，哪里没有惠施？他们固守在狭小的天地，树上长一果，地里结一实，他们都视为己有，牢牢地盯紧铆定，一旦有人靠近，便要奋力驱离，生怕被他人夺取，正如那些捂着口袋的孩子，绝不允许自己的零食损失分毫。

诗之妙用

唐时有个好处，就是大家都喜欢诗，即使写不好，也心向往之。对著名诗人人们都满怀崇敬。诗到唐朝便到了巅峰，天地万物皆可入诗。诗的应用也十分广泛，有些不太好直接表达的意思，人们往往以诗来作答。写的人信手拈来，读的人了然于心。彼此通晓心意，却又不必明说，省了那份尴尬和不必要的麻烦。

自中唐以来，藩镇割据，各镇节度使为了延揽人才，扩张势力，采取各种手段拉拢著名文人和中央官吏。著名诗人张籍时在朝廷为官，自是众藩镇结交的重点对象。平卢淄青节度使、检校司空、同中书门下平章事李师道，就曾致意张籍，希望将他拉入自己的政治集团。因为李师道势大，张籍不敢贸然拒绝，于是写了一首《节妇吟·寄东平李司空师道》相赠·

君知妾有夫，赠妾双明珠。

感君缠绵意，系在红罗襦。

妾家高楼连苑起，良人执戟明光里。

知君用心如日月，事夫誓拟同生死。

还君明珠双泪垂，恨不相逢未嫁时。

乍看之下，像是一首缠绵的情诗。一个有夫之妇在一个真心倾慕者的追求之下，感动得泪水涟涟，但想到自己已名花有主，只好狠心拒绝追求者并退还所赠礼物。实际上，张籍是借妇人之口，婉拒了李师道的盛情邀约。诗中张籍既表达了对李师道信任器重的感激之情，也明确了自己忠于唐王朝的坚决态度。在表明心迹的同时，也没有让李师道感到难堪，避免了给自己树一强敌，张籍的心思可说是十分巧妙，而诗意则更加高妙。

事实上，张籍在任水部郎中的时候，也曾有人以诗试问其意。唐代士子参加进士考试前，时兴“行卷”，即把自己的诗作呈给名人，以求其称扬并介绍给主持考试的官员。宝历年间，诗人朱庆馀参加进士考试，因为张籍当时以擅长乐府而又乐于提拔后进与韩愈齐名，朱庆馀曾作诗《近试上张水部》投赠张籍：

洞房昨夜停红烛，待晓堂前拜舅姑。

妆罢低声问夫婿，画眉深浅入时无。

诗中惟妙惟肖地描绘了一个新入门媳妇拜见公婆时的紧张羞涩心情，实际上喻指作者对张籍评判自己诗作的紧张期待心情。科举考试，对于当时的士子来说，乃是和女孩出嫁一样的终身大事。两者的紧张不安心境极为相似，朱庆馀巧妙地抓住了二者之间的相通之处，生动形象地揭示了这种微妙心理。

张籍何等老辣，当然知道朱庆馀的心意，也欣赏他诗歌的灵性，心中对他已默然应允。当即回了一首《酬朱庆馀》：

越女新妆出镜心，自知明艳更沉吟。

齐纨未足时人贵，一曲菱歌敌万金。

诗中将朱庆馀比作一位采菱姑娘，容貌既美，歌声亦好，虽然并不华丽，却清新动人，必然得到人们的赞赏。暗示他不必为考试担心，一定可以金榜题名。

两人以诗相问，以诗作答，彼此一点即通，明白无误。关键是两诗都借女子之情态，表心中之意愿，巧妙准确，隐约雅致，耐人寻味。

未遇其人

白居易有诗《放言五首·其三》云：

赠君一法决狐疑，不用钻龟与祝蓍。

试玉要烧三日满，辨材须待七年期。

周公恐惧流言日，王莽谦恭未篡时。

向使当初身便死，一生真伪复谁知？

大致是讲人心难测，需要时间的长期检验，不能仅凭一时之表现定好坏。诗中举了两个例子佐证自己的观点。一个是周初的周公，一个是西汉的王莽。两人都曾辅佐幼君，周公最后还政于君，王莽却取而代之。因此周公一直为后世所颂扬，而王莽则长期被作为叛臣的典型，遭到人们无情的批判。

王莽出身声名显赫的王氏家族，族中叔伯兄弟多为将军列侯，生活奢靡，锦衣玉食，声色犬马，不思进取。唯王莽独守清净，生活简朴，为人谦恭，勤奋好学，事母至孝，抚育兄子，行为检点，作风严谨。对内敬重叔伯兄弟，对外结纳文人雅士。用现在的话说是国家栋梁、道德楷模、励志典范。而且几十年如一日地严于律己，踔厉奋发。几乎可以说，他是历史上极少的完人之一。

但因为他后来代汉自立，建立了王莽新政，被忠君卫道士诟病为篡国逆臣，各种脏水都开始往他身上泼。特别是说他虚假伪装，扮成一个忠诚耿介之士，包藏隐忍，目的就是要夺取汉家江山。此论尤为可笑，一个人如果能谦虚谨慎一生，节俭质朴一生，孝亲敬人一生，即便他本意是伪装的，最后也变成真实的了。一时的表演很容易，没见过谁假戏真做一辈子。单凭王莽最后夺了刘家的天下，就全盘否认他的德行人品，实在是一孔之见，不足为训。

王莽的问题在于创新心切，立国未稳，就全面推行改革新政，导致天下大乱，盗贼蜂起，而率兵征讨的人又太过无能，几十万之众竟然溃败于一万余人之手，导致不可收拾，政息人亡。如果王莽主政后坚持稳重扎实、敬士爱民的一贯风格，分步推进体制改革，天下将是另外一番景象。立国成功，后人对他的评价也许会是一片溢美之词了。

历史从来都以成败论英雄，成者为王败者为寇，司马迁能将一败涂地的项羽视为英雄，专门将其事迹列入本纪，无疑具有非凡的历史卓识。假使王莽遇司马迁，或可传盛名于世。

厥功至伟的曹丕

国家强大时代兴盛之时，文学往往也呈现强盛之势。比如两汉时期的历史散文与抒情小赋，唐朝的诗歌散文和宋朝的诗词。但并不意味着时代盛文学就必盛，或者乱世之中就没有好文学。元明两朝不可谓不强大，但文学却显式微之态。有清一代，有著名的康乾盛世，却并未曾见文学如何大放异彩。若不是曹雪芹的《红楼梦》“一力降十会”，与之前诸多朝代相较，几无可称道之处。

最令人惊讶的当属东汉末年三国时期，那是个天下大乱诸侯蜂起的时代。大家都忙于求生存抢地盘，立国称霸，没几个人有作文赋诗的雅兴。诗文写得再好，也攻不下一座城，挡不住一路军。那时最需要的人才是卧龙凤雏那样的谋士、关羽张飞那样的猛将。再多的诗人文章家对攻城略地铲平诸侯也毫无作用。文人在那样的时代实在是没有半点用武之地。按说，文学应该是暗弱衰微才对。但神奇的是，这时的文学却颇具特色，蔚为大观，并形成了被誉为具有“建安风骨”的特有文学风貌，这不能不感谢曹氏父子。

曹操和他两个儿子曹丕曹植本身都是诗文大家，团结了以“建安七子”为代表的一大批文人，经常进行诗文唱和，举办文学盛会，使文化之风得以盛行。也就是曹氏父子有如此雅好，其他如孙权刘备袁绍袁术等枭雄，一心打天下争州郡去了，根本没兴趣与没用的文人谈什么之乎者也。只有曹操，带领几十万大军南下收取荆州，准备攻取江东的时候，于大战之际还要横槊赋诗，文人气十足。曹植是个天才诗人，也是时人公认的建安文学代表。其《洛神赋》表现了高超的艺术水准。其他如王粲、孔融、陈琳等人的诗文也都气势雄强，志深笔长。他们与曹氏三父子共同成就了“建安风骨”。南北朝刘勰在《文心雕龙·时序》中评价他们说：“观其时文，雅好慷慨，良由世积离乱，风衰俗怨，并志深笔长，故梗概而多气也。”

继承了曹操魏王之位的曹丕虽然才华不如弟弟曹植，但其对文学的识见确乎在众人之上。正是他在《典论·论文》中提出了著名的论断：“盖文章，经国之大业，不朽之盛事。”将文章的地位提高到了无以复加的地步，什么年寿荣乐，皆不及文章之无穷。在乱世背景下，能将文章的功用认识得这么透彻，曹丕绝非等闲。虽然他也无时不在想着平蜀灭吴，但他始终对文章抱着敬畏之心，将其作为超越一切世俗的存在，而且大力支持文学发展，并亲自参与创作，与一众文人交往甚厚。也许他算不上是个杰出的君王，但他一定是个卓有见识的文章批评家。

三国时期是历史上出了名的乱世，合该是谋士将军的最好舞台，然而因了曹氏父子，建安文学竟在文学史上占有重要的一席之地。而曹丕则将文章的功用推到了无上之境。对于文学的贡献，整个建安文坛中，曹丕无疑厥功至伟。

绵延的历史

唐朝刘知幾是个博见洽闻、史识深远的史学家，在《史通》中他对唐以前的史书做了一个详细梳理，其时许多史料早已散佚，他能对过去历朝历代的史书成书过程、作者生平进行详细的阐述，殊为不易。不知得收集多少资料、阅读多少典籍。正是在他的深入研究之下，史学的脉络才清晰明了起来。

刘知幾从三皇五帝时期的《三坟》《五典》开始，继而到孔子整理撰写的《尚书》《春秋》及其《春秋》内传《左传》《公羊传》《穀梁传》，《春秋》外传《国语》，记载七国争雄的《战国策》。接下来是著名的前四史《史记》《汉书》《后汉书》《三国志》。西晋灭亡后，司马睿东渡建立东晋，后为刘裕所灭，历经宋齐梁陈四朝。中原大地五胡乱华，先后建立十六国，后由魏统一，魏又分裂为东魏西魏、北齐北周，终归于隋。所以《晋书》之后，南朝有《宋书》《齐书》《梁书》《陈书》，北方各国无论大小，皆有史书流传，最后定于《十六国春秋》。北魏后则有《魏书》《北齐书》《后周书》，隋亡于唐，留有《隋书》。唐武后长安年间，刘知幾与朱敬则、徐坚、吴兢等人修撰了

《唐书》。至此，自有文字记载的上古直到盛唐，史书的修编过程及成果呈现，且不论是否客观真实，但历史基本得以完整地研究梳理出来。让后之史学研究者学有路径，持有实据，确实功莫大焉。

看了刘知幾关于史学研究的宏观勾勒，我受益匪浅。让我震惊的是，每一个朝代，无论运祚长短，都对史书的编撰非常重视，哪怕是天下纷乱战争频仍的五胡乱华之际，少数民族政权也对修史极为关注，居然无一国无史。而且每个当政的国家对灭亡的前朝，都会认真地进行史书修撰，以期获得成败的经验教训。由此形成了重视修史的优秀传统。而作为读书人，几乎都以能参与修史为荣。一般来讲，朝廷会甄拔一些品行端方、才华横溢的人进入编修队伍。纵观那些史书作者，无论是官方指派，还是私自单干者，无不学养深厚、见闻广博。他们不仅将修史作为毕生伟业，也作为成就身后之名的重要途径。

自古以来，正因为国家和个人都对历史高看一眼，厚爱有加，所以中国的史学才得以绵延不绝。

第三辑　碎锦拾遗

吹牛成瘾

吹牛和喝酒抽烟一样是会上瘾的。天天喝酒，哪天突然断了供，嘴上定会淡然无味。烟一支一支地抽，突然没粮了，不仅手指上空落落的，还会口干舌苦，心绪不宁。吹牛也一样，大话讲惯了，要讲几句真话实话，都不知道怎么开口。有时想想，讲话其实是不可逆的，就像人的生活，由检入奢易，由奢入检难。涉世之初，我们心中想着什么，嘴里就说着什么，口舌一致。后来心中想到的是这个，嘴里讲的却是那个。更有甚者，明明只想着一分，舌头一滑，却讲成了十分。泡沫起初很小，吹着吹着，就无边无际。干货原本很多，疯狂注水后便稀释得不见踪迹。从实话实说到大话连篇，用不了很久就可轻而易举地做到；从大话连篇再回到当初的实话实说，可就比登天还难了。经常满嘴跑火车的人，让他说一两句靠谱的话，比折磨他还让他难受。我们常常觉得难以置信，为什么有些人讲起大话来那么自然而然，那么习以为常，实际上那是一直以来毫无节制的结果，乃至于一旦进入吹牛轨道，便像列车那般风驰电掣，不可阻遏。

一直以来，我都讷于言谨于行，与人交流，三言两语便把该说的话说完了。哪来的那么多真话实话！如果彼此开门见山，一针见血，几分钟就能把复杂的问题讲得很透彻。看到别人滔滔不绝口若悬河，着实羡慕。特别是把不着边际无中生有的事，描摹得有声有色生动形象，觉得他们极具想象能力。把一粒芝麻夸成一颗花生，于我已经要绞尽脑汁竭尽才华了；而把一粒芝麻夸成一个西瓜，就完全超出了我的语言表达能力。生活中常能见到把葵花夸成太阳，把池塘夸成海洋的吹牛高手，我想他们不仅具有吹牛的天赋，还需要长期吹牛的实践，达到吹牛入迷成痴的境界，才能如此应用自如。我也曾着力培养自己的“吹瘾”，无奈心拙嘴笨，难有建树。好不容易有点小进步，可以吹一为二，结果因为害怕回不到原点，立即强行闭嘴数日，硬生生戒掉刚刚生成的“吹瘾”。

想来此生我是无法成为吹牛大师了。

雅俗之间

大俗之人是放浪的。酒肉穿肠，美人在怀，得势时便顺势作为，有钱时便挥金如土，做事时也认真，搞关系时也用心，有名就要名，有利就沾利，日日笙歌，夜夜佳肴。他们活着最大的理想就是享受，追求的状态也是享受，实际的行为也是享受，只要可以满足物欲情欲，他们便觉得浑身舒坦。至于思考，基本与他们无关，因为从不思考，自然也就没有关于命运的迷惑，没有更深层次的人生痛苦。他们的生活是单向度的，充满烟火气的。

大雅之人是自足的，超然物外，凌驾众上。身在人世间，心在五行外，他们始终站在云端，俯视着芸芸众生，满怀怜悯，气度恢宏。吃喝玩好并不能给他们带来快乐，粗茶淡饭也不会让他们忧虑。有时学有所成，他们便快乐自足，心中犹如清泉流过；有时思有所得，他们便雀跃欢欣，似云雁穿行长空。城市易主，他们可能无动于衷，花瓣飞落，也许会惊动他们的思绪。他们可能独行于无人的旷野，也许出没于热闹的街区。身外之物于他们都是符号而已，而他们自己任何时候都是气定神

闲，心满意足的。

雅俗兼顾的人是最痛苦的。雅，他们雅得难于出尘；俗，他们俗得难以入世，高不上天低不着地，浮在半空，美其名曰雅俗共赏，其实两头不靠。既不能忘却名利，又不能粪土名利，一边追求物质享受，一边还要讲求精神皈依。本来闷头体味俗世的繁华也就罢了，偏偏要去精神的世界构建美妙的桃花源。结果俗世的快乐不能尽兴，世外的快乐亦不知所谓。无疑，他们是一群心有不甘且又焦虑不安的人。

人活一世，草木一春，快乐地度过一生是每个人的期望。事实上，快乐终身也并非不可企及，只要你甘于做一个大俗之人，或者欣于做一个大雅之人。

宁可信其有

有个朋友声称发现了一种能令人返老还童的奇妙良方，劝我按他的要求好好服用，几年之后将大见成效，我毫不犹豫地予以照办，一来我相信他的为人，毕竟三十多年的交情，不可以价计。二来我心中也确实期盼真能找到一种使自己越来越年轻的办法，虽然理智告诉我这不过是不切实际的幻想。

很多时候我们选择相信别人，并不是因为缺乏判断力或者失去理智，而是要安抚自己固有之善心或良愿。以前街头路边常有残障者哀声乞讨。每次路过时，我都会送给他们一些零钱。其实我知道，一转身他们中有部分人也许就摇身一变为体面人，自由消费，有些人就是因乞讨而发家致富的。但明知受骗，我依然会坚持施舍，因为我不愿硬了自己的柔肠，易了自己的善心，施舍给他们，受益的其实是自己。

以前年少，凡事积极肯干，得到鼓励褒奖，说是只要干出业绩，自然会予以刮目重用，其实，这些都不过是管理艺术。现在听到类似的话，常会淡然一笑，仍会像以前一样奋发努力，不是轻信其缥缈的许

飞，蜻蜓在枝头上静立。一进园内，芳香扑鼻而来，空气清新如洗。微风一过，绿浪翻滚，落叶飘零。景致宜人，人也十分稀少，是个运动散步的绝佳之地。真是踏破铁鞋无觅处，得来全不费功夫，我欣喜异常，决定从此将晨练场景定于此处。

这么多年来，我虽然知道附近有个小公园，而且还常在傍晚时分到这里散步，却从未曾想来此晨练。显然，小公园比社区广场的环境好得多，而且与我家距离约略相等，为何我脑中毫不动念？无疑，是多年形成的习惯性思维使然，认定某个地方，就一头扎进去，直到无法待下去，才想到要另觅他地。

人生之路也是一样，大多数人选定了一条，就没想过要更换，除非进入死胡同。其实，中途尝试着走走新路，没准能找到更加适合自己的路子。

无本生意

农耕时代，牛是农村之宝，农民最珍贵的财富。有耕牛的家庭，才称得上是殷实之家。记得小时候我们村实行包产到户，几家人才共分得一头耕牛，有些家底好肯吃苦的人，很快就独自购买了耕牛，引得他人啧啧称羡，我的邻居就是最早拥有耕牛者之一。遗憾的是，正当他准备大干一场的时候，家里发生了重大变故，他不得不卖掉他心爱的耕牛以救急。赶集的前一天晚上，他反复摩挲着那头牛的牛角，眼中流下了不舍的泪水。第二天，他把牛牵到集市，换回了急需的钱。神奇的是，没过多久，那头牛居然回来了，而且买家竟然也没有过来追问，都说老马识途，没想到老牛也识途。邻居算是白赚了一头牛，全村的人都羡慕得不得了，觉得他做了一次无本生意。那时我便想，长大了如果做生意，就一定要想办法像邻居那样做无本生意。

可惜我并不是做生意的料，所以从未到商海里游过，大半生在体制内蹉跎，也未曾有什么值得夸耀的业绩，方方面面都平平淡淡，内心倒也从未自怨自艾。只是夜来忽梦少年事，邻居卖牛的往事突然清晰起来，于是我突发奇想，做不了实物贸易，能不能贩卖一下知识？知识这东西随时可以免费进货，只要你愿意起早摸黑，古今中外的知识都可大量收集。直接卖或者略作加工后卖，都有人抢着买，市场需求旺盛。知识永远都取不尽，永远也卖不完，这才是真正的无本生意。

于是我决定从现在起，去历史中寻宝，到现实中运货，然后倒给那些有所需求的人，这其间的利润应该是惊人的，因为本钱是零。我为找到一条如此发家致富的路子而欣喜不已，准备接下来全情投入，想来后半生决计不至于像前半生这般潦倒了。

符号

很多时候，我们并不是作为独特的个体存在，而是以一个符号的方式呈现。这个符号可以代表经理、主管、处长、主席，或者单位、部门、街道、城市，总之，并非那个沉静儒雅或者火急火燎的你，正如当你出席某个活动或会议时，那个名位牌写着的机构就是你，你就是那个机构，至于你的高矮胖瘦、美丑老少，根本无关宏旨。一天中的绝大多数场合，我们都是移动着的符号，被摆弄着、借用着，以助力完成某些任务，或者满足某些欲望。

只有当我们回到家里，或者与亲朋好友聚会时，我们才成为与众不同的“这一个”。容貌平平或者出众，性格柔顺或者爆裂，情感浓郁或者淡然，不管怎样，都具有极高的辨析度。我们的父母兄弟妻子儿女绝不会忘却我们的音容笑貌，模糊我们的性情品行，他们的眼中心里，我们不可能是一个只有象征意义的符号。

所以人在江湖，千万不要以为自己是号人物，所有的人都敬你爱你，对你由衷赞佩心悦诚服。其实他们不过是将你看作一个符号，对你鞠躬致礼，点头微笑。随着你的代表身份失效，符号意义彻底丧失，等待你的可能就是冷漠甚至羞辱。许多人错把符号作用当成自身魅力，自欺欺人地生活在美妙的想象世界，突然有一天幻象破灭，便不知所措了。

作为符号的你，终究是要完成符号的使命，彻底回归真我。完全失去符号意义，处处以真面目示人，你也许会变得很不自在。正如《肖申克的救赎》中那个蹲了一辈子监狱的老人，一旦获得了自由，对生活反而无所适从。

说不如写

舌绽莲花不如笔吐珠华。说得再好听，都像是阳光下的肥皂泡，虽然五彩缤纷，终是要破灭的。锦绣文章则不然，落笔生根，摇曳生姿，一长便是千百年。只要够耀眼，普天下的人都能看到。说得天花乱坠，也是空中雪，旋落旋灭，没有几个人能看到。就算站在万人中央，滔滔不绝，也不过是时光刹那，很快就归于沉寂，未若一首简短得只有二十个字的《登鹳雀楼》，跨越千年远播至今。

绝大多数唐朝诗人宋朝词人，我们并不知道他们是善于言辞还是拙于言辞，也许有口吃的毛病，只要没有严重到三国时邓艾那般“期期艾艾”，估计史书对那些说话略有障碍的人不会详细记录。李白杜甫这些大诗人，诗歌精美华丽，表达新奇流畅，焉知他们说起话来不是慢条斯理或者不知所云。韩愈苏轼的文章气势磅礴，酣畅淋漓，他们在生活中未必就是演说家。毕竟辩才无碍的人并不多。孔子孟子这些圣人倒极有可能善于演说，因为他们本来就是老师，经常给一众弟子授课，没道理语言不畅。可他们述而不作，好在弟子们把他们的语言记录了下来，否则，就是金科玉律，现在也找不到半点痕迹。想来历史上这种珠玉之言不知丢失了多少。

所以即使是有一副伶牙俐齿，也抵不上一个烂笔头。就算你妙语连珠佳词迭出，也传不出方圆几里，至少传不出当今时代，而一篇小小的诗文却可以跋山涉水越陌度阡，穿过时光飞渡岁月。从《将进酒》中我们听到的是李白的心声而不是他的歌声，从《江城子》中我们听到的是苏轼悼妻时的悲伤而不是他的哭泣。我想王勃就是口若悬河，也说不出《滕王阁序》那般美的境界；曹雪芹自述身世再生动，也不可能描绘出《红楼梦》那般壮丽的画卷。

生前身后

近几日，两位身边的熟人先后仙逝，虽然跟他们认识，但并无私交，算不上朋友，故无特别悲伤，况且他们都已上了一定年纪。只是惋惜于生命的凋零，慨叹于人生的短暂，有些触景生情，览物自伤罢了。生活就是如此，在滚滚人潮席卷而过之时，总有人要倒在岁月的怀抱，消失在时代的舞台，从此被除名于当世，定格于历史的某个位置，至于是否被人记起，完全取决于在世时留下了什么。有些人一去便烟消云散，恰如春梦了无痕，再也无人问津。有些人虽已身没，灵魂却不灭。他们的思想转化为文字、线条或音符，经久不灭。

很巧的是，驾鹤西归的两位熟人，一个是著名的艺术家，一个是著名艺术机构原负责人。艺术家已成就卓著，名震海内。他的离世被誉为艺术界之重大损失，业内一片哀悼叹惋之声，回忆怀念文章屡见网络报端，大小领导名流都敬献花圈，可谓备极哀荣。可以预测，在将来很长一段时间，他的名字，他的故事，特别是他的艺术风格和艺术贡献，都将不断被提及和赞誉。

而另外一位，虽然曾经领导着一个著名的艺术机构，遗憾的是他自己并非一个造诣深厚的艺术家，而是一个普通管理者，在位时当然有着赫赫权威，离职后便毫无影响了。开始几年，大家总结工作、回忆过去时，还偶尔提及，渐渐地就被人们所淡忘，毕竟工作和生活都是日新月异的，人们习惯于往前看，除了老人，有多少人愿意回头望呢？所以他的去世，只是被身边一些熟人听闻，并不能激起什么涟漪，亲友们转发的不过是则信息而已，形成不了新闻，因此哀荣是不可能有的，普通的丧事一办，一个人的一生便作了了结，从此彻底被人遗忘。

死者已矣，并不知道死后事身后名，却留给了生者无限的感慨：原来人生于世，不仅生前有别，死后更相异。

阿谀之功

以前看金庸的小说《天龙八部》，很是讶异于他的想象，居然能创造一个奇特的反派人物丁春秋。此人武功高强，心地狠毒，创立了西域“星宿派”，门下弟子称其为“星宿老仙”。这些都是正常路数，没有什么稀奇处，最奇葩的是，丁春秋是个特别喜欢门下吹牛拍马的人，每当他出场之时，他的徒弟们都要列队整齐，或弄丝竹，或敲锣鼓，吹吹打打地簇拥而来，并齐声高呼：“星宿老仙法驾降临中原，快快上来跪接！”“恭请星宿老仙弘施大法，降服小妖小丑！”听者无不心生厌恶，无情嗤笑，丁春秋听了却如痴如醉，十分受用。

每当读到此处，总要生起质疑：世上果有如此厚颜无耻之人？没想到，近日真有关于类似的消息刷屏，说是一个公司的老总走到哪里，员工们都训练有素地极尽阿谀美化之能事，完全像丁春秋一样，生活在一个满是好言好语的美妙世界。怪不得他说发明了保持年轻的好办法，也许每时每刻听着溢美之词，真不失为一种心情愉悦青春永驻的绝佳处方。

事实上，谁都喜欢听好话。只是客观地承认人家的优点是赞美，而虚美他人的特点则是阿谀。讲的人肯定分得清是赞美还是阿谀，但听的人多已完全失去判断能力，肉麻的话听起来也很顺耳。要获得他人的好感，达到自己的个人目的，阿谀比送礼有时更管用，精神上的贿赂比物质上的贿赂更有威力。

金钱、美女对普通人可能具有极大的诱惑力，但对那些物欲淡薄的人来说可能不起什么作用。阿谀奉承就不一样，成年累月地赞美歌颂，任谁也招架不住。古代的皇帝富有四海，送什么金银财宝也引不起他们的兴趣，但小人们一通猛拍，一定会让他们心旷神怡。以乾隆皇帝的英明，照样经不住和珅的奉承，乃至于终生离不开和珅。

听好话是会上瘾的，道古今而誉盛德的话再多，入耳也不烦。这就是为什么掌权者身边常有小人，因为君子是不愿阿谀奉承的。

深根固柢

西学东渐，在鸦片战争之后，已逞不可阻遏之势，到了民国初期，其势益张，可谓滥觞。很多学子基本抛弃传统，完全西化。二十世纪八十年代，西学再次席卷而过，很多领域诸如哲学、文学、美学、社会学的学子，传统底子本就不够扎实，经此冲击，更是薄如蝉翼。许多人甚至不知四书五经为何物，经史子集几乎从不触及。写起文章来都是时尚洋气一路，就是沉不下去。乍一看，很是新鲜活泼，可经不起回味，就像雨前茶，泡了两三次就没味了。

早在十九世纪中叶，张之洞就曾对中西学之间的关系作了明辨。他在《劝学篇》中指出："今日之学者，必先通经，以明我中国先圣先师立教之旨。考史，以识我中国历代治乱、九州之风土。涉猎子集，以通我国之学术文章。然后择西学之可以补吾阙者用之，西政之可以起吾疾者取之，斯有益而无其害。"通经，考史，涉猎子集，再辅之以西学，这便是张之洞倡导的为学之序。只有把中学的底子打好了，西学才能发挥作用。没有根底，实行拿来主义，很有可能换来邯郸学步的结果。正如一个体虚气弱的人，不去设法固本培元，却滥用补药猛汤，不死也要得一身的内伤。

今日回望，张之洞的循序观仍颇富洞见。通经考史，遍览子集，佐以有益西学，如此便再也不至于头重脚轻，步态虚浮。体健身正，气足神完，信心自生。

动静得宜

我的居处虽略嫌偏远，但依山傍水，是个安静所在。平素偶或深夜回家，车入月影深处，两旁树茂花香，仿佛自俗世回到仙都，身上红尘被荡涤一空，那些烦心之事瞬间被冲淡乃至忘却。所以一旦踏进归来的林荫道，我便百般不愿再返身外出。在这个城市，热闹我没怎么去体验，安静倒是享受了不少。闹处得静，实在是天予我取，最是顺应自然。

平日里以静为主，滤心养神，颇得意趣。到了周末，便常驱车至繁华处，看人群络绎，物华天宝，感受时代的风起云涌。置身其中，随波逐流，行于兴起，止于意阑。时不时到最前沿走走，看生活进入了第几重境界，不至于游离于世外，成为一个活着的古人。

而每当我返回自己的天地，我发现那里被许多寻静的人侵入。也许他们平时热闹惯了，想找个地方安住心神，我所居之地正好是他们的理想之所，于是他们从四面八方赶来徒步登山，临湖而钓，将自己从热闹的场景中硬生生地拔身而出，然后纵身跃入这片宁静，一如我从宁静中站起，汇入滚滚洪流，去体味缤纷喧哗的味道。

人不能一直处于宁静之中，一生波澜不起，那种生活注定毫无趣味。当然也不能像隙中驹石中火，匆匆忙忙心神不定，回头一望尽在奔跑。所以在云上躺久了，一定要翻身按下云头，去人间好好看看。在红尘中来回打滚，须寻个僻静处，任凭风吹雨打，将灵魂冲个干净。

虽然总的来说，动静算是得宜，但近来事多务繁，心事颇为动荡，该是日暮掩柴扉，临风听暮蝉的时候了。

以柔克刚

虽然家住老旧小区，但因为居于顶层，有一小块天台可资专用，心下还是颇为满意的。烟雨之朝，星月之夕，我每每独往，张臂迎风，开胸纳气，觉天地顿然辽阔，人间无限美好。居高望远之豁然，登临送目之慨叹，皆拜天台之所赐。

当初迁居于此，正是看中此处地僻人稀、环境幽静，特别是楼顶登眺，四无阻碍，令人心旷神怡。旧主人移交时，房屋一空，唯天台遗留一株三角梅。这棵梅树一看便有年头了，弯曲盘旋，伞状怒张，枝叶茂盛，繁花似锦。梅花沿着屋檐铁栅，于空中倒悬而下，丛丛簇簇，煞是艳丽。尤其是春夏两季，花开最盛，恰如雨后瀑布，其势益张，远远望去，就像天空飘着一个大花球。数里开外，见有花红一片飞落者，其下正是我家。

初时梅树必是倚着铁栅生长，渐渐地，枝叶缠绕着栏杆，与铁栅融为一体。时光流逝，树干变得曲折环绕，显得苍劲老辣。有些地方，枝干已将铁栏扭曲，缠抱在一起，难分彼此。原本横竖分明坚硬冷漠的铁栏杆，竟有了脉脉温情，与树枝相倚相偎起来。柔弱与刚强，在岁月中互相转化。这里，我目睹了坚持的韧性和力量。

是的，什么都抵挡不了日复一日的坚持，“何意百炼钢，化为绕指柔”，只有那些顽强的生命才有如许的功力。也许最初他们并不强大，甚至是脆弱的，但在岁月的磨砺中不屈不挠，在不辍的坚持中日益刚强。那株梅树正是无声的示范，从弱小到坚强，她告诉我想要做好一件事，那就一如既往地坚持，岁月自会见证。

唯冬天不可辜负

深圳素来被称为没有冬天的城市，且别说见不到大雪纷飞银装素裹，就是寒风凛冽的感觉也只能更多地想象。有一年春节，有人制作了一幅深圳市民中心飘雪图，并在微信上发布，立即引起了全城轰动，时值气温骤降，很多人信以为真，真的前去求证，结果自是失望而归。雪基本与深圳无缘，寒总是那么遥不可及。那些家在北方、在江南的人，还能借春节之机，回去体验一下冬季与寒凉，而生长于岭南一带的人，只能到别人的故乡去看雪。

我本是江南人，来到深圳久了，回老家渐渐就少了，冬天变得陌生起来，很多季节带来的心灵体悟和情感变化，日益模糊缥缈。所以冬天里偶有凄风冷雨之日，我便如获至宝，深觉不可辜负。一定要穿得单薄简略，在狂风中漫步穿行，体会那种瑟瑟发抖的滋味。时光会瞬间把我带回江南，雨打梧桐的声音一时清晰可闻，湿身的寒鸦在光秃的树林中哀鸣，枯黄的细草在寒风中摇曳，溪流冷涩，炊烟不起，昏暗的光线下，城市村庄都少了些生气。这时最令人想念的是被窝中的温暖，特别

是细雨蒙蒙，湿衣不见，却将寒气直逼肌肤，让人遍体生寒，这时进入温室，盖上暖被，沉沉进入梦乡，而在雪花飞舞的早晨醒来，挣扎着起来看一个洁白的世界，还有什么比这更美妙的事呢？

可是在深圳，一年到头多是夏天，有时时序已是冬令，走在路上仍然挥汗如雨，穿着衬衣过春节的日子不在少数。情感上没有冬天，无疑是件幸运的事。季节里缺少冬天，总令人感觉少了些人生况味，就像酸甜苦辣咸样样都有才是真实完满的生活。有时，我宁愿被寒风刺骨，骤雨抽身，也要努力恢复关于天寒地冻的记忆，所以一旦寒冬来了，我一定不会辜负那些弥足珍贵的日子。

遗忘

其实，人们真的不必遇事就觉得天要坍塌，急着寻死觅活。时间就是麻醉剂，一剂下去，再深刻的记忆，都会渐渐变得麻木无感。遗忘似乎是人的天性，如果不是经常唤醒，我们甚至会彻底混淆自己的前世今生。

俗话说，好了伤疤忘了痛。大部分人都有生病入院的经历，甚至上过手术台，饱受病痛折磨。在医院发誓赌咒，出院后一定要以身体为重，看淡一切，决计不能再进医院经受痛苦。然而过不了几天，生活便一切照旧，痛苦也好，誓言也罢，都抛到了九霄云外。

痛易忘，穷也一样。四十多年改革开放，进入全新的小康社会，生活早已变了模样，过惯了富裕日子的人们，有几个还记得家徒四壁、饿得前胸贴后背的艰苦岁月？过去缺吃少穿，如今营养过剩；过去经常饥肠辘辘，如今要努力培育饥饿感。所谓的穷，不过是相较而言，绝对贫困已被完全消灭。曾经穷苦的日子，人们已经记不清是什么样子了。

情好像遗忘得要慢一些，但也因人而异。有些人的初恋花一生都难以忘却，有些人一分手便找到了新欢，一段了却迅速另起一段，正如某些娱乐明星，就像喝了忘情水，昨天还如胶似漆，今天便形同陌路。至于父母之情，是终生难忘的，忘了，便不算是人了。

最不该忘记的是仇恨，特别是民族屈辱之仇。虽然我们不必时时生活在仇恨之中，但一定要清晰地牢记异族入侵杀我同胞掠我财货之仇。以史为鉴，才能更好地防患于未然。现在看到的历史，更多的只是文字记载，从中很难体味到我们父辈祖辈所经受的巨大苦难。此时我们只是读起来心情沉重而已，彼时他们却无时无刻不在以性命相搏。我们有什么理由忘记那些辱国毁家的仇恨！

生活中的贫穷与伤痛，内心里的情感与仇恨，都不应该轻易忘却。保持清醒，加深记忆，是确保不再饱受折磨屈辱的前提。

融入自然

每日清晨，我都会一如既往地来到社区公园，在绿树掩映中，闻花香，听鸟鸣，开始吐故纳新。绿色盈盈欲上人衣，空气清新沁人心脾，转眼之间，仿佛目光多了几许湛然；呼吸之间，仿佛胸中作了一次清洗。眼中的混浊一扫而空，心里的淤积一吐而尽。我站在树林草地中，感觉自己就在自然的怀抱里，与自然融为一体。微闭双目，我能听到竹露滴清响，我能听到枝条拔节声。时间久了，我便不知身在何处。继而忘却了时间，甚至忘却了身体，只有一缕思绪，时隐时现，在林中盘旋。我知道，就在此时，我把自己从社会中弄丢了，遗忘在自然的一个小角落。

事实上，我一直想把自己遗忘在自然之中，无论是树林草地，还是江河湖泊。可是每次意识都把我硬生生拉回现实世界。我深刻体会到了苏轼“长恨此身非我有”的痛苦，我并不能完全控制自己的身体，否则我一定会隐身在木叶之下，只在清风朗月中暴露自己。

我很是不满自己为何好似与自然之间隔着一条鸿沟，非要努力跨越，才能从所处的社会到达彼岸。好在我每天都会坚持到公园漫步，否则不知要过多久才能想起自然，然后又不知要过多久才能接近一次自然，更毋庸说融入自然。

与花草树木为伍肯定比与人为伍要轻松愉悦，花草树木会给我新鲜氧气，翠绿颜色，让我心旷神怡。而跟人打交道，需要谨慎小心，常常紧张焦虑，让我神疲意倦。

我渴望到大自然放逐，行到水穷，坐看云起，最好迷失在奇花异石中，忘情于林泉花海里，一去不返。“小舟从此逝，江海寄余生”也是非常不错的选择。

上帝视角

智者都喜欢登高。登高不唯可以望远，更重要的是可以俯瞰。杜甫《望岳》云：“会当凌绝顶，一览众山小。”只有登顶，才能全方位广视角将所有景致尽收眼底。否则，只见冰山一角，岂可妄言其巨细方圆？苏轼说“不识庐山真面目”，是“只缘身在此山中”，王安石放言“不畏浮云遮望眼”，是“自缘身在最高层”。站在山中看山，哪能看清山的全貌。站在最高层，树木岩石溪流蜂蝶皆历历在目。故游山览胜，人人尽知奋力登顶，没有任何遮挡，自可放眼四眺，饱览大好河山万千风物。

可是在生活中，却不是人人都能找到至高点，更毋庸说居于至高点。我们常常被万物迷花了眼，不知身在何处，不是陷于事件，便是羁于人情，总是看不远看不全看不清看不透，兜转于生活深处不能自拔。只有少数人能像孙行者一样，一个旱地拔葱站在空中，驾起一片祥云，手搭凉棚俯视人间。来从何处去往何地，转几道弯过几道坎，谁是同道谁是路人，皆一目了然。山自此挡不住视野，雾自此遮不住身形，惑自此迷不住心灵。

恰如全知全能叙述一场战争始末，战机出现在何时，胜负决定于何处，叙述者早已预先作了设定。站在上帝的视角俯瞰人间万物亦复如是，所有隐藏的、模糊的、未定的、难解的，都变得清晰明白纤毫毕现，人生透明如薄纱，还有什么好苦恼、好怨愤、好猜疑的呢?

问题是，如何才能站在空中？如果纵身一跃都能上天，也不至于那么多人会在俗世中意乱情迷。也许像老子说的“绝圣弃智”“清心寡欲”，才有可能轻身便体，不借于物而浮于半空。

预兆

老家农村有个说法，新年第一天的生活情形预兆着全年的大致光景。第一天要是忙忙碌碌，全年都要辛苦劳碌。第一天要是有吃有玩，全年都轻松快乐。于是，新年元旦，正月初一这两天，大家把该干的事都往后推延，相互邀约着打牌喝酒，开心玩乐。只有几个每天起早贪黑干活成性的老人，实在是闲不住，还是要扛起锄头挑上箩筐往田地里赶，似乎不去田间地头待上一会，日子就不知道怎么过。年轻人恨不得类似的风俗越多越好，吃喝玩乐还有十足的理由，天地间爽快事莫过于此。越吃预示着越会有，越玩预示着越有得玩，新年第一天谁不愿吃喝着开场玩乐着度过呢？

可事实证明，那不过是个美丽的谎言。第一天如何度过，跟全年的运程并无多大关联。就算第一天玩出了花，后面不努力也是白搭，幸福始终是靠干出来的，不是凭运气碰到的。沉浸在自己美妙的设想中，欣喜于亲友们美好的祝福中，达不成任何实际的效果，锦绣梦想是以踏实的步伐作为针织编制而成的，生活来不得半点虚假，也没什么侥幸。坐等，永远到达不了远方；缓行，哪怕一次寸步，终将至千里。

我当然祈盼老家的俗话灵验，只是不信也不愿以吃喝玩乐肇始，而获一年的清闲畅意。我的脑海中固执地保留着一幅画面：几个农民伯伯在新年第一天踽踽行于田地之中。所以祈盼归祈盼，我绝不至于以祈盼替代行动。我会在新年第一天养足精神，然后像往常一样出发，正如农民走向田地，我将走向历史的天空，走向无垠的未来。我希望在新起点上，依然以勤奋为开端，换得全年的丰收大结局。

解释

有一种强大叫不解释。生活中，人们会因为各种原因彼此之间产生误会，如果适当地作个解释，很容易冰释前嫌。除了亲人，人们本来就互不相识，因了一起学习，一块共事，成为同学或者同事，慢慢熟络起来。既在生活工作中常有交集，难免有些意见相左情感不合，如果加强协调及时沟通表明心迹，相互之间的矛盾误解自是易于化解。但并不是每个人都愿随时袒露心扉，或者为自己的行为详细注解。解释有时意味着大度，有时意味着怯弱，不同的人有着不同的理解，也就表现出不同的态度。

不为自己言行做任何解释的人，一定是个自信的人。不管别人如何理解，有何看法，都不会丝毫影响他的惯有风格或行事方式，议论也好，反对也罢，他始终保持本色。为什么要作解释？解释其实是说明在乎，当其心不在焉，无所谓有、无所谓无的时候，解释就是多余的了。一个人如果对一切都不放在眼里，名利都不留于心头，哪里还用得着多费口舌，作毫无意义的说明？

解释首先费时，其次费力。有那些解释的时间，对于有所作为者来说，还不如实实在在做点事。一有误会就去解释一通，生命哪里承受得了那么大的浪费？为了廉价的理解而将宝贵的时光用于解释，无疑是得不偿失的。而且就算你花费大量时间精力去解释，也未必就能说得清楚，听者也未必能听得明白。有时对牛弹琴，艺术水平再高，牛也照样无动于衷。

最好的办法就是不作任何解释，一意孤行就好。当然要强大到耳中有镗鞳之声，掩盖呕哑之音；眼中有巍峨之山，遮盖匍匐之坡；心中有辽阔之境，覆盖方寸之地。江湖上，人狠话不多的人才是大角色；生活中，不作任何解释的人，才是大人物。

故地重游

故地重游是最易产生伤感的，特别是一别多年的故地，最好不要轻易重游。岁月最是毁人损物。时光快逝，无端地都会让人感慨，更别说触景念人。重回故地，前后两相比较，有时差异惊天动地，物是人非，一睹能让人肝肠寸结。

故地重游之叹，无非因数种情形而生。

一是境迁。再见时旧场境已损毁殆尽，不复旧时模样，美好的事物已破灭了，鲜活的场面也消失了。苏轼的《和子由渑池怀旧》正是这种情形的生动写照：

人生到处知何似，应似飞鸿踏雪泥。

泥上偶然留指爪，鸿飞那复计东西。

老僧已死成新塔，坏壁无由见旧题。

往日崎岖还记否，路长人困蹇驴嘶。

当年一起论道的老僧已圆寂，题写诗句的墙壁也倒塌了，看到一幅萧条破败景象，苏轼不由痛感“人生到处知何似，应似飞鸿踏雪泥”。

二是人非。当日游玩，知己在侧，自是心花怒放，兴致勃勃，无处不妙，无往不乐。再往时已是孤身一人，感怀伤逝，情何以堪。欧阳修《生查子·元夕》说尽了这种前喜后悲的心境：

去年元夜时，花市灯如昼。

月上柳梢头，人约黄昏后。

今年元夜时，月与灯依旧。

不见去年人，泪湿春衫袖。

三是情逝。心境这东西，来如春梦几多时，去似朝云无觅处。也就是说，心境是变化不居的，往日是一种心境，今日或许是另一种心境，时隔多年，经历了人生蝶变，昔日的心境再也难以寻觅。李清照的《偶成》准确地表达了这种心境情感变迁的无奈：

十五年前花月底，相从曾赋赏花诗。

今看花月浑相似，安得情怀似往时。

即使故地景致相似，赏景赋诗还是故人依旧，当年的情怀也未必有，更何况此时不见当年人，平添了无限伤感。

四是境迁人非情逝。再次重游，时代变了，景致变了，人物变了，心境也变了，一切都恍如隔世，往事只堪哀，对景难排。陆游重游沈园时就是这种心情，有《沈园二首·其一》为证：

城上斜阳画角哀，沈园非复旧池台。

伤心桥下春波绿，曾是惊鸿照影来。

阔别四十多年，陆游再次来到沈园，园中景物早就面目全非，表妹唐婉也去世多年，自己已是风烛残年，忆故人，念旧情，除了伤感，还是伤感。

故地，从地理的意义上说是可以重游的，但从人事情境的意义上说，是永远回不去的。心理上不够坚强者，建议不作故地重游之计。

应酬

在这个经济社会高度活跃，人们心扉全面打开的时代，应酬成为不可或缺的交流沟通方式。隔三差五出去应酬一下，再正常不过。每日深居简出没有饭局，反而显得不太正常。据说在日本，男人到了晚上没有应酬，说明社会地位低，事业无所成，一到下班时间就回家，连妻子都会嫌弃蔑视。想想也不无道理，创业的洪流席卷而过，你没有立于潮头也就罢了，至少也要随波逐流跟得上趟，没事人一样与主流无关，可不就是混得不怎么样？事业有成者必然要广泛交流洽谈，而要广泛交流洽谈，免不了经常吃饭应酬。虽然应酬多未必就代表事业蓬勃，但应酬少无疑说明交情清简冷淡。

参加应酬，有人是主角，有人是配角；有人欣然而往，有人勉强而至；有人目标明确，有人漫无目的。坐在应酬席上，其实每个人的心境是很不一样的。官员们因找到价值存在而意足，商人们因获得商业机会而窃喜，穷人们因看到食物浪费而心痛，书生们因觉得生命消耗而不安。虽然觥筹交错，欢声笑语，但都各怀心事，所虑有别。

我虽不善饮酒，但并不厌恶应酬，偶尔也参加一下朋友聚会，毕竟人具有社会属性，终究割裂不了社会联系，非不得已者，不必终老林泉。再说，多了解一些物情世态，多增加一些人生际遇，也不是什么坏事。年轻时，应酬时也很热烈，甚至很淋漓。渐渐地，便不好作声，但只微笑，默看人情冷暖。现在却又不同，忧喜叹惋，民胞物与，不热切，不冷漠，不作无谓之争，不发虚美之辞。兴来痛饮酒，兴阑只端茶。虽云应酬，实高下在心，收放在我，谓之人间云游亦可。

酒

人才

二十世纪八九十年代，我在内陆的一个城市按部就班地工作生活，日子波澜不起。但那时候的东南沿海，改革浪潮已经高及千尺，正逐步席卷全国。虽远隔千里，其流风余浪也时有波及。我所在单位是个科研机构，高学历高职称人员不在少数，时闻有人南下北归，把一向平静肃穆的院子搅得喧闹缤纷，把一直安于现状的人们激得热血沸腾。最先勇敢辞职南飞的是那些既有想法又不安分的年轻人，他们虽自负才高，却为老一代科研专家所不容，从未以人才视之。既然无用武之地，他们自然就思忖着远走高飞。所以毅然决然离去的，多是郁郁不得志者。那些处境平顺颇有前景的人，虽然心里也有所活泛，但始终犹豫着下不了离去的决心。

那些在单位混得不上不下没有回旋余地的活跃分子，一到南方，却找到了施展身手的绝妙空间。未几，便能在各自的领域有所建树，崭露头角，成了掌管一方的英才。在原单位表现平平且又不甚安分的多余人，到了新天地却如鱼得水、频传捷报，成了不可多得的宝贝。早期的特区建设者成就者似乎多是这种人物，他们有胆识有想法，却囿于陈旧的体制和观念，不能奋发有为。一到没有框架约束的特区，恰如脱缰的野马，驰骋在一望无际的草原，自然跑得欢跃得远，瞬间恢复了千里马的本性。

其实，任何时候，我们身边都不乏这种敛藏着奔驰之性的千里马，只是缺乏任其纵横的腹地，或者饲之不能尽其道。不能腾空而起，他们当然无法以千里马称呼。某一天他们脱缰而去，从此海阔天空，任意飞驰，我们倒成了不识不解千里马的“奴隶人”。故如遇名马，且修大道，任其驰骋。

情淡

随着科技越来越发达，经济越来越富裕，人们的情感似乎越来越淡。记得以前让人伤心流泪的时刻还真不少。要么为自己的遭遇心酸，要么为别人的不幸流泪。在艰苦的岁月，处处埋藏着悲伤，只要随意一挖掘，就能让人泪流满面，甚至痛断肝肠。如今我们很难得掉一次眼泪，更别说泣下沾襟。或许有抑郁，或许有焦虑，或许有忧愁，但很难有忧伤。从某种程度上讲，我们的心正在硬化，情正在干涸。当然，这并不能完全怪我们自身，不是我们变得冷漠，而是可令人移情动性的事情越来越少。

古时离别是伤感的重要源头，因为一别就是数年甚至一生，天涯海角再也难以相见。“浮云一别后，流水十年间。”“难相见，易相别，又是玉楼花似雪。”“相逢一醉是前缘，风雨散、飘然何处？”“放眼暮江千顷，中有离愁万斛，无处落征鸿。”与亲人离，与友人别，生离死别，安得不黯然神伤，涕泪横流？现在的离别，不再有什么感伤，乘上飞机火车，朝发夕至，千里江陵一日还，再见只是想不想而非能不能的事了。如此一来，思念难免不减，情感难免不淡，游子之意，羁旅之思，皆荡然无存，伤感自是无因，泪流当然无由。

过去家国穷困，老一辈多缺吃少穿，含辛茹苦，种田打工，持家育儿，即使是日常生活，也有许多感人至深的故事。回忆艰难岁月，父母深情，挣扎情形，至今都会让我们迎风流泪。这几十年来，生活发生了翻天覆地的变化，贫穷落后的日子已一去不复返，抚今忆昔仿如隔世。我们忧虑的不再是设法脱离贫困而是如何更加富裕，焦虑的不再是能否生存而是怎样大踏步发展。欲望屡屡增多，情感渐渐减少。除了亲人离去，已经没有什么值得我们痛苦流泪了。

因为没有多少理由动情，我们甚至都忘却了深情款款的模样，伤心落泪的滋味。我怕长此以往，我们情似枯河，心如死灰，对一切生动的景象、感人的场面都无动于衷。

依靠

人老了，难免会有些心慌胆怯。从生理上说，身衰力竭，气短神减，以前轻而易举就能完成的动作，已难以做到。攀高迈远，矫健敏捷，都是昔日风采。怕风怕雨更怕艰难险阻，忌吃忌喝更忌长夜不眠。从心理上说，权威降低，影响趋弱，越来越没有纵横的气势，睥睨的信心，头上的光环日渐黯淡，身上的霸气荡然无存，慢慢还原为普通的老者。没有了掌控力、威慑力，不知不觉中就远离了社会，淡出了人们的视线。最初还有人礼节性地问候，不久就是冷漠地视而不见，直至最后无人问津。

因为害怕被人遗忘，行将老去的人总要想尽各种办法找到依靠，尽量体现自己的存在。

有些官员自以为聪明，偷偷培养自己的亲信，破格提拔重用年轻人，以延续自己即将交付的权力，保留一定的话语权，维系一点可怜的尊严。然而，铁打的营盘流水的兵，将帅一换，情形尽变，没有人是一成不变的，大部分人都要图谋自己的前程，必然改弦易辙，向着光明处去，有多少人会矢志不移地跟随一个日薄西山的老者？不过彼此敷衍罢了，岂可作为凭恃？

商人们比较讲求实际，他们觉得人不可信，唯钱可靠，于是拼命储蓄，积累金银财宝。诚然，许多问题有了钱便可迎刃而解，不必屈尊求人，更无须为手下的背叛而愤怒。但钱再多，也避免不了老去时的寂寞孤独冷。且老迈之时更需要的是尊重而非享受。显然，钱可靠却不可全靠。

学者们认为学识可作依靠。确实，学识随身，不会遗失，不可抢夺，得便时可以套现，发挥时受人尊崇。也许不足以换取物资任意挥霍，但却可供无穷精神享用。相较而言，学识似乎比钱更值得依仗，因为它不像钱财那样随时会化作灰烬，海晏河清时还能有效地实现经济转化。可见，学识比金钱更能化解老去时的恐慌。

当然，最可依靠的是身体。只要身体健康，既不需要人壮胆，也不需要钱撑腰，独行江湖，遍历天下，皆无所畏惧，如果兼有学识在身，那就更加天马行空了。

畏史

史官在封建时代的官僚体系中是个特殊的存在，其官职其实不高，世俗权力几乎没有，但地位却备受尊崇，常出没于皇帝身边，发挥着举足轻重的作用。普通百姓也许不觉史官有何大用，帝王将相可都对史官敬让三分。因为史官手执如椽之笔，掌管着每个人的身后之名。子曰：“君子疾没世而名不称焉”，也就是说，每个有着家国情怀的士子，都希望建当世之功，留万世之名，但若无史官的成就，就是功名盖世，也无法进入简册，光照后世。所以但凡欲图不朽之事者，史官是无论如何都不能得罪的。

《左传・襄公二十五年》记载了一则史官故事：齐国权臣崔杼谋杀了国君齐庄公。太史如实记录：崔杼弑其君。崔杼看后大怒，将太史杀了，太史的弟弟接任后，仍是坚持如实记录，结果又被崔杼杀了。太史的另外一个弟弟也是史官，继续沿用两个哥哥的说法，崔杼无奈，只好作罢。孟子说，孔子作《春秋》而乱臣贼子惧。崔杼恐怕此时真有点恐惧了，虽然手握生杀大权，也连杀了两个太史，希望阻止史官的秉笔直书，然而根本无济于事，继任者毫不在乎生死。想想将要遗臭万年，崔杼岂能不惧？杀得愈多，后世骂名愈盛，倒是被杀者成就了千秋万世名。崔杼无奈只好作罢。

史官一职，由来已久，春秋战国时期大国皆置史官，有太史有小史，有内史有外史，有左史有右史，各司其责。帝王君子，凡有志于天下者，无不珍惜自己的羽毛，希望青史留名，故对史官均高看一眼，即便是可以随意贬撤甚至捕杀史官的君王亦不敢任意妄为。他们再作恶多端，对史官始终还是保存一份尊重。

现在一些人缺乏史学意识，没有竹帛概念，更为重要的是，作为芸芸黎庶，根本没有书入简册的机会，当然也就没有什么言行道德底线，对于历史，必然缺乏起码的尊重和应有的敬畏。

助人

助人无非两种方式。最直接的办法是给钱给物，帮其解决问题，助其送穷脱困。这是最为常见的一种助人模式，条件具备时，做起来方便快捷，迅速让人得到实惠，改变现状，摆脱困境。应该说，这种帮助，社会上绝大多数人都有能力提供。现实中，也确实会有很多人付出实际行动，助人一臂之力。因为人皆有恻隐之心，路见不忍之事，一般都愿施以援手。

更高层次的帮助，不是给予实物馈赠，而是为其创造成长空间。对于一个身体健康思维正常者，若要相助，更好的办法是让他有个发挥自己特长的环境。人各有所长，但不是都能碰到好机遇，千里马须得有伯乐才行，鸣之通其意，饲之以其道，才能驰之尽其能。英才俊杰，最希望的是充分发挥潜力，尽量为他们提供自由的工作氛围和广阔的驰骋纵深，比给他们什么物质配备都要来得重要。但话说回来，能给这些人提供帮助的人不是身居要津，就是手握重金，否则，凭什么给予别人优质的平台。然而终极的帮助远不止这些，而是解开其心结，破除其思想桎梏，让其了无滞碍，身心舒畅。只是这种帮助是最为高级的形式。

首先被助者要到达一定的层次，具有较好的文化素养，而且抱有强烈摆脱金钱名利诱惑的愿望，苦于不得其法。助人者自然要亭亭物表，皎皎霞外，立于云端，俯视人间。通古今天地之变，悉物理人情之奥。否则，拿什么开示于人。助人精神思想开悟犹如佛学中的法布施，必须自己首先善于讲经说法。

《金刚经》云：“若三千大千世界中，所有诸须弥山王，如是等七宝聚，有人持用布施。若人以此《般若波罗蜜经》，乃至四句偈等，受持读诵，为他人说，于前福德，百分不及一，百千万亿分，乃至算术譬喻所不能及。”意思是，对人讲解佛法，比拿须弥山那般大的一座宝库做慈善还要功德远甚。可见思想上的悟道何等重要。现在助人，多停留在给人些许钱财解决物质贫乏之类。为人提供发展空间让其奋发有为，客观上具备这种能力的不多，主观上愿意无私这么做的更少。至于助人锁心猿收意马，穷物理悟大道，绝大部分人想都不敢想，更不用说做。

两重天地

从家里走到街区，须得左转右拐，经行很长一段林荫道和繁花盛开地，过了一组红绿灯后，才算是到了外面的世界。每次乘出租车或者搭朋友私车回家，他们都会由衷赞叹：这里真安静，空气太好了。这或许是我来到这座繁华城市二十多年所作最正确的决定：居于闹市之静处。当然这也是我物质上唯一所获，然已意足。

那组红绿灯，我总觉得好像是仙都与红尘之间的闸门开关。每天早晨，我储存好足够的精气力量，以及必备的寒暄词汇，还有放之四海而皆可的笑容仪态，身披霞光或者迎一袭轻雨，来到两个世界的接壤处，一俟绿灯亮起，便步入烟火人间。霎时顿觉心中尘土飞扬，噪声四起，即使来到庄严肃穆的大厦，一样会听到喧闹一片；漫步开阔疏朗的广场，一样会感到狭隘不堪；参加欢声笑语的聚会，一样会听出虚情假意。虽然我早已做好思想准备，把随身携带的各色工具一一派上用场，一切都处理得妥妥帖帖，有时甚至是游刃有余，但我仍然深感疲惫万分，因为这种身心消耗不可以每秒多少牛顿计算，而是以每秒几许生命计算。我不愿在这个看似光鲜实则暗哑，看似丰满实则露骨的世界停留太久，只要不是必须坚守，我一定会早早撤出阵地，就像一个刚刚参与过决战的将军，脱下铠甲，倒提长枪，放马南山。

我将以最快速度返回世界转换的闸门处，驾车飞快驰越那组红绿灯，然后慢慢松开油门，打开车窗，接受林荫道上长风的轻拂，欣赏鸟儿们奏起的欢乐颂，一路有暗香盈袖，远处见光影浮动，山峦耸翠，花色含烟，窗中远岫，舍后长松，天地突然安静，心中波澜不起。这是个寂然的世界，也是个丰盈的世界。一切尽在不言中，一切无声胜有声。我以花草树木之灵气疗我心伤，以天地万物之妙理实我穷思，于是我又饱满如初，光彩如初。

在两个世界转换，必是彼消此长，我只把握一点：就是尽量多居于此而少留于彼。任他两轮日月来往如梭，到头来，我定是欢欣渐多。

准备变老

因为有晨练的习惯，我经常会跟老人打交道。老人和孩子其实很相像，都喜欢成群结队，很怕被孤立而落单。我锻炼时好清静，所以常独来独往。老人们则多三五成群，结伴而行，人越多越好，他们最怕的是孤单。无论是公园还是广场，我们见到的都是一伙一伙的老人，很少见到那种独行侠。这点跟孩子们游戏时完全一样，孩子们很喜欢凑在一块，捉迷藏，踢足球，听故事，只要人多，似乎干什么都兴致勃勃。独自一人肯定是没精打采，毫无乐趣可言的。

老人活动队伍的领头人具有绝对的权威，甚至是说一不二的。到了此时此处，可不管你以前当多大官，现在有多少钱，是教授也好，是工人也罢，一切行动听指挥，领头人发话了，就要绝对服从，没有任何讨价还价的余地。就像小时候一起玩耍的孩子王，各种游戏和活动都由他策划组织和指挥，违者轻则出局，重则驱出队伍。一旦遭到整个群体的冷落，也就意味着没有一个玩伴了，从此也就失去了乐趣。大抵孩子们都明白不听指挥带来的后果有多么严重，所以基本上都会遵守规则，服从孩子王的调度。

老人也一样。到了一把年纪，人生基本已成定局，其他已没什么可祈盼的了。只希望找到一些玩伴一起锻炼身体，或者参加一些文娱活动，所以无论之前多么风光，或者多么普通，加入了群体就处在同一起跑线了。谁有某方面的特长，谁就是这个团体的佼佼者，最强者自然为王。比如太极队、舞蹈队、歌唱队，专业能力最强的人才可能被推为领头人。其他人当然唯他马首是瞻，谁敢违背其意愿，则很可能被清除出去。

我曾亲眼见到过团体的领头人训斥那些不听指挥的老人，就像领导训斥那些没完成工作任务的下属，可以说毫不客气，不留任何情面。也许被训斥者以前就是个不小的领导，而训斥者以前并未在领导岗位上待过。此一时彼一时，老了有些东西也就清零了。以前的种种，到了这时根本无济于事。有时见到这种场景，很为那些被训斥的老人不平，心想若是换了我，肯定就拍屁股走人了，彼此又没有任何约束关系。但奇怪的是，那些被训斥的老人并不多作反驳，也不愤然离去，而是虚心接受。

我想，老人们之所以委曲求全，极有可能是不愿脱离群体，他们害怕放单独行，正如孩子害怕没有玩伴。从这个意义上讲，每个即将老去的人，还真得为将来的生活认真考虑，否则哪怕现在指挥千军万马，到时也只有听命于人。

衬托

读研时，有个师妹不仅学术底蕴一枝独秀，而且一米七五的身高也一松独挺。一次我笑问她，是否在班上女生中“海拔”最高，结果她告诉我她在全班都无人相匹。然后她表情复杂地叹了口气说：“其实一米七五并不高，只是他们太矮罢了。”我颇替她班上的男生感到遗憾，虽然身高并不能说明什么。

毕业后南下深圳工作，在大街小巷、楼顶路边到处看到一种三角形的既叶且花的植物，春来甚是繁盛，即便是冬天亦不甚衰。后来才知道，这便是深圳市花簕杜鹃，也叫三角梅，外形上最大的特点就是花瓣像叶片，而且枝叶特别繁茂。在城市处处盛开，一丛丛，一簇簇，绚丽多姿，煞是动人。平时总觉得她颜色特别红艳，一次到公园的花园中赏花，立于玫瑰、月季之侧，簕杜鹃的色彩便略显黯淡了，毕竟前二者皆是正宗的大红，而簕杜鹃只是紫红，若论光彩夺目，勒杜鹃就要稍逊风骚了。平时之所以感觉簕杜鹃的色彩无与伦比，实在是那繁盛的绿叶烘托得好。

后来接触过一些所谓的国学大师，其名也著，其声也显，听其讲学论书，实则不过“授之书而习其句读者”，绝非“传道授业解惑者”也。心下十分疑惑，这些人最多能授人以鱼，而不能授人以渔，为何被时人誉为大师？细思之下才明白，听众多是些连句读都断不了、意思都弄不明白的外行，忽见有人能将“之乎者也”念得很是流畅，焉能不心惊？不是讲述者有多强，而是听讲者太弱。

又有许多所谓著名作家者，这里拿过大奖，那里作过演讲，俨然文章妙手诗家谪仙，观其要旨，往往不知所云；考其行文，轻浮飘忽，只是文从字顺，差堪连贯而已，但读者往往是些连基本语法都没过关，逻辑关系还理不顺的人，当然视之若神人。不是作家真的跑得有多快，而是读者还没学会走。

仔细想来，一米七五的师妹确实算不上出奇，但同学们的矮衬托出了她的“伟岸”。对比之下簕杜鹃真不能算是花中艳丽者，但有了团团绿叶的众星捧月，就显出了她的非凡气度来。而一些国学大师著名作家之类，之所以得盛名于一时，则是读不懂书作不了文的人太多之故。

人与事皆如此，有时还真不是本身有多好，而是余众衬托得佳。为什么“古来材大难为用”？因为一些掌权者不喜欢身边的人太强，你高了，就显出他们的小来。只有在一群弱者当中，他们才找得到叱咤风云的感觉。正如与一群矮如武大郎者为伴，即使身材并不高大魁梧，也会生出武二郎的气概。

年终总结

人的一生不过是时光的有限绵延。在这一段属于我们个人的时光区间中，并无任何间隙。就像一条奔涌向前的河流一样，水流是不断的。将其分为少青壮老、年月日时是人为使然，与抽刀断水无异，只是表面形式复杂其实没有任何内在意义。我们将时光分段，也许是为了更好地警醒自己，不要浪费生命，哪怕是一秒这样一小截时光。

年是我们用来计量生命的基本单位，一个人的生命再长也不过是一百多年。所以对于每年的结束，人们都要举行各种仪式以表纪念，以示郑重，毕竟，生命经不起几次翻页。总结是现代人在岁末年关必须进行的仪式流程之一。单位有单位的总结，个人有个人的总结，一年来做了哪些事？取得了什么成绩？出了哪些问题？还有什么不足？原因到底是什么？未来有什么计划？将要采取什么措施？这些方面单位总结固然是严肃认真的，个人总结也要求准确到位。当然个人在工作总结之外，往往还会在心中默默地盘算一年的得失损益，获得一些妙处难与君说的体悟，作出一些不足为外人道的决定。比如说因为处理人际关系方面还不够灵活，致使本该获得的晋升机会泡了汤，以后一定要吸取教训，多长个心眼。在与贸易伙伴谈生意时，因为之前进行过多次场景演练，将对方的性格好恶研究了个透，所以才能顺利地拿下项目，挣了个盆满钵满，明年要继续发扬这种细致入微的工作作风。诸如此类，都是非常微妙而又实际的经验教训，不好用文字表达，只能在心中梳理。所以人们在年终总结的时候其实都有两本账，一者示人，一者自留。

既然众人都将年作为一个时间段，在新旧交替之际，将过去进行彻底的盘点，我自然也不能例外。按照要求，我会好好地将工作进行全面总结，如实地道成绩，找问题，究原因，以供上级循名责实之用。同时，我也会在心里列出一份只给自己参阅的不成文总结，只是这份总结与人际关系无关，与权钱名利无关，只与快乐与否有关。我会将一年中快乐占比、快乐缘起、快乐程度等计算清楚；当然也要对忧愁日子、忧愁事项、忧愁原因分析研判，做到心中有数。如此，我在筹谋明年的计划时，将采取有效措施，努力将忧愁消灭于萌芽状态，而将快乐日子尽量增多，着力延展。

吾谁与归

天空中飞翔的不仅有燕雀，更有雄鹰；丛林中奔跑的不仅有狐兔，更有虎豹；而人世间行走的不仅有凡夫庸卒，更有卧龙凤雏。鹰击长空的时候，快如闪电，转眼即逝，漫天飞舞的多是燕雀。虎豹隐于深林，常常敛迹隐踪，四处乱窜的多是狐兔。浪迹人世间的人长得都一个样，不像天空中的鸟、丛林中的兽，一眼即可辨别优劣勇怯。有时看着高大威猛的人，也许是个懦夫；有时看着聪明伶俐的人，可能是个蠢才。相貌丑陋的凤雏，即便是英明如孙权者，也完美错过。躬耕于南阳的孔明，若不是刘备求贤若渴，哪有机会闻达于世？

大师也许就在身边，正是你千百朋友中的一个。英才也许就在街头拐弯处，悠然地喝茶赏花，他们脸上并没有印上卧龙凤雏的标记，也是两个肩膀上长着一个脑袋，走起路来也并非总是虎虎生风，但他们身上一定有一股无形之气，敏感的人越靠近越能感受那股气的强大；迟钝的人即使天天与之相处，也无法感知。

芸芸众生中，平凡者始终居多，他们以己之平凡猜度他人亦平庸，

是以得出结论：杰出魁伟者，都在远方陌生处。就是让他们放胆想象，他们也绝对不能相信，那个经常晨练的邻居，或者自己经常光顾的那个咖啡店店主，正是传说中的非凡人物。他们总喜欢天真地认为，比他们更高层面的人理所当然应该更加英明神武，潇洒出尘。殊不知，他们只是我们身边平常人物的升级版，本质上无甚差别，只是飞得高一点的燕雀，跑得快一点的狐兔而已。而真正的雄鹰，有时也在枯草中逡巡；真正的虎豹，有时也在灌木丛中出没；真正的英杰，有时就在人群中藏身。

看着大街上川流不息的人群，我经常陷入沉思：其中应有一个两个出群者？我也同样会审视身边的诸位同仁：其中应有三五个可与言者？耳边不禁响起范仲淹留下的千年一叹：噫！微斯人，吾谁与归？

角色转换

将某一角色演得神形兼备、活灵活现，令人印象深刻且过目不忘的，无疑是一个优秀演员，不管这个角色是正派还是反派，是主角还是配角。而不限于某类角色，演什么像什么，既有快速代入感，又给人强烈真实感的演员，则是一个天赋演技兼备的杰出演员。

我们经常将演绎银幕中人物、舞台上形象的人们称为演员，其实我们每个人在生活中都是演员。而且扮演着不同的角色，在单位里，我们是领导是上级，是处长科长、董事长总经理之类，或者是僚属是部下，是科员职员、秘书司机之类。在家里，我们是父母老一辈，或者儿女新生代。在社会上，我们化身为知交好友、生意伙伴、城市过客、乡村闲人。有些人是很优秀的演员，演什么角色都入木三分。在家里是好父亲好儿子，在单位也是好领导好下属，在社会上是好朋友好伙伴，而且角色转换毫无滞碍，绝不将某一角色的特点带入另一角色的戏中。有些人可以将某一角色演得很好，可情境一变化就完全无法入戏。比如有人在单位当领导当得很成功，决断果敢，深孚众望，在家里却颐指气使，不可一世，变成了一个武断的父亲，或者不孝的子孙。还有人作为父亲很慈爱和善，而作为领导却显得软弱无能；作为儿女很孝顺听话，作为下属却显得庸庸碌碌。有些人更糟糕，演什么都演砸。在单位做不了领导，做不好下属；在家里既不是慈父母，也不是乖儿女；在社会做朋友不靠谱，做市民无公德。这种人就像那些有着明星梦想却不肯琢磨演技，也不愿意投入真情的演员，永远入不了戏，演不好角色。

成熟的舞台银幕演员，不管什么角色都轻松胜任，拿捏准确。有趣的是，很多演员在舞台银幕上演得令人拍案叫绝，却在生活中演得一塌糊涂。真正的好演员，是在生活这幕戏中，在人生这个舞台上，于单位、家庭、社会的角色流转中变换自如，成功刻画，把每个形象都演绎得生动立体，深刻隽永。

论史

中国最早的典籍该是《三坟》《五典》《八索》《九丘》，虽然典籍的内容已散佚，但名称幸得以保留。《左传·昭公十二年》记载，王（楚灵王）曰："（左史倚相）是良史也，子善视之，是能读《三坟》《五典》《八索》《九丘》。"说明春秋时这些典籍尚有保存，也有人能读得懂，事实上这时去夏朝就已经一千多年了，更毋庸说更早的三皇五帝时期。

《尚书序》称："伏羲、神农、黄帝之书，谓之《三坟》，言大道也。少昊、颛顼、高辛、唐（尧）、虞（舜）之书，谓之《五典》，言常道也。"意思是三皇时期的典籍《三坟》讲的是宇宙天地的大道，而五帝时期的经典《五典》讲的是通常之道。孔子将之前的四大典籍加上夏商周的相关书籍整理编辑成《尚书》，可惜后来秦始皇焚书坑儒，把《尚书》都给抄没焚毁了。现今所用《尚书》乃后在孔宅颓壁中发现的古文《尚书》，加上西汉伏生口述流传的今文《尚书》汇编而成。所以并不完整，且内容存疑，后世多有争议。

中国历史可上溯大致五千年，而有文字记录者始于公元前841年，不到三千年。也就是说两千多年里有文字论及而无真实档案，实在是可惜。正是因为没有典籍遗留，很多说法都很难令人信服。

孔子一直推崇尧舜禹汤文武周公，对过去的那些时代向往推崇，认为那才是人类社会的典范形态。事实上真的如此吗？因为没有真实的文字记录，我们不得而知。孔子对于先贤的溢美，未必不是为了构建一个理想国度而虚设几个完美的政治形象。缺失记载的两千多年，或许有清明美好的大同世界，但肯定少不了暴虐压榨的苦难时代。

没有典籍遗留，固然难以知晓历史的轮廓。其实，即便是有了史书流传，也未必真实可信。

不是每个朝代每个帝王都有真实记录历史的勇气，否则，为什么杀害逼迫史官的事时有发生？但无论是无惧还是畏惧，是让人秉笔直书还是逼人弄虚作假，总的来说，对历史尊重敬畏，倒是历代帝王大致相同的心理。

心平气和

我答应过自己从此以后要心平气和，毕竟已人到中年。不仅要学会与自然万物和谐共存，更要学会与自己达成谅解。世间不平事十有八九，人生不得意者十之八九，如果因此导致不快乐时十有八九，那我无疑成了《悲惨世界》里的冉·阿让。保持平静淡然并不容易，我下了很久的决心才实现了艰难的自我承诺。我知道，要达到预期的目标，必须努力具备两个前提条件，一个是洞穿人间，一个是看清自己。

洞穿人间必须练就一双慧眼，能看清波平如镜下的暗流涌动，风和日丽下的山雨欲来，亦能预感温柔一笑中藏着寒气森森的刀锋，甜言蜜语中透出置人死地的毒素。关键是洞悉一切后还要若无其事，与低智商者一样表现得低智商，与伪君子一样表现得很真诚，断不可像《皇帝的新装》里那个诚实的孩子一样，看到皇帝赤身裸体还要直陈己见。在具有洞穿能力者的眼中，人间就是一个玻璃墙壁的阳光房，什么都纤毫毕现，什么都一目了然，看到了隐处，预见了结果，自然心中不起波澜，情感不再跌宕。

如果说洞穿人间需要智慧，看清自己则需要勇气。有些人瞧不起这个看不上那个，以自己为能，但到底是个什么货，能成多大事，实践一检验，是驴是马就立即见分晓了。即使自己看不清自己，从别人的眼里话中也可掂量得出来，只是不愿承认自己是个凡人罢了。说到底，就是缺乏自我客观批判评价的勇气，即使在心中骂了自己一万遍笨蛋，还是要以一个智者自持。看不清自己永远都无法摆正位置，居非其所，焉能心安?

既然我已决定心平气和，那我定要立志荡胸张目，直视无碍，把万里浮云一眼看穿。同时勇于输肝剖胆，洗污涤秽，然后把透明的自己看得清清楚楚。

玉树后庭花

唐朝诗人杜牧有首著名的诗《泊秦淮》："烟笼寒水月笼沙，夜泊秦淮近酒家。商女不知亡国恨，隔江犹唱后庭花。"借陈后主陈叔宝故事，咏史感怀，慨叹兴衰。诗中所提到的后庭花是指《玉树后庭花》，乃陈叔宝代表性诗作，曾被谱成曲，在坊间广为传唱。因为陈为隋所灭，《玉树后庭花》被称为亡国之音。仿佛听了此曲，有国者将灭国，有志者将沉沦，故凡志士仁人皆以为警示，生怕像陈后主那样沉迷在靡靡之音中不能自拔，忘了初心泯了理想。

我一直很是好奇，是什么样的诗歌有如此功效，能让人们磨灭意志，耽于享乐，甚至把国都丢了；乃至于要以之为前车之鉴，始终保持警惕之心。若果其然，则此诗之艺术影响力也太深远。后数读详品陈叔宝之《玉树后庭花》，确实造诣非凡：

丽宇芳林对高阁，新装艳质本倾城。

映户凝娇乍不进，出帷含态笑相迎。

妖姬脸似花含露，玉树流光照后庭。

花开花落不长久，落红满地归寂中。

陈叔宝一向被誉为艳词高手，但此诗却丽而不艳，甚至可以说是清新雅致的。诗中对于美女容貌、身材、服饰、神态之描述可谓细致入微惟妙惟肖，不唯如此，最后两句是在眼前实景下的艺术升华，是日常生活下的深刻思考。花开正盛，终要落红满地；青春妙龄，终要美人迟暮。诗人显然意不止于对美人的生动描摹，而在于得出“美好总是短暂的”伤感结论。这无疑是一首思想精深艺术隽永的好诗，与唐朝那些诗歌圣手的大作相比也不遑多让。如果此诗出于元稹李商隐之手，肯定会被欣赏赞誉。可惜的是作者是个君王，而且是个亡国之君。而诗中之主旨与亡国之音十分契合，《史记·乐书》云：“亡国之音哀以思，其民困。”可不正是说的《玉树后庭花》？

历代君王中写诗者不在少数，偏偏精于此道者多是亡国之君，像隋朝的杨广，南北朝陈朝的陈叔宝，南唐的李煜，个个都是才华横溢、诗艺高超。他们失了国破了家，其实是因为他们贪图享乐、奢侈荒淫、治国乏术，跟诗歌本身毫无关系。正如许多人将国破家亡归因于红颜祸水，而不究其根本。对此，宋花蕊夫人《述国亡诗》道出了真相：“君王城上竖降旗，妾在深宫那得知。十四万人齐解甲，更无一个是男儿。”灭国是男人们的无能，跟我一个深宫弱女子有什么关系呢?

隋灭陈，自然是陈后主治国无能、无力御敌的结果，跟几首关于美少女的诗歌似乎扯不上什么联系，非要把《玉树后庭花》定为亡国之音而加以批判，实在是一种诗歌的冤屈。政治所犯的错误，绝不能让文学艺术来承担；正如男人们所犯的错误，绝不能由美女们来承担。

珍惜光阴

即便是家庭殷实的人，花起钱来也多少会有心痛惋惜之感，更别说家境一般的人。所以绝大多数人对于花钱都是有计划有节制的。那些一掷千金挥霍无度的人，要么继承了父母的巨额资产，要么通过权力寻租积累了大量钱财，他们在获取财富的时候未曾付出丝毫汗水心血，当然花钱起来痛快淋漓，毫不可惜。然而人们花钱的时候觉得心中隐隐生痛，花起光阴来往往毫不吝惜。虽然自古以来就有一大堆诸如“尺璧非宝，寸阴是竞”“一寸光阴一寸金，寸金难买寸光阴”的警世通言、醒世恒言，可人们依然大段大段地浪费光阴，一年一年地虚度青春。钱花完了，大家都知道难挣，因此会省着花；光阴花完了，大家心中其实也知道不可再生，可仍然屡屡豪掷。

不同于钱财的不可限量，每个人的光阴都是封了顶的。钱财可以腰缠万贯，可以价值连城，可以富可敌国，没有规定说钱财积攒到什么程度就不能再增加了。光阴却不同，一个人了不起能度过一百多个春秋，大限到了的时候，向上天再借三五年，得阎王爷同意才行。显而易见，光阴比钱财宝贵。如果光阴可以买卖，那些垂暮之年的富翁绝对愿意出高价收购。遗憾的是，光阴不是商品，无法流通交易。岁月永远不可逆转，时光永远无法再生。费在酒桌上的光阴，耗在争斗中的光阴，花在愁苦里的光阴，早已一去不复返了。

好在我并不是个对光阴慷慨大方的人，虽然在青春年少时也曾快意地虚掷过，但总体上还是用得其所，不至于如雁过无声踏雪无痕。好歹，我在每段光阴的页面都留下了明显的刻痕，迄今犹能讲述每段光阴的故事。曾经月白风清，今已忧患凋零，老去光阴速可惊。我更不愿轻易浪费自己余下的稍许光阴。好钢都要用在刀刃上，钱财都要用在紧要处，比其更金贵的光阴理所当然要用在心仪兴至处，如此方不负余生。

春来新发

我不知道春是从海那边越山渡水而来，还是从地底下穿石破土而来，总之她一定是来了，且是款款而来，御风而来，虽然看不到她的身影，但她特有的气息已经弥漫在天地之间。或许她从未走远，就在白雪下隐身，在寒风中等待，在枯枝上蓄势。随时准备挺身而出，接掌时序。

春是力道遒劲的，她扫残雪，破凛冽，驱寒意，除破败，掩荒凉，一改江山颜色。春也是品性温柔的。她吐鹅黄，开繁花，垂杨柳，铺绿茵，布和煦，温暖大地怀抱。放眼一望，满目皆是绿色。沉心一闻，鼻中溢满花香。凝神静听，耳边鸟鸣如歌。山由肃穆而破颜，水由凝重而雀跃，远岫含烟，云蒸霞蔚。不论江南塞上、乡村都市，一体都以绿为主色调，以柔为主情调。走在路上，渐渐地便绿上人衣，柔满心田。阳春烟景，大块文章，看不足，游不够，化人于无形，醉人于不觉。蜂飞蝶舞，花瓣纷披，于草中仰卧，于溪头放歌。芳洲拾翠暮忘归，秀野踏青来不定。春就像一盏浓酒，就像一壶酽茶，一饮便绵软无力，一眠便不觉天晓。

我爱春之繁茂，我爱春之柔媚，我更爱春之欣欣向荣，春之生机勃发。春雨分明就是甘露，滋润了萎谢的万物；春风分明就是麈尾，拂却了心头的阴霾。枯树寒枝长出新绿的时候，幽咽泉流破冰迸发的时候，销声黄鹂欢然吟唱的时候，总有一种感动油然而生，总有一种希望勃然萌发，总有一种力量自然集聚。仿佛定要做出一番事业，或者完成一种爱恋，方不辜负了这美好的季节。

春天里播种，春天里发芽，春天里拔节；春天里酝酿，春天里规划，春天里出发。我喜欢一切都从春天开始，一路繁花似锦，一路暖风扑面，一路笛声飞扬。

禀性难移

人的某些特质是与生俱来，生长在骨子里头的。比如傲气，比如势利。有些人接触起来谦虚低调，有理有节，可并不平易近人，相反，倒常感到有股气势逼人而来，拒人千里之外。这种气势带着冷漠，带着傲然，带着某种孤芳自赏，某种居高临下，颇有视众生若无物之意。他们就像个内力雄浑的武林高手，武功平平的人站在他们身边，马上就会感到一种巨大的压力，觉得浑身不自在起来。只有那些功力相当的人才能坦然面对。

骨子里长着傲气的人，天生就是才情纵横的。他们的傲气是靠学识支撑的，不恃才，如何傲物？这种先天具有的傲气跟后天培育的傲慢截然不同，虽都带着傲性，但前者凭借的是才气学识，后者依仗的是家世权钱。前者是自身生发的傲气，是以永在。后者是依外物而生，外物丧则傲气自灭。天生傲气的人显然是内心强大的存在。这种存在看起来并无特别之处，但只要一靠近，便能感受到一种压迫感。做他们的朋友是件不容易的事，做他们的上司实在是件不幸的事情。就像关羽一样，谁在他的眼中都是土鸡瓦犬，只有刘备曹操这样的英雄才配与其论交。所以在现实生活中，天生傲气的人虽或才华横溢，但往往不得志，无他，自身不肯屈，上司不能容耳。

势利是绝大多数人骨子里都具备的基因，有些人不知不觉，或者明知而不肯自认。有几个人有勇气坦承自己是个势利之人呢？势利是普通人皆有的秉性，没什么可避讳的，只要不做势利小人就好。在一群生意人当中，我们更愿意与最富有者交流对话，表示尊重敬意。其实，我们很清楚，这群人无论贫富都与我们无关，再富有，他们也不会分给我们一分一毫钱财，本当对他们一视同仁。可是我们往往会看重其中的佼佼者，这本身就是一种势利。也许在我们潜意识当中，有着某种获利图好的用心。而在一群官员们当中，我们更愿意奉承讨好官职最大的那个，实际上，哪个官大哪个官小跟我们可能都毫不相干，我们就是个局外人，别想得到他们的照顾提拔。可我们依然更愿意与官最大的人结识交友，这无疑就是一种势利之心，只是我们不愿承认罢了。

天生的秉性，要人为地磨灭，谈何容易？但可以通过不断地强化修为，让其变淡磨平。比如让傲气不那么逼人，让势利不那么明显。

总策划/出版人：
胡洪侠
策划编辑：
郭洪义
责任编辑：
钟婷
校对：
杨杰 程晓玲 崔华林
装帧设计：
周舒婷
插画：
冯大美

图书在版编目（CIP）数据

江山犹是 / 王国猛著. -- 深圳 ： 深圳报业集团出版社，2022.11
（深圳文典）
ISBN 978-7-80774-029-2

Ⅰ. ①江… Ⅱ. ①王… Ⅲ. ①散文集 - 中国 - 当代 Ⅳ. ①I267

中国版本图书馆CIP数据核字(2022)第191587号

江山犹是
Jiangshan Youshi
王国猛 / 著

深圳报业集团出版社出版发行
（深圳市福田区商报路2号 518034）
深圳报业集团印务有限公司
新华书店经销

开本：889mm×1230mm 1/32
字数：155千字
版次：2022年11月第1版 2022年11月第1次印刷
印张：7
ISBN 978-7-80774-029-2
定价：58.00元